FOUNDATIONS OF EXPERIMENTAL RESEARCH

D0110001

FOUNDATIONS

HARPER'S EXPERIMENTAL PSYCHOLOGY SERIES

UNDER THE EDITORSHIP OF H. PHILIP ZEIGLER

OF EXPERIMENTAL RESEARCH

BY ROBERT PLUTCHIK

HARPER & ROW, PUBLISHERS

NEW YORK, EVANSTON, AND LONDON

TO MY DAUGHTERS LISA AND LORI

CONTENTS

APPENDIXES

INDEXES

PREFACE

As an undergraduate majoring in physics I came to appreciate the role of theories and models in helping us understand the nature of the world. At the same time I recognized that experiments and concepts could not be considered in isolation, but were part of an historical, intellectual process.

When I went on to graduate training in experimental psychology, I found that these same ideas were also applicable to psychology. Subsequent participation in research concerned with electrical stimulation of the brain, psychophysiology, and clinical problems enabled me to see that experimentation in all areas of science had many common aims as well as methods.

Over the course of time I gradually came to recognize that experimentation in any science is a complex *decision-making process* that starts with the initial conception of a problem and continues until the ultimate publication of a report. The decisions concern such issues as: definitions of key concepts, sampling of subjects as well as conditions, measurement, scaling, instrumentation, design, and statistics. This book is an attempt to analyze the many decision-making problems faced by the experimenter, and to suggest, wherever possible, rational considerations for solving them. In order to accomplish this, I have drawn liberally upon research reports in various fields to illustrate different problems, and I have proposed some solutions. Because of the emphasis on issues of methodology and decision-making this book should be useful to students in all the areas of psychology as well as those in related fields such as psychiatry and sociology.

This book is not intended to be a summary of research in different areas; it seems to me that the student can develop an appreciation for research only by going to original experimental reports published in contemporary journals. The book is not intended to be a statistics text, although two chapters have been included which deal with basic statistical procedures in the light of certain decisions the experimenter makes. Finally, although the book does not propose a philosophy of science, several important philosophical issues are critically explored; for example, the problem of operationism and the nature of measurement and scaling.

I am indebted to the Literary Executor of the late Sir Ronald A. Fisher, F.R.S., Cambridge, to Dr. Frank Yates, F.R.S., Rothamsted, and to Messrs. Oliver & Boyd Ltd., Edinburgh, for permission to reprint Table No. III from their book *Statistical Tables for Biological, Agricultural, and Medical Research*.

My indebtedness to other people is great. Richard Trumbull, Gilbert Tolhurst, and James Prescott of the Office of Naval Research provided me with some support for the preparation of the manuscript through an ONR contract. Philip Zeigler and Joseph Lyons were very helpful with their suggestions. Fred Lit provided generous counsel on my chapter on psychophysics and helped improve it considerably.

In addition, various others contributed comments on one or another aspect of the book. I should like particularly to thank

Bernard Aaronson, Sherman Ross, John Paul Scott, Sherwin Klein, Jack Werboff, Solomon Kugelmass, Joseph LaLumia, Joseph Zubin, and my wife Anita. Needless to say, the responsibility for the final form of the book rests entirely with me.

ROBERT PLUTCHIK
Department of Psychiatry
College of Physicians and Surgeons

July, 1967

I shall begin by making some experiments before I proceed any further; for it is my intension first to consult experience and then show by reasoning why that experience was bound to turn out as it did. This, in fact, is the true rule by which the student of natural effects must proceed.

—LEONARDO DA VINCI

THE ROLE OF OBSERVATION

AND DESCRIPTION

Many of us are harassed by relentless and importunate cravings for
scientific maturity, which incline us to leap over all the tedious stages
of observation, description, and classification through which
chemistry and all the biological and medical sciences have
passed.

—HENRY A. MURRAY

This book is concerned with the nature of research and experimentation in psychology. The word *research* has its origin in a term which means "to go around" or "to explore" and was derived from an even earlier word meaning "circle." *Experiment* means to "try" or "test" and refers to some of the procedures used in trying to discover unknown facts and procedures. As the definitions of these terms suggest, research and experimentation refer to the process of exploration and testing used to achieve a fuller understanding of the nature of the world.

Such definitions emphasize two important aspects of research: First, it involves actively trying to find new facts; and second, it implies an attempt by scientists to order the facts they discover into meaningful patterns.

The purpose of this book is to describe some of the basic experimental methods used by psychologists to gather information about living organisms. These methods are applicable to almost all kinds of problems, from those associated with aesthetic preferences to those concerned with the analysis of international conflicts. In describing these various procedures, illustrations from many different areas of psychology will be used to clarify the generality of approach.

The integrating theme of the book is the idea that each experiment requires a series of decisions, from the initial definition of a problem to the final analysis and presentation of results. The chapters that follow are organized around this idea with each chapter devoted to a major class of decisions that must be made. In Chapter 2 the concept of experimentation as a decision-making process will be described in detail and will be followed by chapters on definitions, sampling, statistics, design methods, etc.

Before any laboratory research is undertaken, however, a great deal of information has usually been informally acquired either by careful observation or by "pilot" studies. In fact, all science starts from observation. Before formal experimentation is begun, we must have some idea, even if not very precise, about what to search for, what to observe, and what to measure.

The process of searching, observing, and describing has sometimes been called "naturalistic observation" and has been thought of as a rather primitive kind of research procedure. Although this is often the case, there have been some important improvements in recent years in the techniques concerned with accurate observation. Because of the fundamental role of observation in experimentation, this first chapter will illustrate, through a series of examples, the nature and significance of observational techniques. It will become evident that the basic problems of sampling behavior and establishing categories of analysis are part of the larger, general problem of observing and describing people, animals, and their environments.

SOME HISTORICAL EXAMPLES

DARWIN AND THOMPSON

Most of biology until about 1900 was concerned primarily with description. Animals and plants were observed and grouped into species, families, orders, genera, and phyla on the basis of structural or morphological characteristics. Animals or plants having many similar characteristics were considered closely related; those having few similarities were considered only remotely related. Careful description provided a basis for classification or taxonomy.

Based on previous observations by other biologists as well as many of his own, Darwin proposed his theory of evolution in the middle of the last century. To this day, his theory has had a profound influence on most sciences—both the descriptive and experimental aspects. It stimulated the extensive work in comparative anatomy, neurology, and physiology, and excited an interest in the comparative psychology of animals.

Although comparative psychology in America has been limited to a few species, European ethologists have provided many interesting descriptions of species-specific behaviors in diverse animals. Recent issues of ethological journals contain articles dealing with the feeding habits, sexual behavior, care of the young, and aggressive behavior of such animals as the fly, the ant, the bee, the fish, the chicken, the sea lion, and the elephant. These studies usually involve systematic observations of these animals in their more-or-less natural surroundings. Such detailed descriptive information provides a background for interpreting in a meaningful way the results of laboratory experiments.

To take one interesting example, there has been a good deal of research dealing with "hoarding" tendencies in rats. In most cases, these interpretations are based on rats studied in isolation under food-deprived conditions. It was not until fairly recently that a study was made of the Norway rat under naturalistic conditions. In this observational study it was found that rats are highly social animals who live in groups with well-established dominance hierarchies.

If there is but one source of food in the territory of a group, it is usually controlled by the dominant animals, which, however, carry the food away to various outlying points. Such stores may be visited by the less dominant rats when unable to reach the central supply. . . . Is this hoarding, or is it food storing or possibly even food sharing? Since the food is always concealed in burrows or shelters, it is perhaps most likely that the behavior trait has adaptive value in that the food is placed in positions where it can be eaten by others as well as the carrier—in comparative safety from predators (Scott, 1955).

Naturalistic studies may thus throw new light on laboratory investigations.

There is nothing, of course, to prevent the combination of a naturalistic study with an experiment in which some of the conditions affecting the animal are varied systematically. A simple but interesting example of this is provided in the work of Darwin dealing with the sensitivity of worms to light, an excerpt of which is presented here.

Worms are destitute of eyes, and at first I thought that they were quite insensible to light; for those kept in confinement were repeatedly observed by the aid of a candle, and others out of doors by the aid of a lantern, yet they were rarely alarmed, although extremely timid animals. . . .

When the light from a candle was concentrated by means of a large lens on the anterior extremity, they generally withdrew instantly; but this concentrated light failed to act perhaps once out of half a dozen trials. The light was on one occasion concentrated on a worm lying beneath water in a saucer, and it instantly withdrew into its burrow. In all cases the duration of the light, unless extremely feeble, made a great difference in the result. . . .

From the foregoing facts it is evident that light affects worms by its intensity and by its duration. It is only the anterior extremity of the body, where the cerebral ganglia lie, which is affected by light. . . . If this part is shaded, other parts of the body may be fully illuminated, and no effect will be produced. As these animals have no eyes, we must suppose that the light passes through their skins, and in some manner excites their cerebral ganglia. . . . One thing was manifest, namely, that when worms were employed in dragging leaves into their burrows or in eating them, and even during the short intervals whilst they rested from their work, they either did not perceive the light or were regardless of it; and this occurred even when the light was concentrated on them through a large lens. . . .

. . . The different effect which a light produced on different occasions, and especially the fact that a worm when in any way employed . . . is often regardless of light, are opposed to the view of the sudden withdrawal being a simple reflex action. With the higher animals, when close attention to some object leads to the disregard of the impressions which other objects must be producing on them, we attribute this to their attention being then absorbed; and attention implies the presence of a mind. Every sportsman knows that he can approach animals whilst they are grazing, fighting, or courting, much more easily than at other times. . . . The comparison here implied between the actions of one of the higher animals and of one so low in the scale as an earthworm, may appear far-fetched; for we thus attribute to the worm attention and some mental power, nevertheless I can see no reason to doubt the justice of the comparison.

On the basis of the careful observation of a relatively small number of worms under conditions which are partly naturalistic and partly experimental, Darwin notes, first of all, the variability of response of the animals under given conditions. He then sees that sometimes when no reactions are observed, the worms are doing something else, like eating. Darwin notes a parallel between this observation and the fact that higher animals will act in a similar way, i.e., ignore certain stimuli if their attention is directed elsewhere. Reasoning by analogy, Darwin concludes that these observations therefore indicate the existence of a "mental power" in the earthworms.

Regardless of whether a contemporary psychologist would

agree with each step of this chain of reasoning, it is fascinating to see the interaction of observation and inference in Darwin's thinking. It is also interesting to note that his observations combined with simple experiments led to conclusions which can provide the basis for future research.

One other example taken from biology deals with the work of the mathematician-biologist Sir D'Arcy Thompson, who wrote a remarkable book in 1917 (*On Growth and Form*) dealing with the way things grow and the shapes they take. The presentation, although using mathematical concepts, is based almost entirely on careful observation and the identification of similarities and relationships between different kinds of animal and inorganic shapes.

In one section Thompson describes the horns of a number of animals as being essentially spiral shaped, and adds that this basic form is also found in many shells and also in teeth, beaks, and claws.

In a fashion similar to that manifested in the shell or the horn, we find the equiangular spiral to be implicit in a great many other organic structures. . . . Nail and claw, beak and tooth, all come under this category. . . . When the canary-bird's claws grow long from lack of use, or when the incisor tooth of a rabbit or a rat grows long by reason of disease or of injury of the opponent tooth against which it was wont to bite, we know that the tooth or claw tends to grow into a spiral curve, and we speak of it as a malformation. But there has been no fundamental change of form, only an abnormal increase in length; the elongated tooth or claw has the same curvature which it had when it was short, but the spiral becomes more and more manifest the longer it grows. It is only natural, but nevertheless it is curious to see, how closely a rabbit's abnormally overgrown teeth come to resemble the tusks of swine or elephants.

After noting these many basic similarities, Thompson shows that such spiral shapes will always be formed if there are unequal rates of longitudinal growth of a structure and where each new growth is added on as a permanent part of the entire form.

Thus, Thompson goes from a series of observations to the recognition of a common form, and to a mathematical analysis of the problem. All this without any experimental work in the laboratory at all. Perhaps a more accurate way of saying this is that Nature often provides us with unusual conditions which are like experiments, and if an observer is present and able to see and record the changes that occur, far-reaching conclusions may be drawn.

KRAEPELIN AND FREUD

At the beginning of the nineteenth century, several physicians noticed that there were certain patients in the mental hospitals who had fairly similar symptoms. These patients often had poor memory, defective speech, and difficulty in walking or doing skilled movements and yet, at the same time, maintained that they were capable of the greatest deeds. Invariably, these patients got worse and eventually died in the hospital.

During the course of the next 60 years it was gradually learned that more men than women were affected, that onset of symptoms was usually during middle age, and that certain reflexes were abnormal. It became increasingly evident that this complex of symptoms had a typical *onset*, a typical *course*, and a typical *outcome*. By the end of the nineteenth century it had been fairly well established that this disease, later called paresis, was caused by damage to the spinal cord and brain due to syphilitic infection. Once this was known, various methods of prevention and treatment were instituted.

During the latter part of the nineteenth century, a German psychiatrist named Emil Kraepelin began to study large numbers of case histories in the mental hospitals. His aim was to establish various groupings of symptoms that were associated by virtue of a common onset, common course, and common outcome; just as had been done previously for general paresis. Kraepelin eventually classified mental diseases into two major groupings which he called the manic-depressive psychosis and dementia praecox (or schizophrenia). Within each major grouping he proposed several subgroups.

This system, with relatively few changes, has been in use by psychiatrists up to the present time. It is used as a basis for the legal determination of insanity, the establishment of wards for custody, the screening of military personnel, the preparation of census data, the estimation of prognosis, and the treatment of patients. Experimental research with patient populations usually uses these categories as the descriptive basis for selection of subjects and evaluation of results. Here again, description and classification precede experimentation.

While Kraepelin was achieving renown as the great classifier of mental hospital patients, Sigmund Freud was beginning his studies of hysteria. Hysteria seemed to be a strange malady, recognized many centuries before, and characterized by a large assortment of symptoms which could include blindness, deafness, paralysis, anesthesia of parts of the body, and convulsions. For a long time it had been believed that hysteria was due to a disorder of the nervous system, but then some surprising observations came to light.

It was discovered that most of the symptoms of hysteria could be produced by hypnotic suggestions and then eliminated by further suggestions. It was then possible to show that in some actual cases of hysteria the symptoms could be removed by hypnosis. Other peculiar facts were the existence of anatomically meaningless symptoms and a lack of occurrence of certain symptoms while the patient was asleep.

In an effort to clarify these issues, Freud published an essay in 1893 which described the differences between paralyses due to organic lesions and those due to hysteria.

After giving a detailed description of these differences between organic and hysterical paralyses, Freud noted that the particular symptoms that develop seem to depend on common, popular ideas about the organs and parts of the body. He then predicted that no one would find hysterical symptoms in patients that mimic certain well-know effects of brain or nerve injury (e.g., certain visual field defects, or certain kinds of partial facial paralyses) because the symptoms seem strange to the unscientific mind. Finally, Freud concluded that in all cases of hysterical paralysis there is a strong subconscious emotional feeling associated with the organ whose function is lost, and that cure requires the elimination of the connection between the emotion and the organ.

It is interesting to see how Freud moved from acute observation, to generalization, to prediction, and finally to speculation. What is also interesting is that it is just these kinds of speculations which have stimulated a good deal of subsequent research.

SOME RECENT EXAMPLES

LANGUAGE DEVELOPMENT
IN THE CHILD

A number of years ago, the Swiss psychologist Jean Piaget set himself the task of trying to learn about the development of language and thought in the child. He approached the problem from the point of view of a naturalist. His method, in his own words, is as follows:

Two of us followed each a child (a boy) for about a month at the morning class at (a private school), taking down in minute detail and in its context everything that was said by the child. . . . The children work individually or in groups, as they choose; the groups are formed and then break up again without any interference on the part of the adult; the children go from one room to another (modelling room, drawing room, etc.) just as they please without being asked to do any continuous work so long as they do not themselves feel any desire for it. In short, these schoolrooms supply a first-class field of observation for everything connected with the study of the social life and of the language of childhood. . . .

Once the material was collected, we utilized it as follows. We began by numbering all the subject's sentences. As a rule the child speaks in short sentences interspersed with long silences or with the talk of other children. Each sentence is numbered separately. Where the talk is a little prolonged, the reader must not be afraid of reckoning several consecutive sentences to one number, so long as to each sentence containing a definite idea only one number is affixed. In such cases which are rare enough, the division is necessarily arbitrary, but this is of no importance for statistics dealing with hundreds of sentences.

Once the talk has been portioned out into numbered sentences, we endeavour to classify these into elementary functional categories (Piaget, 1955).

On the basis of these sentences Piaget proposes that the language of these children, who are both 6½ years old, may be classified as: monologue, repetition, commands, requests, questions, answers, etc. He notes that these categories are reliable since four different judges agree within three percent on the scoring. He then points out that all these categories can be subsumed under two broad classes which he calls *egocentric* and *socialized* language. In the former case the child does not address himself to anyone in particular nor does he know whether

Table 1-1. Total sentences used per category

| | Percentage of Subjects' Responses | |
Categories	Pie	Lev
Egocentric		
1. Repetition	2	1
2. Monologue	5	15
3. Collective monologue	30	23
Socialized		
1. Adapted information	14	13
2. Criticisms	7	3
3. Commands	15	10
4. Requests	13	17
5. Answers	14	18
Egocentric language	37	39
Spontaneous socialized language	49	43
Sum of socialized language	63	61
Coefficient of egocentrism	0.43 ± 0.06	0.47 ± 0.04

SOURCE: J. Piaget, The language and thought of the child. New York: Meridian, 1955.

he is being listened to, while in the latter case, the child exchanges his thoughts with others.

The results of about 1500 remarks for the two children, Pie and Lev, are summarized in Table 1–1. The figures represent the percent of the total number of sentences used in each category.

On the basis of data such as these, Piaget proposed a number of hypotheses and interpretations which have had considerable influence on subsequent research using methods other than the ones he described.

AGONISTIC BEHAVIOR IN WOODCHUCKS

The branch of biology which is called ethology has tended to rely largely on naturalistic observation as a method for gathering information. One example of such an ethological study is given by Bronson (1964) in his attempt to study agonistic (i.e., fight and flight) behavior in woodchucks.

Observations were made on a 10,000-acre area where woodchucks were living in natural populations. Seven small subareas were chosen for detailed observation, and, on each, five neighboring woodchucks were trapped, marked with dye, and released. Then, for a period of 3 to 4 weeks each subarea was observed by the experimenter during the morning and afternoon activity periods of the woodchucks. At the end of each minute of observation a notation was made of the location and type of behavior exhibited by each woodchuck observed. The observations were made from May to September, producing a total of 11,648 "minutes" of data.

After the observation periods were over, the woodchucks were retrapped and subjected to a paired competitive situation for water, in order to compare the dominance-subordination relationships determined in the laboratory with those seen in the field.

In this study, the categories of analysis were established

before the field observations were made and were based upon the prior decision to study only those behaviors which related to fighting or avoidance. Therefore such things as nuzzling, visual threat, vocalization, fighting, and social avoidance were all observed and recorded. In addition, signs of alerting with the head up or with the head down were also noted.

One of Bronson's observations was that there was only about one aggressive interaction per day for each animal, and that agonistic behavior accounted for only about four percent of the behavior of the woodchuck in the period after reproductive behavior had occurred. In contrast to this, in the laboratory tests using water competition, fights occurred in 50 percent of the encounters. This difference, it appeared, was largely related to the fact that subordinate animals simply avoided their dominant neighbors in the field. It is thus evident that laboratory studies alone do not permit generalizations to the natural setting unless there is an established relationship between the variables present in the laboratory and in the field. It is also worth noting that this study used a time-sampling plan; that is, recordings were made once every minute during each of the observation periods. A final point of interest in this study is the use of *both* field and laboratory techniques with the same population. This highlights the fact that these two methods of approach are supplementary and interrelated, and may often contribute valuable insights when used together. Another example of the interaction of theory, field description, and laboratory research may be found in Plutchik's discussion of the nature of emotion (1962).

BRAIN STIMULATION
IN MONKEY COLONIES

The overlap and interaction of laboratory and naturalistic studies are illustrated very nicely in a study by Delgado (1965). It has been known for some years that electrical stimulation of certain subcortical areas in the brain will evoke behaviors of various kinds, for example, flight, biting, attack, erection of the penis, eating of food, and vocalizations. When large animals such as monkeys are used in these studies they are usually kept fairly restricted to prevent them from pulling on the wires to their heads. In order to minimize limitations on an animal's freedom, Delgado developed a technique for stimulating the brain of an animal by the use of implanted intracerebral electrodes and small radio receivers mounted on the head or back of the animal. This allows stimulation of the brains of free-ranging animals in natural settings without the experimenter being present.

From an established colony of eight rhesus monkeys, Delgado selected four animals and implanted 12 electrodes in each animal in various subcortical areas. One of the selected animals was "boss" of the colony; that is, he was at the top of the dominance hierarchy. The selected animals were placed back into the colony one or two at a time for periods of four to ten weeks. Stimulation was carried out for five seconds every minute for an hour, but in some cases for as long as 14 days.

In order to measure and evaluate the complex social behavior of the colony, time lapse motion pictures were taken, that is, one frame was exposed every 10 or 15 seconds. When the film was later run at normal speed, a condensed but reasonably accurate record of the activities of the colony, both before and during stimulation, was obtained.

By the use of this technique of radio-controlled brain stimulation and time-lapse photography it was found possible to change the dominance hierarchy in the colony, to induce hostility between previously friendly animals, and to enable subordinate monkeys to modify the aggression of the "boss" by allowing them access to a lever controlling the radio stimulator.

The technique of radio telemetry undoubtedly holds great promise as a way of combining experimental manipulations and naturalistic observations.

THE PROBLEM OF SAMPLING BEHAVIOR

Since behavior is a more or less continuous matrix of actions and interactions, only through some kinds of analytic, abstractive processes can it be grasped, recorded, and understood. One aspect of this abstractive process is the use of categories of analysis; another is the use of sampling procedures.

Many different kinds of observational methods have been developed for obtaining data on complex social events; a number of the more common ones are summarized by Wright (1960) in the context of the study of child behavior and these are also relevant here. He describes several types of sampling plans which he calls *diary description, specimen description, time sampling,* and *event sampling.* These are outlined below on the basis of Wright's description.

Diary descriptions are designed to trace in sequence the procession of behavioral events including all that the observer can manage to record. In essence, the use of motion pictures and tape recordings are diaries which can be broken down later in any of a number of ways. Such records have been used mainly to study longitudinal day-to-day development and to provide the basis for extensive data collection in an area where the investigator does not have any strong presuppositions about what to look for.

Specimen descriptions are generally based upon a shorter time span than diary descriptions and refer to a particular context. It could be used, for example, to describe the free cage behavior of monkeys, or the process of interaction of pairs of animals. The records, however, must still be examined and categorized in some ways before they are useful.

Time sampling utilizes short time intervals (ranging from a few seconds to as much as twenty minutes) which are sampled at regular intervals. Descriptive categories are generally established in advance and judged during the sample period. One limitation of the method that has been suggested is that it can be meaningfully used only for events that happen fairly often, at least every 15 minutes on the average. A second limitation relates to the fact that certain sequences of behavior may last longer than the sample time period, thus producing judgments on "fragmented" sequences of behavior. A third criticism that is sometimes raised about the method is that it does not usually record situational factors as well as individual behavior. Despite these criticisms this general method has probably been used more frequently than any of the others.

Event sampling requires that a particular type of event such as aggressive acts, or fear reactions, be defined and that each such event that occurs within a given time period be recorded and described as fully as possible. This method is limited in that it is applied only to one or two types of behavior while all other types are ignored, but its advantages include the fact that natural units of behavior are examined and that it can be applied to events that occur quite infrequently.

Wright notes that the various sampling plans do not differ generally in terms of reliability of observer agreement, and that it has been found that broader, vaguer categories are not necessarily judged with less reliability than more specific, smaller items of behavior. From the descriptions given above it can be seen that any one or more of these sampling strategies may be used in studies of behavior in natural environments.

WHY CATEGORIZE?

The various examples that have been cited above emphasize the fact that scientists continually seek to establish meaningful categories for the description of events. What function do these categories perform?

In a general sense, the categories scientists use are designed to group large numbers of observations into a smaller number of classes. The more the members of the class have in common, the more satisfactory is the classification. People can be grouped by the color of their eyes, but this is related to very few other properties of a person. Whales, seals, and dolphins could be considered fish because they live in the ocean, but they have far more properties in common with mammals (e.g., warm blood and suckling of their young).

Sometimes categories are made too broad and many important differences are ignored. This is illustrated by the attempts to classify all people as introverted or extroverted, and the attempt to classify them by body types such as ectomorph, mesomorph, and endomorph.

Classifications are arbitrary to some extent and depend on the purposes of the scientist. For the fisherman, whales may be considered as fish, but this is not satisfactory for the marine biologist. The psychiatrist in a mental hospital may consider his patients in terms of such categories as schizophrenia and manic-depression, but such a system has little value for a psychologist who is director of personnel in a large business. A music teacher in a public school may be content simply with distinguishing the "listeners" from the "singers"; the same teacher in a music school might want to make much finer distinctions in musical talent.

However, it must not be assumed that categories are completely arbitrary. In many cases, they do reflect consistent natural groupings of properties and may thus be thought of as "laws." Metals tend to have different properties from nonmetals (although there is some overlap); the symptoms of tuberculosis tend to be different from those for malaria; and the expressive behavior in anger is different from that in depression.

Bruner *et al.* (1956) sum up the value of categorizing in the following ideas:

1. categories make the environment seem less complex;

2. categories enable us to label parts of our environment so that they seem more familiar;
3. categories reduce the need to learn new things each time we encounter a new situation since there are usually some relations between the new event and our older experiences;
4. categories help us to determine appropriate and inappropriate action in new situations;
5. categories enable us to relate different classes of events.

Categories also provide a basis for new research.

To illustrate some of these points we might consider studies that have been concerned with the social behavior of nonhuman primates (Plutchik, 1964). In this research there has been a tendency for each investigator to make up his own set of descriptive categories. Quite often no rationale for the selection was given, and sometimes the reliability of observations between different observers was not obtained. Some examples of suggested category systems for social behavior of primates are presented in Table 1–2. The number of categories used varies from five to eleven and the type of behavior considered also varies.

In the face of such variation, is there any way of justifying one category system rather than another? The answer to this question can only be tentative, but a number of possible criteria are available. In connection with primate social behavior studies, category systems will be of maximum value if (1) they use a relatively small number of categories, (2) they are based upon theoretical (rather than practical) considerations, (3) they have a wide range of possible application (throughout the mammalian kingdom, for example), (4) they are exhaustive, that is, are able to incorporate all existing data into the system, (5) they are reliable, and (6) they are sensitive to certain experimental operations, such as reinforcement, deprivation, or stress. Although these criteria are meant to be applied in the context of primate research, it is evident that most of them are relevant to any category system.

Table 1-2. Some suggested category systems for social behavior of primates

Chance, 1956	Scott, 1958	McDowell, Davis, and Steele, 1956	Mason, 1960	Hammack, 1960	Plutchik, 1962
Sounds	Ingestive behavior	Self-oriented units	Approach	Shifts in location	Incorporation behavior
Agonistic behavior	Agonistic behavior	Other-animal-oriented units	Aggression	Aggression	Destruction behavior
Display of dominance	Shelter-seeking	Inanimate-object-oriented units	Sexual presentation	Cage manipulation	Reproduction behavior
Copulatory behavior	Sexual behavior	Rapid-energy-expenditure units	Mount	Block manipulation	Orientation behavior
Play	Investigative behavior	Visual survey units	Play	Visual activity	Exploration behavior
Bathing	Care-soliciting behavior		Visual orientation	Self-grooming	Deprivation reactions
Grooming	Care-giving behavior		Groom	Resting	Protection behavior
Erotic behavior	Eliminative behavior		Social investigation		Rejection behavior
Running	Allelomimetic behavior		Thrusting		
Huddling			Social facilitation of exploration		
Social space			Withdrawal		

A SUMMING UP

Naturalistic studies, sometimes called field studies or clinical studies, are usually concerned with an accurate description of an individual's behavior as it is found to occur outside of the laboratory. They are concerned with relations between the individual and his environment as well as with relations between individuals. The ideal of such studies requires the observer to interfere as little as possible with the ongoing behavior. In attempting to carry through this aim, instruments are often used to extend the range of events observed, to record them more reliably, and to provide permanent records.

In an effort to make more manageable the continuous flow of behavior, the observer selects categories of events to be observed. These categories are selected either on theoretical grounds, practical grounds (e.g., ease of observation), or empirically by grouping observations that have something in common (as is done by factor analysis). In addition, various sampling plans are used to condense the total flux into a workable portion. Time sampling and event sampling are examples of such plans.

Naturalistic studies are important in that they provide us with some idea of the nature of the world as it exists. Barker and Wright (1955) point out that

Geologists, biologists, chemists and physicists know in considerable detail about the distribution in nature of the materials and processes with which they deal. . . . In contrast, psychologists know little more than laymen about the frequency and degree of occurrence of their basic phenomena in the lives of men—of deprivation, of hostility, of freedom, of friendliness, of social pressure, of rewards and punishments. Although we have daily records of the behavior of volcanoes, of the tides, of sun spots, and of rats and monkeys, there have been few scientific records of how a human mother cared for her young, how a particular teacher behaved in the classroom and how the children responded, what a family actually did and said during a mealtime, and how any boy lived his life from the time he awoke in the morning until he went to sleep at night.

As such observations are made, the observer begins to suspect possible relationships between variables. These variables may then sometimes be tried out in the laboratory. Knowledge of this sort will help decide whether the results of laboratory research can be validly generalized to the typical situation.

Another value of naturalistic studies is that they sometimes provide the basis for theories and broad speculations. The work of Freud was entirely clinical and his theories were based on inferences from observed behavior, yet there is little doubt that he has had considerable influence on modern psychology. Darwin's work was almost entirely descriptive, and yet evolutionary theory has become a firm basis for much of modern science. It seems to be true that theories affect men more than do facts, and bitter controversies are more likely to occur over differing theories than over differing facts. Perhaps it is because of the lack of control over variables or perhaps for other reasons, but observational studies seem more likely to engender broad theoretical speculations than do laboratory studies. To the extent that this is true, they provide a stimulant for further research.

One final point needs to be made. The distinction between naturalistic studies and laboratory studies is not always very sharp. For example, Piaget's naturalistic study of language development was done at a special private school for children where they were free to come and go and do whatever they pleased. This is certainly an "artificial" situation relative to the ordinary school classroom where the children are not free to talk or wander about and where classes are large in size. Similarly, Delgado's study of radio-controlled brain stimulation began with eight monkeys in a cage, certainly an unusual situation for most monkeys. Within these limitations, it was assumed that "normal" social relations would develop.

These remarks serve to point up the fact that we do not

have an unequivocal way of specifying what is natural and what is artificial since manipulations and restrictions of all sorts occur in everyday life. In a sense, experiments in Nature occur all the time. There are disasters, floods, wars, concentration camps, prisons, slums, large schools and small ones, segregated schools and desegregated ones. These kinds of situations provide natural laboratories of a sort, with interacting variables. Imaginative investigators using experimental and observational techniques may yet produce rich yields of data and theory from the study of such situations, just as astronomers and geologists have advanced their sciences by carefully observing naturally occurring events. Scott (1955) has emphasized this point in relation to studies of development in animals:

> While experiments are designed to test new ideas, new ideas rarely come from them. Many of the important psychological ideas come directly from clinical observation, and the most original discoveries come from the observation of a curious fact and the inevitable question, why should this happen? As observation is improved there should be a corresponding improvement in the quality and depth of psychological research.

2

EXPERIMENTATION AS A

DECISION-MAKING PROCESS

Science, as its name implies, is primarily knowledge; by convention it is
knowledge of a certain kind, the kind, namely, which seeks general laws
connecting a number of particular facts. Gradually, however, the aspect
of science as knowledge is being thrust into the background by the
aspect of science as the power of manipulating nature.
—BERTRAND RUSSELL

FOUR REASONS FOR DOING EXPERIMENTS

Besides the general aims which all experiments share, that
is, to increase our understanding of and our ability to control and
predict events, there are a number of specific reasons why an
experimenter might perform a particular experiment.

One basic reason experiments are done is simply to *determine the relations between two or more variables*. Sometimes this
is referred to as exploratory research, or as research designed to
determine the conditions under which certain events occur. Occasionally the impetus for beginning such a study is the appearance of new or improved technical instruments. If an investigator
is interested in the effects of rewards on learning, or the effects
of room color on mood, or the effects of the racial background of
an examiner on the IQ of children, he is studying the relation between two variables. He may study such questions because of
curiosity or because he thinks the answers may have practical

importance, or for any other reason. The gathering of such data in systematic ways is the primary function of experiments and it provides the basic data of the science of psychology. A theory can only be developed in the light of well-established empirical generalizations which experiments provide.

The second reason particular experiments are performed is *to extend the range of study of a variable.* Frequently in psychology studies are done under limited conditions; a stress condition might be compared with a no-stress condition, a drug might be given to see if anxiety is produced, visual threshold might be determined for white light only, or transfer might be measured for just one level of practice. In most such cases a negative finding could conceivably mean that the magnitude of the independent variable was not sufficient to produce an effect. More stress, more of a drug, more practice might produce positive results or unexpected findings. The completion of any experiment almost invariably poses further problems for exploration, even if it only means going beyond the limits already studied.

Frequently, new phenomena are discovered as one pushes beyond the usual limits of observation. For example, with small increases of muscular tension, learning is facilitated; with large increases, learning efficiency drops. For short periods after learning a task, a "reminiscence" effect sometimes occurs; with longer intervals recall decreases. Changing the color of the light used in a threshold experiment shows that the eye is maximally sensitive to green light and least sensitive to red. Such examples could be multiplied. Thus one of the important reasons for experimenting is to explore beyond a range already tested.

Another reason for experimenting is *to increase the reliability of reported findings.* This simply involves the exact replication of previously reported experiments. This is common practice in any science. When, for instance, a physicist several years ago reported the discovery of a magnetic unit of matter comparable to the electrical unit of matter, a dozen investigators throughout the country quickly repeated the experiments and within a relatively short time had shown that a misinterpretation had occurred in connection with the original data. Replication is a very important function of experiments, since one can never be certain that all possible precautions have been taken to avoid bias. If different investigators, using different samples of subjects, are able to verify a reported finding, confidence in that finding is greatly increased. This is a function of the scientist that should not be underrated or looked upon with scorn, since lack of replication is a common enough occurrence in psychology.

A fourth general reason for doing experiments is well recognized and that is *to test theory*. Many studies have been done in an effort to test psychoanalytic propositions, the views of Gestalt psychologists, and the concepts of reinforcement theory, as well as many other hypotheses. Quite often, attempts to test broad theories of the type mentioned above do not produce clear-cut results. The reason is that such theories tend to be rather vaguely formulated so that no crucial experiments can be performed. This is not too surprising, since most theories have value as sources of stimulation for research rather than as exact predictors of new facts. In this context it is important to remember the point made by Conant (1947) in his discussion of the history of science. He wrote, "A theory is only overthrown by a better theory, never merely by contradictory facts."

EXPERIMENTAL VERSUS CORRELATIONAL STUDIES

A great many studies have been done using what is called *correlational methods*. This means simply that the researcher tries to measure the relations between two or more phenomena that have been observed or measured. For example, a correlational study might determine the correlation between the IQs of identical twins or the relationship between success in college and certain personality traits. What these examples have in common is an acceptance by the investigator of whatever he finds. No attempt is made, as in experimental studies, to manipulate or change conditions.

A second characteristic of correlational studies is that the time sequence has no particular relevance. It makes no difference which twin's IQ is measured first, or whether the personality traits are measured before or after the college grades. By contrast, in an experiment the values of the independent variable (i.e., the one manipulated by the experimenter) are established and measured *before* the values of the dependent variable (i.e., the response measure) are determined. In order for an investigator to study the effects of drugs on mood, he must *first* administer specified amounts of drugs to the subjects and *then* measure the reactions.

A third point of distinction is the fact that a correlational study does not imply causation, whereas an experimental one does. The fact that cigarette smoking is correlated with frequency of lung cancer does not necessarily mean that it causes it. For example, it may be that people who smoke the most also live in the larger cities where smog and exhaust fumes exist in great concentrations, which in turn increase the chances of lung cancer. Perhaps heavy cigarette smokers have a diet which is different from that of nonsmokers again affecting the probability of illness. Because a large number of hypotheses are possible, any correlation does not enable a direct statement of cause. In a good experiment, it is possible to say that the conditions manipulated by the experimenter caused the reactions which were obtained.

This raises a fourth point of distinction between the two kinds of studies. If the correlation between two variables turns out to be high and reliable, then we can use this for prediction. For example, some employee aptitude tests will predict with a high degree of accuracy how well a person will do on a given job. These tests can be of great help in selecting or rejecting individuals for those jobs. However, they do not tell us what variables influence good or poor performance. Thus, their use is limited to choosing the proper person for a job.

To use another example, it is well known that school success is correlated with intelligence only to a limited degree and that emotional factors play a role. If we can learn in detail just what experiences bring the necessary emotional factors into play, we could presumably influence school success. In other words, by identifying the individual causal factors at work in a given situation, we gain increased control over our subject matter.

There is one further point that can be made with regard to the distinctions between experimental and correlational studies. To the extent that an experimenter can control the conditions under which an event occurs, he is prepared to make more accurate observations in contrast to an observer who simply records events as they occur. In addition,

Controlled conditions being *known* conditions, the experimenter can set up his experiment a second time and repeat the observations; and, what is very important in view of the social nature of scientific investigation, he can report his conditions so that another experimenter can duplicate them and check the data (Woodworth, 1938).

In correlational studies this is often not possible.

The differences that have been described do not mean that correlational studies are of no value; on the contrary, in some areas of research they represent the only ways of getting reliable information. This is particularly true in clinical, educational, and industrial psychology where the most common approach is to collect test, questionnaire, and rating data of various sorts and subject them to statistical analyses. In addition, correlational studies frequently suggest hypotheses that may be tested by means of experiments. This book, however, will be concerned primarily with experimental studies rather than correlational ones.

INDEPENDENT AND DEPENDENT
VARIABLES

Two concepts frequently used by psychologists are the *independent variable* and the *dependent variable*. The independent variable is usually defined as that factor or variable which is manipulated by the experimenter, such as amount of drug administered, level of electric shock used, or amount of food reward given. The independent variable can also refer to the absence of external stimulation, such as the amount of time an animal is deprived of food. The dependent variable is defined as the measured changes in the subject as indicated by his responses, for example, mood changes, frequency of avoidance responses, or speed of learning a task. These terms are widely used in the psychological literature in connection with the design of experiments, but the terms have been used in several different ways.

For example, in studies of maze learning, the subject learns to go through the maze to gain food reward. The subject reacts to such stimuli as the food object and the actual size and shape of the maze. But the animal's responses can be greatly modified by making him hungry, although the amount of hunger is not a stimulus in the same sense that the food reward is. Food deprivation is essentially the absence of stimulation, and yet the time of deprivation can be thought of as a variable. The food reward is a directly manipulated stimulus to the subject. In current usage, both the food and the deprivation time are conceived as independent variables.

It should be noted that the independent variable is only one sufficient condition among many which can affect the phenomenon being studied. For instance, maze learning will be affected to varying degrees by the size of the maze, as well as the amount of food reward that is given. In any experiment it may be possible to manipulate more than one variable at a time, and in such a case we would refer to two or more independent variables.

All experiments also require that certain conditions be kept constant. This is done, of course, for the very reason that these conditions might affect in some way the responses being measured. In most experiments, timing is carefully kept constant, apparatus is checked or calibrated, environmental conditions are kept fairly uniform, and any definitely known variables (other than those under study) are kept fixed at some value. It should be evident that the factors kept constant may all potentially change the response being measured, and, therefore, may all be thought of as *potential independent variables*. These factors that are kept constant are called *parameters*.

An important point to be remembered in this context concerns correlational studies. In such studies, we do not generally talk about independent and dependent variables since both of the recorded measures may be dependent on a third factor (just as changes of skin resistance and changes of heart rate may both be brought about by stress). From this point of view it would be incorrect to say that the IQ level of a group of parents is the independent variable in a study *correlating* parents' IQ with the IQs of their children.

In recent years, there has been a tendency to extend the terms independent and dependent variable to relatively broad, complex social situations. In such cases, it is often very difficult to specify in any detail the particular parts of the situation to which the subject is responding. There have been studies, for example, concerned with the effects of psychotherapy in which "type of therapy" has been called the independent variable. Since therapy may go on for years and involve a continuous interaction between the patient and the therapist, it is almost impossible without many detailed studies to talk about the specific conditions which bring about changes.

In conclusion, it may be said that the concepts of dependent and independent variables are useful, so long as we all learn to use the terms in the same way. As science progresses we discover more of the independent variables affecting and modifying the events with which we are concerned. At the same time we are enlarging our conceptions about the applicability of those ideas in a regular progression from the simple stimuli of the psychophysical world to the complex patterns of social interaction.

DECISION-MAKING IN EXPERIMENTATION

Experiments are generally performed in order to find out what causes events to happen as they do. If we can determine causes, we can often learn to arrange conditions so that the events we are interested in will occur whenever we wish. Successful experiments therefore increase our control over events.

The aim of establishing cause and effect connections is simple and clear, yet in practice it is often very difficult to be sure that we have been able to do this. Let us take a simple example from the folklore of psychology. Does a bull really get angry when he sees the color red? In order to answer such a question quite a few decisions have to be made. For example, we have to decide whether we mean all bulls or only certain breeds, and then we have to decide how many of each type to measure. Then we must choose some red objects. Should they be red sheets waved at the bull, colored pieces of cardboard, a red fence, or perhaps colored lights? The words *red* and *angry* have to be clearly defined. If an animal being tested reacts to a waving red cloth, we still have to make sure that he does not react the same way to a white cloth or a blue one, and obviously we cannot compare a blue fence with a red cloth. Furthermore, we have to match the colors for intensity so that we do not inadvertently compare light blue with dark red since a difference in brightness rather than in color could be the reason for a difference in behavior. It should be evident that a great deal of work and care would be necessary before we could unequivocally answer the question that was posed.

There are some general lessons that may be learned from this example. In any experiment whatsoever, an experimenter must make a series of decisions. These decisions concern such matters as how he defines the key concepts connected with his problem, how he selects subjects to be used, how he measures their behavior, what factors he keeps constant, what kind of statistics he uses, and how widely he generalizes his results. *All experimenters must make these kinds of decisions, explicitly or otherwise, in carrying out any experiment.*

Sometimes these decisions are made with full recognition of the implications; sometimes they are made simply as a matter of convenience, or by rules of thumb; and sometimes they are made implicitly without recognition of the implications. This is true whether the research deals with the influence of different schedules of reinforcement on behavior or with the problem-solving ability of small groups. What makes a man an expert in one field rather than another is that he is more aware of what factors to control, what variables are most effective, what kinds of definitions are most likely to be fruitful, and what kinds of measurements are most meaningful.

The preceding decisions have been given only for illustration. In the next section we will look more closely at the general types of decisions that are implicit in every experiment.

GENERAL CLASSES OF DECISIONS IN EXPERIMENTATION

The following descriptions are meant as a bird's-eye view of the kinds of decisions an experimenter makes from the time he conceives of a problem until he writes his final report of the research. The sequence listed here does not necessarily imply that the decisions are made in this exact order; there is a complex interaction between the different classes of decisions, and those made at any time automatically restrict or affect those made later.

Decisions about Definitions. Most of the theoretical terms of psychology have been defined in a number of different ways. For example, changes of motivation or drive are defined sometimes by the operations used to produce them, such as hours of deprivation, or by their effects on behavior, such as rate of bar pressing to acquire food. Motivation means one thing in a school situation, another in an industrial plant, and something else in a study done with lower animals. The use of different definitions sometimes prevents the different situations from being comparable and limits the generalizations possible from experiments.

It has occasionally been suggested that the use of "operational definitions" and "intervening variables" will solve some of these problems. However, many criticisms have been leveled at these philosophic points of view. Some interesting questions concerning the philosophy of science are implicit in this whole matter of choice of definitions and some of these will be examined briefly in Chapter 3 in order to clarify the issues involved.

Decisions about Sampling. In all experiments, decisions must be made about the number of subjects to be used and the number of measurements to be made. Is taking 100 measurements from one subject the same as taking a single measurement on 100 subjects? Why is it that in some areas of psychology such as vision and audition research, generalizations are based on just a few subjects, while in other areas of psychology such as personality research, reliable conclusions often require the use of dozens or even hundreds of subjects? What are the considerations that enable us to decide to use 2 or 200 subjects, 20 or 2000 measurements?

Decisions about the Type of Experiment. A great many of the experiments reported in the literature are concerned simply with a comparison of two conditions. Is school A better than school B in the teaching of reading? Does group discussion affect consumer buying more than formal lectures? Will psychotic behavior be decreased more by reserpine than by a placebo? Is the eye more sensitive to blue light than to red? Studies of this sort compare two conditions or compare an experimental with a comparison or control condition (or control group). They provide a limited insight into the question of whether a factor or variable is or is not affecting the behavior or event measured.

A second type of experiment attempts to extend the kind of study described above by comparing several different conditions instead of only two. Thus it might involve a study of the effect of different dosages of a drug on bar-pressing behavior, or the effect of different amounts of punishment on learning. A great deal more information is obtained from this type of experiment, and a functional curve or graph may usually be plotted showing the relation between the variables which are studied.

A third type of experiment extends the functional study described above by systematically varying one of the other factors which had previously been kept constant. This produces a family of curves rather than a single one. An example of this type of experiment might be a study of the effect of different dosages of drugs on skilled performance for various age groups.

All of these types of experiments have different properties with regard to (a) the possibility of making generalizations, (b) the applicable mathematical techniques, and (c) the appropriate design method. Chapter 4 will be devoted to this analysis.

Experimental Design Decisions.   In all research, decisions have to be made about the number of groups to use and in what sequence to study them. Sometimes groups or individuals are matched and then exposed to different conditions; sometimes random groups are used; and sometimes one group is studied under a variety of conditions. Each method that is used requires that certain assumptions be met. These assumptions vary for the different design methods. The explanation of these methods and assumptions is necessary, since different design methods do not always yield the same results.

Decisions about Measurement. There has been increasing recognition in recent years that the conclusions we draw from an experiment depend on what and how we measure. In learning and memory experiments, for example, the different measures used have different properties; theories which may be developed to account for one set of relations would therefore be unable to account for another set. This means that different experiments frequently are not directly comparable. For example, one investigator may measure learning in terms of the number of errors a subject makes, another by the speed or rate of response. The results of experiments using different measures of the same concept (such as learning) do not generally correlate in any simple fashion. Therefore, interpretations will vary. How one might choose the most adequate measure from a set of alternatives is a basic problem in doing experiments.

There is also the problem of the units of measurement. The kinds of statistical analysis permissible with a given set of numbers depend upon what sort of scale they represent. But how is an investigator to know whether a set of measurements that he makes represents a scale with equal units, and if it does not, how might he construct one?

Another important issue related to the problem of measurement concerns the properties of the instruments and apparatus used. Psychologists have come to depend to an increasing degree upon the instruments made for them by the engineers, particularly upon electronic equipment. These must be understood in order to be used properly. It is simply not sufficient to read numbers from a dial and assume that some psychological variable such as "emotionality" is being measured. The path from the black box to the person is a long one and must be carefully examined before meaningful conclusions may be drawn.

Statistical and Mathematical Decisions. In any study, the experimenter must make a decision on the way in which the specific information which has been gathered is to be handled.

What kinds of statistical analyses are to be used? Are the assumptions of the statistical methods met by the data? Shall empirical curves be fitted, or is there a theory which predicts a specific kind of outcome?

Some methods of analysis are much more general, or useful, or sensitive than others. It is necessary to understand the specific assumptions, uses, and limitations of the various statistical and mathematical methods in order to be able to use them intelligently. There have been cases in the history of science where a later investigator reanalyzed the data of a previous worker and discovered unsuspected relationships. The proper choice of mathematical technique is very important.

Decisions about Generalizing. Once the data have been gathered and analyzed, it is necessary to draw conclusions and implications from the findings and attempt explanations. The kinds of generalizations that are made depend upon the type of experiment that has been performed, the design method used, the sampling procedures followed, and the adequacy of the instruments used for measurement. They depend also upon the experimenter's concept of what an explanation is, and what he means by the term *lawful*. Philosophic assumptions of this sort are inseparably linked to the conclusions drawn from experiments.

SUMMARY

These seven broad classes of decisions implicit in experimental research provide a framework for considering the steps involved in research. Various chapters to follow will take up each of the major classes in turn and try to analyze the nature of the decisions to be made and their implications for research. Not all questions can be given a simple answer and some difficult and controversial problems will be raised. This is why experimentation today is partly an art.

DECISIONS CONCERNING

DEFINITIONS OF CONCEPTS

Too great haste in defining is almost as much a fault as failure to define at all; and there is a peculiar fallacy which attempts to bar the way to all fruitful discussion by remarking that "it is all a question of definition, and if the terms had been first defined, all this argument would be unnecessary." The remark is perfectly true, but it overlooks the fact that any fully adequate definition is the product of thinking, not its point of departure.

—JAMES E. CREIGHTON

Although science may start from common-sense ideas, the gathering of new information quickly creates the need for new concepts. These new concepts introduced into the language of science serve various purposes.

For one thing, *new terms are introduced in order to make old ideas more precise or more general*. In the early 1930s, Skinner, for example, introduced the terms *operant* and *respondent conditioning* to distinguish more precisely between several types of conditioning situations. The term *respondent conditioning* was to refer to those cases where the unconditioned stimulus (the food, or the electric shock) *elicited* a response which then became conditioned to a previously neutral stimulus. The term *operant conditioning* was to refer to those situations where the response to be conditioned was spontaneously *emitted* by the animal and then reinforced by some kind of reward.

35

A second reason for introducing new terms into the scientific language is for the *labeling of new observations*. Ethologists are zoologists who are especially interested in behavior which is specific to each species of animal. Since the turn of the century they have known that in order to cross certain species of wild birds, it is necessary to have the young of one species reared by the adults of the other. When these birds reach maturity they prefer to mate with birds of the same species as their foster parents. It was also discovered that many birds reared from birth by humans develop social responses to the human caretaker which are normally reserved only for their own species. This phenomenon was given the name *imprinting* and was later reported to occur in insects, fish, and some mammals.

New terms are also introduced into the scientific language *to provide a theoretical explanation of some observed fact*. Psychologists have known for a long time that the apparent extent of certain illusions decreases gradually as an observer continues to look at the figure. More recently, a new phenomenon was discovered which was also related to the inspection of certain geometric figures. For example, if an observer looks at a bent arrowhead for a few minutes and then fixates on a straight vertical line, he usually sees the line bent slightly in the opposite direction. This phenomenon is called a *figural aftereffect*. Some of the Gestalt psychologists have suggested that both the decrease in the magnitude of certain illusions and the figural aftereffects can be explained by assuming the existence of so-called *satiation currents* in the brain. The new term is designed to provide an explanation, in some sense, of certain observations.

The fourth reason new terms are introduced into the scientific language is *to conveniently summarize in one word several related concepts*. One of the important learning theories of the present time, developed by Clark Hull, uses the term *excitatory potential*. The greater an animal's excitatory potential, the greater the chances are that he will respond to an appropriate conditioned stimulus. It is assumed in the theory that this variable depends on the number of rewards an animal has had and on his state of drive. However, the term excitatory potential does not mean anything more than these particular variables which are interacting. It serves simply as a convenient summary word for these variables and can be dropped at any time and be replaced by them. Such a term, which is used only as a summary for a group of other terms, is usually called an *intervening variable*.

Some psychologists (MacCorquodale and Meehl, 1948) have suggested that such summary terms be distinguished from other kinds of theoretical terms which are meant to imply something "real." For example, does the concept *gene* refer only to certain observations which are conveniently summarized by the word, or does it refer to some underlying reality? Similarly, does a word like *memory* function simply as a summary term for certain kinds of observations, or does it imply certain underlying brain mechanisms or even more fundamental biochemical structures? If a concept is used in the latter sense, it should be called a *hypothetical construct* rather than an *intervening variable*.

This kind of distinction has actually been part of the history of physics since the last century (Plutchik, 1954) and is still reflected in current psychological usages. For example, a word like *drive* is sometimes used as a convenient summary word to describe certain procedures used in depriving experimental animals of food or water, but it is also sometimes used to refer to certain physiological changes inside the body. In the former sense it may be thought of as an intervening variable; in the latter, as a hypothetical construct. However, the essential criterion of the adequacy of any hypothetical construct is that its assumed properties can be measured and checked in several independent ways. For example, in the case of the concept of drive, it is possible to record changes in blood chemistry, stomach acidity, and muscular tension as independent measures of that state. If the independent measures corroborate the properties of the state being studied, this increases our confidence in the "reality" of the construct.

ON CHOOSING A DEFINITION

In this section we will examine several examples of decision-making problems associated with definitions. The first concerns the concept of *fear*.

In the many studies dealing with fear (sometimes labeled emotional response) there have been few attempts to specify its nature in general terms. Most investigators have simply chosen one particular method for producing or measuring this state and then performed all their experiments using the one method. Yet Miller (1957) has described eight different methods for producing or studying fear in animals. They are as follows:

1. Avoidance conditioning. In this method the animal is made to turn an activity wheel, or run from one box to another, or press on a bar in order to avoid a painful shock. The usual measures are the speed of response or the percent of avoidance responses made relative to the total number of trials.

2. Strength-of-pull. The animal tries to get away from a noxious stimulus and his strength-of-pull on a special harness is measured.

3. Sidman technique. The animal presses a bar in order to postpone the occurrence of a shock for a set period of time. Bar-pressing rate is measured.

4. Approach-avoidance conflict. A conflict is induced in the animal between the desire for food and the desire to avoid an electric shock.

5. Conditioned-suppression. A clicking sound is presented for a period and is immediately followed by the onset of electric shock. After some trials, the animal will decrease his rate of bar pressing during the clicking sound even though the shock is not given.

6. Startle technique. A signal is followed by a shock for a number of trials. On the test trials the shock is omitted and a sudden loud noise is given. The degree of startle measures the amount of conditioned fear.

7. Physiological measures. The animal's heart rate or skin resistance is recorded as a measure of fear.

8. Naturalistic observations. The spontaneous behavior of the animal is observed either under natural conditions or in a laboratory setting. Examples of flight and withdrawal behavior are noted.

In view of the existence of these many techniques for measuring or producing fear, which one should be used? In most cases, the key terms involved in any inquiry are usually general, theoretical terms. A concept like *fear* is a theoretical term implying some general state or condition of the body. This is also true for such concepts as learning, memory, hunger, thirst, psychosis, emotion, and drive. Such general states *cannot* be measured completely by a single index any more than a person can be completely described by a single personality trait. The very essence of a general concept is that there are many different ways in which the various aspects of it can be measured. Any one method is simply one index, or indicator, but it never can provide a complete understanding of the concept. Different indicators may sometimes even give apparently contradictory results.

An example of this is seen in a study by Miller *et al.* (1950) who compared several different indices of hunger drive in rats with lesions in the part of the brain called the hypothalamus. Rats with such lesions had been found in the past to develop obesity when they had free access to food. It was therefore assumed that such brain lesions produced increased hunger or appetite. However, when four different measures of hunger were used, a different picture emerged. Rats with hypothalamic lesions pressed the bar for food at a slower rate than control animals who were without any brain damage. They also ran more slowly to get food, and they were stopped by lower levels of electric shock. They also worked less hard than the control animals in order to get food. All these measures seemed to imply that rats with hypothalamic lesions were less hungry than the controls, even though they ate more when given free access to food. These findings suggested that the brain lesions produced a more complex state than one simply connected with hunger.

We must be careful to recognize that results obtained by use of only one measure are always tentative. Thus, learning has been measured by speed of response, number of errors, trials to reach a criterion, rate of response, percent of animals responding on a given trial, and magnitude of response. These measures do not correlate with one another in any simple way, and in addition, very few attempts have been made to determine their interrelationships. Although any one measure may serve as an indicator of learning, at best it will provide insight into only one aspect of the hypothetical state we call *learning,* just as any one method for measuring fear provides limited insight into its nature. Ideally, most studies should use multiple measures, even though this may be difficult from a practical standpoint.

This same general viewpoint has been proposed in connection with attitude measurement (Cook and Selltiz, 1964). Attitudes may be thought of as underlying *dispositions* that an individual has for acting in certain ways toward certain kinds of objects. An attitude cannot be measured directly any more than learning or emotion can, but it can be *inferred* on the basis of what an individual says or does in a variety of situations. Each question on a questionnaire or each test used may be thought of as an indicator or index of the attitude, but no one question is fully adequate alone. The investigator generally tries to combine the different answers or measures into a single index which then provides the best inference available at the moment.

This process of defining concepts in general terms and then looking for indices may be illustrated by one further example.

In recent years, a good deal of research has been directed at the nature of risk-taking attitudes in adults. Such attitudes have been measured in many different ways, for example, (a) by extremity of judgments, (b) by willingness to take risks in hypothetical military situations, (c) by preferences for jobs with high risks and large stakes, (d) by gambling behavior, (e) by questionnaire tests, and (f) by attitudes toward competitive sports. Any one procedure will measure risk-taking attitudes only to a limited degree. This is supported by the fact that several studies have shown that these different indices correlate only slightly (Slovic, 1964).

OPERATIONISM:
ITS HISTORICAL BACKGROUND

In their attempt to understand the language of science, philosophers and logicians have suggested that there are many types of definitions that are actually used. To take a simple example, we may use a dictionary definition to define a word by giving other terms which may be used to replace it. Thus, someone might say that a definition of the word *drive* is "motive" or "impulse," and that we may use these terms interchangeably. Such dictionary definitions may be helpful in some cases and not in others, depending on the context.

Far more important in the thinking of psychologists are *operational* definitions. These definitions seem to play an important role in discussions of the philosophy of science, and the concept itself has an interesting origin and history.

In 1927, a physicist named Bridgman wrote a book called *The Logic of Modern Physics,* in which he discussed the philosophic significance of Einstein's theory of relativity. In his book, he indicated that physicists had been embarrassed by Einstein's theories because the theories had called for some fundamental revisions in thinking about old concepts which had been taken for granted. Bridgman then proposed a solution which he hoped would prevent such a revolution in our thinking in the future.

He proposed that our concepts should be defined by the operations we use to measure them. For example, he said, "The concept of length involves as much as and nothing more than the set of operations by which length is determined." This apparently simple idea actually has some far-reaching implications. It means, for example, that if we measure something in two different ways, we actually have two different concepts. This would imply that if we measured the temperature of an object by a mercury thermometer and also by an electric resistance thermometer, we would actually be measuring two different kinds of temperature. Similarly, it would mean that if we measured the intelligence of a person by two different tests we would be measuring two different kinds of intelligence. Furthermore, if someone requested a definition of intelligence, it would be sufficient simply to say "Intelligence is what my test measures."

This idea of Bridgman's, to define concepts by the operations used to measure them, seemed to appeal to psychologists. During the 1930s and 1940s they wrote about *operationism* (as this point of view came to be called) with great enthusiasm. They claimed that operational definitions of terms would help us avoid contradictory notions and hazy ideas and would lead to clarity and precision in our thinking.

After a number of such favorable reports had appeared, a reaction set in and several philosophers began to criticize this general point of view. Unfortunately, by this time operationism had already developed several different versions, and it was not always clear toward which one the criticisms were directed.

One point of view that developed proposed that operationism meant that the statements of scientists are valid only insofar as we can verify their truth by means of certain operations. Later on Bridgman himself (1950) decided that the word *operation* could refer not only to actual physical measurement procedures, but also mental, or paper-and-pencil operations; in other words, to the theoretical and computational procedures scientists actually use. What this means, simply, is that the physicist does not take his raw data at face value. In most instances, the raw data consist of numerical readings on dials. These readings are then assumed to measure the properties of certain unobserved structures such as electrical charges or nuclear forces, usually on the basis of complex theoretical or mathematical procedures. Raw data are often entered into equations which provide new hypothetical quantities.

A sociologist named Lundberg, in 1939, enthusiastically stated that by using only physical operations in defining concepts we could avoid "metaphysical problems" in science. In 1945, at a symposium devoted to the problem, Skinner proposed that "Operationism may be defined as the practice of talking about (1) one's observations, (2) the manipulational and calculational procedures involved in making them, (3) the logical and mathematical steps which intervene between earlier and later statements, and (4) nothing else." He also added, "Operationism is not regarded as a new theory or mode of definition." This last note was echoed by Feigl, a philosopher who participated in the 1945 Symposium on Operationism. He wrote, "Operationism is not a system of philosophy. It is not a technique for the formation of concepts or theories. It will not by itself produce scientific results." This sample of comments on operationism suggests that it has become a somewhat ambiguous idea to psychologists.

Another variant of operationism has centered around the question of whether an operational definition describes operations needed to *measure* a concept or operations needed to *produce* a phenomenon. How, for example, can we operationally define a "chocolate cake"? Using Bridgman's original ideas we would describe the operations used to measure the properties of the chocolate cake: its texture, color, taste, and so on. However, some writers on the subject have suggested that an operational definition can be given by simply providing a recipe for baking the cake. To take a psychologically relevant example, the word *drive* may be operationally defined by some measures of the behavior of a hungry animal, such as his restlessness, his bar-pressing rate to get food, etc. On the other hand, it might also be defined in terms of the procedures that have been used to produce a state of hunger, such as keeping the animal deprived of food for a certain number of hours. Now, although these two kinds of procedures may be related, they are not necessarily equivalent. One philosopher (Benjamin, 1955) has objected to the latter method of defining on the grounds that "operationism is a device for creating and defining *concepts*, not for producing *things*."

During the past few years, a number of criticisms of operationism have been advanced (Plutchik, 1963). Some of the more important of these will be briefly summarized here.

CRITIQUE OF OPERATIONISM

MEASUREMENT PRESUPPOSES A CONCEPT

Operational definitions have often been illustrated by examples of the following sort, "Intelligence is what an intelligence test measures." Actually, this is a very inadequate way of defining any concept, because it can produce results which are obviously meaningless. This was shown by Adler (1947) in terms of his so-called C_n test, which he operationally defined by the answers to a series of questions, as follows:

1. How many hours did you sleep last night? _____
2. Estimate the length of your nose in inches and multiply by 2. _____
3. Do you like fried liver? (Mark 1 for Yes and −1 for No.) _____
4. How many feet are there in a yard? _____
5. Estimate the number of glasses of ginger ale the inventor of this test drank while inventing it. _____

Add the above items. The sum is your crude C_n score. Take the test daily at the same hour as long as you can. Then calculate your refined C_n rate by . . .

It is obvious that such a test does not make sense, regardless of the statistical formulas used or methodological refinements involved in the statement of items or categories of analysis. The statement that "C_n is what the test measures" is not satisfactory on the two grounds that we are unable to form any meaningful concept of it, and that all criticism is excluded, since "The test measures C_n and C_n is what the test measures." It is also clear that an infinite number of such "tests" could be formed in this arbitrary way. Operationism provides no basis for distinguishing between meaningful and meaningless concepts.

Before we can adequately measure anything, we need to know, at least in general, what we want to find out, even if there is some vagueness to our concept. Science develops its measuring tools, typically, by a series of successive approximations in which the concept gradually achieves greater precision, the ambiguities are eliminated, and the relations between the concept and other concepts are more clearly formulated. Observation and measurement presuppose objects with properties as well as previous theory. We never start from operations.

This means, for example, that before we can measure the length of something we need to have some idea that a ruler is appropriate for such measurement rather than, say, a magnet. Similarly, we form an idea of what we mean by a concept like *habit strength* before we measure it, and then we recognize that several different kinds of indicators, such as number of errors made, or speed of response, can all measure habit strength. Sometimes these different indices do not correlate very well, but operationism does not provide any basis for selecting which is a "better" measure.

THE PROBLEM OF GENERALITY

Several critics have raised the question of whether operationism does not make all general concepts impossible since even the smallest variation in the procedure of measurement would imply a new concept. Does the concept of *length* change if we measure the length of an object by a micrometer rather than a wooden ruler? Is *heat* different if it is measured by a mercury thermometer rather than a thermocouple?

Such variations in procedure are commonplace in science, and yet it is generally believed that these different procedures or operations are designed to measure the same concept. It is also recognized that certain sources of error may operate for one measuring procedure that do not operate for another. These sources of error are gradually discovered and eliminated, and the different measurement procedures converge to produce a single consistent answer.

Operationism literally interpreted would imply that the use of many different methods to determine the properties of the synapse, for example, means that many different and unrelated concepts are being studied. This, of course, is contrary to the spirit of the whole series of observations made in connection with this problem. If there are many independent operational definitions, how is it possible to arrive at general constructs? The fact is that most scientists are interested in finding general explanations and general concepts that will account for a large number of apparently isolated or unrelated observations in terms of a small number of terms or constructs. Operationism, literally interpreted, would move science in the opposite direction, greatly increasing the number of unrelated concepts and actually providing a new concept for each new kind of measurement. Such a situation would make scientific teaching and prediction very difficult.

THE PROBLEM OF ERROR

The fact that in actual scientific practice there are often several ways of measuring a given phenomenon poses several problems for the operationist. One concerns the problem of equivalence of operations, but a second question which arises is whether one measure is in some sense "better" than any other. To be able to judge the relative value of measurements or of operations requires criteria beyond the operations themselves. If a concept is nothing but an operation, how can we talk about being mistaken or about making errors? If *heat* stands for certain measurement procedures, there is no sense in talking of better ways of measuring it or of being mistaken in such measures. Similarly, from a definition such as "intelligence is what the IQ tests measure," one cannot construct a new test or judge how good the old one is.

One of the facts of science is a continuous tendency to modify existing methods of measurement so that certain properties can be evaluated with greater and greater precision. New instruments and new designs are continuously being developed, yet we do not identify the concept being measured with the measurement procedure or instrument being used. If we did, then improvements and changes of method would produce new concepts, which they generally do not.

Over the past half century, skin resistance, or the galvanic skin response, has been measured with dozens of different instruments using different circuits, designs, and procedures, and although many of these operations have had various sources of bias associated with them, the common element which binds all this research together is the fact that the particular concept *skin resistance* is being measured. As science develops the sources of error are gradually eliminated. Operationism has never adequately taken into consideration this problem of the improvement of measuring procedures and the elimination of error. Feigl (1945) has pointed out that thermometers and IQ tests did not arise in an historical vacuum, but that there were repeated redefinitions. "It makes perfectly good sense to ask whether a mercury thermometer measures temperature adequately." The same, of course, may be asked of psychological measurements.

THE PROBLEM OF THEORETICAL TERMS

The criticisms raised against operationism under this general heading are of three sorts: (a) very few terms have in fact been operationally defined, (b) some theoretical terms *cannot* be operationally defined, and (c) some terms can be operationally defined which are not usually thought to be included in the scientific universe of discourse.

Considering the first point, it has been noted that there is actually a dearth of illustrations in the literature of operational definitions of terms, and that the few examples usually given, such as "Intelligence is what the intelligence test tests," are not fair samples of the terminology of psychologists. Very few, if any, attempts have been made to define operationally such currently used terms as *field, synapse, emotion, cognitive map, Oedipus complex, drive, superego,* etc. Almost none of the terms in any dictionary of psychology are defined operationally.

That there are some meaningful concepts which are not operationally definable is also clear. Many of the terms used in science refer to ideal states such as perfect gases, point masses, frictionless engines, instantaneous velocities, etc., which represent the limiting condition of an infinite series of approximations. Mathematical concepts used in science also often refer to conditions not realizable in the actual world; this is illustrated by the concepts of the calculus which use notions relating to infinity. In addition to this, there are concepts employed in science which cannot be measured by currently available techniques; for example, the earth's core, the neurophysiological basis of memory, the fossil link between man and the higher primates, etc., yet these concepts are not meaningless or invalid (Ginsberg, 1955).

In relation to the third point, it may be said that the way operationist thinking has developed, it is possible to "operationally define" almost all the terms of our language, even those usually called metaphysical. Operationists have extended the term to include paper and pencil, mental, and logico-mathematical operations, which dilutes operationism to such a degree that almost anything a scientist does to get knowledge can be included. Even a metaphysician uses mental operations, and *God* and the *soul* can be defined in these terms. Feigl also notes (1945) that such a broad definition of operationism can be applied to the speculations of theology and metaphysics. It is not evident that operationism can avoid or solve metaphysical questions as has sometimes been claimed.

IMPLICATIONS

The preceding remarks have been meant to indicate some of the problems implicit in the classical operationist position which has undoubtedly claimed too much. It is possible, however, to accept an important idea contained in this view, and that is that *all experimental and theoretical reports should be as explicit as possible in describing the methods used to obtain and analyze the data.* The methods section of any experiment should be clear enough and complete enough so that the experiment can be duplicated from that description alone (or with the aid of other published references). That the description of the experiment is clear and unequivocal does not mean that the concepts used in the experiment are nothing but the measurement operations. The concept always comes first, and then certain procedures (or operations) are selected from a larger possible number and used as *indicators* of the concept.

It is not consistent with actual usages in science for a particular investigator to simply say that his method of measuring something provides an operational definition. If this were done, then each investigator might have his own private operational definition of each concept and communication between researchers would completely break down. *In practice, each scientist's procedures for measuring concepts must relate in some reasonable way to the work of other investigators as well as to the history of that idea.* Science is basically a highly social enterprise in which new developments in knowledge are almost completely dependent upon the existing state of knowledge. This is why scientists are always eager to disseminate their findings and why they continually maintain communication with other scientists through journals and other channels.

The actual definitions used in psychology, or any other science, may be any one or more of a large number of types, because scientists introduce concepts into the scientific language by a variety of procedures. Textbooks of logic often distinguish a whole variety of types of definitions, for example, verbal, heuristic, operational, genetic, real, classificatory, extensive, intensive, systematic, circular, coordinating, dictionary, and literary. [The complexity of the problem of what a definition is and which one to use may be seen in the paper by Scriven (1958).]

Scientific dictionaries do not generally use operational definitions; they more often define concepts by the use of theoretical terms or by listing properties associated with the concept. The desire to be precise and restricted may unnecessarily limit the productiveness of research. It is interesting to note that early in the present century, Sigmund Freud made a statement that is quite relevant. He wrote:

The view is often defended that sciences should be built up on clear and sharply defined basal concepts. In actual fact no science, not even the most exact, begins with such definitions. The true beginning of scientific activity consists rather in describing phenomena and then in proceeding to group, classify and correlate them. . . . It is only after more searching investigation of the field in question that we are able to formulate with increased clarity the scientific concepts underlying it, and progressively so to modify these concepts that they become widely applicable and at the same time consistent logically. Then indeed, it may be time to immure them in definitions.

SUMMARY

Just as there are many different reasons for introducing new terms into the language of science, so there are many different types of definitions. In most cases, the key concepts involved in experiments (e.g., learning, motivation, attitudes, etc.) are theoretical terms referring to general states of the body or inferred conditions. Such general states cannot be measured by a single indicator, but require many separate indices in order to provide a fairly complete understanding of the concept which has been defined.

Some psychologists have stressed the importance of operational definitions. Although some important ideas are implied by this notion, many criticisms have been directed at *operationism* and its claims. The major criticisms were presented and the point was emphasized that although the measurements used in any experiment should always be clearly stated and explained, it is not the case that the concepts used in the experiment are *nothing but* the procedures of measurement. Measurements are usually partial indicators of theoretical constructs. The use of different indicators of a concept often provides increased insight into its nature.

4

TYPES OF EXPERIMENTS

The uniformly certain and completely universal laws of science can be realized only in the carefully guarded conditions of the laboratory and are never found in the world outside.
—NORMAN CAMPBELL

One of the decision-making problems any scientist faces when starting an experimental investigation concerns the type of experiment to be performed. The expression *type of experiment* refers essentially to the problem of the number of variables to be manipulated and to the number of values of each variable to be used. Thus it is possible to perform an experiment designed to compare two methods for learning French verbs or, in contrast, to develop a functional relation between two variables, such as is illustrated by Weber's law. Weber's law simply states that the relative sensitivity of a sense organ is approximately the same at all intensities of stimulation. Differences in the type of experiment performed lead to different design methods used and different analyses of the data, as well as to differences in the possibility of generalizing. This chapter will describe three types of experiments, their functions, properties, and limitations.

BIVALENT EXPERIMENTS

A type of experiment frequently performed in psychology is one in which two conditions are compared. The effects of "success" on a task may be compared with those of "failure," reinforcement with nonreinforcement, drugs with the absence of drugs, electric shock against no shock, "authoritarian" families with "democratic" ones. All these studies involving a comparison of two conditions, or two points, may be called *bivalent* (i.e., two-valued) experiments. Andrews (1948) has suggested that such experiments are most useful at the beginning of a series of studies in that they help identify important variables or factors which may be examined more systematically later on. There are, however, certain serious shortcomings in this type of experiment which greatly limit the kind of conclusions that may be drawn from them. These points will be illustrated by some examples.

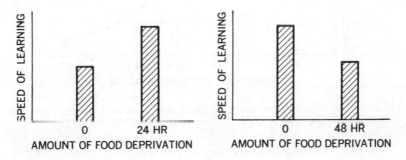

Fig. 4-1. (left) A hypothetical illustration of a bivalent experiment: speed of learning a task under two conditions of food deprivation.
Fig. 4-2. (right) A hypothetical illustration of a bivalent experiment: speed of learning a task under two conditions of food deprivation.

Suppose a bivalent experiment is contemplated dealing with the effect of food deprivation on speed of performance. Assuming everything is carefully done, the results may look somewhat as shown in Fig. 4-1. The bar graph shows quite clearly that 24 hours of food deprivation leads to an increase in speed of performing some given task. If the difference is significant, the result may be quite reliable. The experimenter is often tempted in such a case to say, "Speed of performing increases with amount of food deprivation."

Suppose, however, that another investigator unknown to the first tried this experiment in exactly the same way except for one slight modification: he used 48 hours of food deprivation instead of 24. His results might look somewhat as shown in Fig. 4-2. If the difference is significant, this investigator would be tempted to conclude, "Speed of performing decreases with amount of food deprivation."

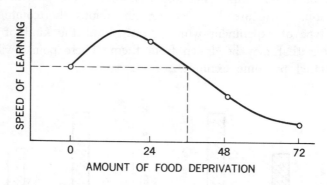

Fig. 4-3. A hypothetical curve showing the relation between speed of learning a task and amount of food deprivation.

Both investigators may be said to be guilty of *overgeneralization*. The data may be reliable for each limited set of conditions, and yet both investigators could arrive at opposite conclusions. Such a situation might occur any time the relation between two variables is *nonlinear*; i.e., when it cannot be represented accurately by a straight line. Figure 4-3 shows such a nonlinear relationship.

A number of interesting facts may be determined from Fig. 4-3. If a food deprivation period of about 36 hours had been chosen instead of the other values, then *no* difference between the two conditions would have been found. Any deprivation time up to 36 hours produces an increase in speed of performing whereas any deprivation time after 36 hours produces a decrease in speed of performing. Thus, the conclusions drawn from the experiment depend on the arbitrary choice of the particular comparison conditions. Since, in any exploratory study, the experimenter does not know the shape of the total curve, any decision about conditions must be an arbitrary one. Quite obviously, if the results show no significant difference between the two conditions being compared, this does not necessarily mean that there is no relationship between the two *variables*. In any U-shaped or inverted U-shaped curve, there are many pairs of points which are at the same height. This means that there are many possible comparisons that would show no differences. Therefore, negative findings in bivalent experiments are never conclusive; positive findings are usually ambiguous.

There is another aspect of the problem. In many studies a comparison is made of a high condition with a low condition, for example, a high anxiety group with a low anxiety group, a high shock condition with a low shock condition, highly permissive parents with slightly permissive parents. The same general problems exist here as before, but in addition the following problem may arise. Many relations between variables show a plateau or *asymptote*. This is indicated by the portion of the curve between B and C in Fig. 4-4. If the high and low anxiety conditions in our example happen to fall along the asymptote, no difference between the two conditions will be found. If they happen to fall somewhere between A and B, then the experimenter will be tempted to conclude that an increase in anxiety leads to an increase in speed of performing.

Thus it may be seen that bivalent experiments are particularly subject to two dangers: (a) concluding that no relation exists between two variables being compared when in fact all that has been demonstrated is that no difference exists between two conditions; and (b) concluding that the effect of one variable on another is to cause an increase (or a decrease) when, in fact, this is true only over a small portion of the total curve. The actual relationship may be nonlinear and asymptotic. Both these dangers relate to the tendency to overgeneralize.

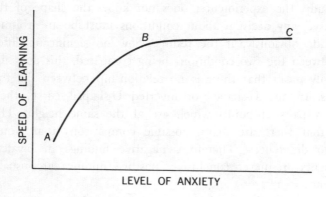

Fig. 4-4. A hypothetical curve showing the relation between speed of learning and level of anxiety.

Another important point to be made about bivalent experiments is the fact that they give limited information about the relationship between two variables. If we discover that students of school A tend to get better grades than those in school B, or that a person can learn a poem faster with 10-minute rest periods than with 1 minute ones, there is very little else that we can add. Such findings will presumably indicate that the condition tested affected the dependent variable, but accurate interpolations are hardly possible. In other words, since one of the aims of science is to develop a body of laws or principles and theories which cover as wide a realm of phenomena as possible, we try to use the specific findings of any one experiment as a basis for *generalizing* to conditions and values not yet tested. We try to *predict* the outcome of untried experiments. In order to be able to do this with some hope of success, it is necessary to go beyond the simple bivalent experiment and to determine the functional relation between the two variables. This can be approximated more satisfactorily by means of a multivalent experiment.

MULTIVALENT EXPERIMENTS

The term *multivalent* experiment is used synonymously with the term *functional* experiment. Such experiments are designed to determine the relation between two variables and require that at least three values of the independent variable be used. This is because at least three points are necessary to determine the shape of a curve. The more points that are employed, however, the more reliable the resulting curve is likely to be, although only five to seven values of the independent variable are typically used.

Figure 4-5 is a graph illustrating a functional or multivalent experiment showing the relationship between learning time and amount of material to be learned. In this experiment, seven values of the independent variable were used: 8, 12, 16, 24, 32, 48, and 72 syllables in a list. These seven values actually represent a sample taken from a potentially unlimited range of values of the independent variable. Thus it would be possible to repeat the experiment with lists of 4 items, or 14, or 55, or 155. The experimenter is generally as interested in these other values as he is in the particular ones he selected. Since we assume that there is a continuous relationship between the independent and dependent variables, a continuous line can be drawn connecting all the points in the simplest way possible. From such a continuous curve it is possible to *interpolate* an estimated learning time for any amount of material, including those values not directly tested. It is also possible to make an estimate or prediction of the value of learning time for a syllable list either shorter or longer than the original range of values.

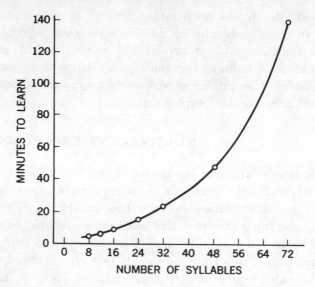

Fig. 4-5. The relationship between learning time and number of syllables to be learned. (Adapted from T. G. Andrews, 1948.)

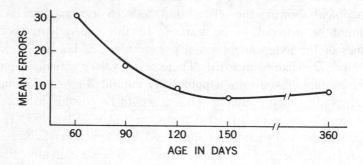

Fig. 4-6. Learning as a function of age in terms of errors before attaining the learning criterion on initial discrimination problem. (Adapted from H. F. Harlow, **et al.,** 1960.)

Figures 4-6 and 4-7 present two illustrations of multivalent experiments taken from the psychological literature. Figure 4-6 shows the mean number of errors in learning a discrimination problem made by groups of monkeys differing in age. The curve is quite smooth and regular and would enable an interpolation for any other age group that has not been tested. For example, a group of monkeys 75 days old would be expected to make an average of about 22 errors in learning this task. In fact, from the curve it is possible to estimate (or interpolate) the mean errors for any group between the ages of 60 and 360 days.

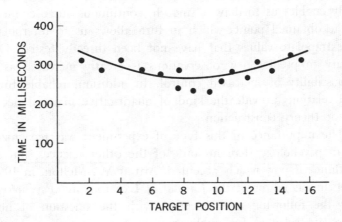

Fig. 4-7. Reaction times to each of the targets in a 16-alternative task. Data are for one **S**. The curve is fitted by eye. (Adapted from P. M. Fitts, 1954.)

It is possible to go one step further. The curve is so regular that an estimate of performance of 40-day-old animals can be made, as well as that of animals 400 or more days old. These *extrapolations* beyond the range of data originally tested must be made with some caution, but they can be made. In general, the further the extrapolation the greater the possibility of error.

Figure 4-7 shows the reaction time to each of the targets in a task having 16 alternatives. The curve that is drawn is called a best-fitting curve for the obtained data. This best-fitting curve is usually drawn in such a way that there are as many points on one side of it as on the other, and the sum of the distances from the points to the line on both sides are equal. This idea will be discussed in greater detail in Chapter 7. On the basis of this multivalent curve, interpolations and extrapolations may be made just as was done in the previous case.

Multivalent or functional types of experiments are of fundamental significance to experimental psychology. When we compare a whole series of conditions, we are, in essence, sampling the independent variables over a wide range of values. This usually enables us to draw a smooth, continuous curve connecting the obtained points which in turn allows us to interpolate and extrapolate values that have not been directly tested. Our capacity to predict new observations is greatly increased as is the possibility of increased control. In addition, reliable functional relations provide the kind of quantitative material necessary for theory construction.

The importance of this type of experiment was recognized later in psychology than in some of the other sciences, but its importance is now widely accepted. Arthur W. Melton, in 1962, on retiring as editor of the *Journal of Experimental Psychology,* wrote the following in connection with the question of how articles are selected for publication in that journal:

. . . The investigation should not merely identify the effect of a variable, but should move beyond that simple demonstration to either the determination of a *function* relating levels of the variable to levels of the effect or the assembly of further information about the demonstrated effect. . . . We believed that the day of the archival report based on a simple experiment with an experimental and control group or with a 2 x 2 design was past in many mature areas of psychological research, and that each published report should make a more substantial contribution to the problem. In particular it seemed desirable for experimental psychology to move toward the determination of quantitative functional relationships between independent and dependent variables, especially since so many of these quantitative relationships in behavior turn out to be nonmonotonic.

In the light of these various considerations and comments,

it seems that in many areas of psychology bivalent experiments are rarely defensible and should, if possible, be avoided. The extra time and effort needed to do a multivalent experiment is amply repaid by the gain in unequivocality and by the increased prediction that is made possible.

PARAMETRIC EXPERIMENTS

This type of experiment is a further extension of the multivalent experiment. If the latter is conceived of as two-dimensional because it relates two variables, then the parametric experiment may be described as three-dimensional because it interrelates three variables. The term *parameter* is borrowed from the field of mathematics, where it refers to a constant in a given equation, but one which may have different values. The different values of the parameter produce a family of curves.

In order to apply this concept to psychological research, it must first be recognized that all experiments keep some conditions constant while the relation between the independent and dependent variables is explored. For example, to study the relative sensitivity of the eye at different intensities of light, the duration of the flash of light used is kept constant at some value (e.g., half a second). To study the relation between serial position of a group of nonsense syllables and the speed with which each one is learned, the amount of trials used is kept constant. At any one flash duration or for any given number of trials, a functional relation will be obtained. However, at a different flash duration or for a different number of trials, a different functional relation will be obtained. This will usually produce a family of curves as shown in Figs. 4-8 and 4-9.

Each family of curves shows the connections between three variables. In Fig. 4-8, the variables are relative sensitivity of the eye (the dependent variable), intensity of light used (independent variable) and duration of light flash (independent variable). In Fig. 4-9, the variables are percent correct anticipations

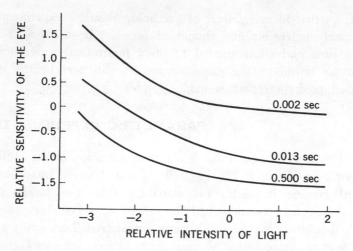

Fig. 4-8. The relative sensitivity of the eye as a function of the intensity of light used (logarithmic units). Each curve is based upon a different duration of the flash of light. (Adapted from C. H. Graham and E. H. Kemp, 1938.)

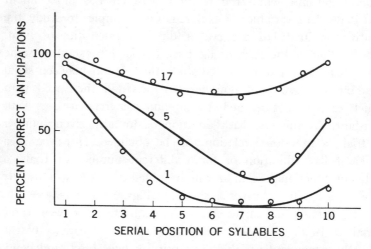

Fig. 4-9. The learning of nonsense syllables as a function of the serial position of the syllables. Each curve is based upon a different number of trials used. (Adapted from E. S. Robinson and M. A. Brown, 1926.)

(dependent variable), serial position of the nonsense syllables (independent variable), and number of trials (independent variable). These relations may also be represented by a three-dimensional type of figure as illustrated in Fig. 4-10. This graph

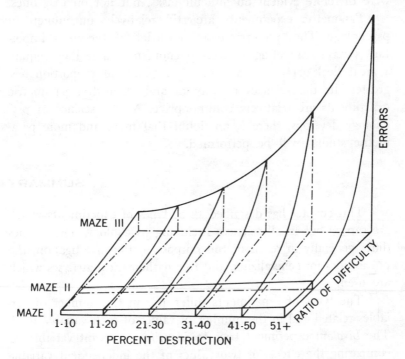

Fig. 4-10. A three-dimensional graph showing how the errors made in a maze depend upon both the difficulty of the maze and the amount of cortical damage that has occurred (Adapted from K. S. Lashley, 1929.)

is based on the classic study by Lashley in which he destroyed various amounts of cortical tissue in rats and tested them on mazes of different degrees of difficulty. The dependent variable was the number of errors made, while the two independent variables were the percent of the cortex destroyed and the relative difficulty of the maze. Figure 4-10 should be thought of as a three-dimensional solid. It shows at a glance how the three variables are interrelated. It shows that performance on easy mazes was about the same for all degrees of cortical damage, but that performance rapidly grew worse (increased errors) as the maze became more difficult. The effects of brain damage were therefore evident on difficult tasks, but not on easy ones.

Parametric experiments are still relatively uncommon in psychology. They presuppose a knowledge of the most important variables affecting a given phenomenon, and they require a great deal of time and effort, but gains are proportionately greater. In the sciences of physics and chemistry, parametric experiments are relatively commonplace. As the science of psychology develops, there is no doubt that more and more parametric studies will be performed.

SUMMARY

This chapter has described three types of experiments which are carried out in all sciences including psychology. These types differ generally in terms of the purpose of the investigation, the possibilities for generalizing, and the mathematical analyses which are used.

The types of experiments differ also in the number of variables related and in the number of values of each variable used. The *bivalent* experiment tries to *identify* a relevant variable by comparing the effects of two values of the independent variable on the dependent variable. If a change in one produces a significant change in the other, then a factor has been located. Generalizations from bivalent experiments are greatly restricted. A further extension is the *multivalent* experiment utilizing three or more values of the independent variable in order to determine the functional relationship between two factors. This greatly increases prediction by allowing more meaningful interpolations and extrapolations. When one of the conditions held constant in a multivalent experiment is systematically varied, that is, kept constant at a new value, while the multivalent experiment is repeated, a family of curves is obtained. Such a three-dimensional structure is called a *parametric* experiment and from it maximum information is obtained with which generalizations can be made. Other chapters will describe the specific experimental and mathematical procedures used with each of these types of experiments.

5

SAMPLING IN

EXPERIMENTAL RESEARCH

Proper sampling of situations and problems may in the end be more important than proper sampling of subjects, considering the fact that individuals are probably on the whole much more alike than are situations among one another
—EGON BRUNSWIK

One of the most important aims of the research scientist is to be able to make general statements about the events he studies. This is simply another way of saying that the scientist is usually interested in finding "laws." Although rats may be used as subjects, the researcher will usually say that he is interested in the "laws of learning," and although college sophomores are frequently used in social psychology experiments, the aim is often to find out about how attitudes may be developed or changed in the general population. How is it possible to do a limited experiment and come to a general conclusion?

In principle, the answer is simple. Generalizing depends upon adequate sampling. Only when the conditions of an experiment can be considered an adequate sample of a larger set of conditions can generalizations be made. Although this notion of sampling as a basis for generalizing is well recognized with regard to the subjects of an experiment, it has not always been made clear that it applies also to many other aspects of an experiment as well. For example, it applies as well to the variables which are studied. If a "high anxiety" group of subjects is compared with a "low anxiety" group, it is not at all evident that the results, whatever they are, apply to a "moderate anxiety" group or a "very high anxiety" group, or in fact, to any conditions other than the ones actually tested. This is one of the reasons for the emphasis, in earlier chapters, on multivalent and parametric types of experiments which greatly increase the validity of generalizations.

The present chapter is concerned with a more detailed description of the many ways that sampling issues arise in experimental research.

POPULATIONS AND SAMPLES

At one time the word *population* referred only to people. Later it was used to describe any large group of objects that could be counted. As mathematical statistics developed, the word became progressively redefined so as to refer to any group of numbers, finite or infinite, which usually referred to real or hypothetical objects or events. The term now is used to refer to such varied things as the number of school children in a given class, the entire set of records of mental hospital admissions in a given decade, or the total range of auditory frequencies which human beings can hear. "The term population implies that in principle one can catalog, or display, or index all possible members, even though the population is infinite and the catalog cannot be completed" (Loevinger, 1965). The important aspect of all populations used in research is that it is possible to select samples from them.

A sample is simply part of a larger population and, when appropriately chosen, can be used to describe the larger population with a high degree of accuracy. Although it might seem desirable to count or measure all members of the population whenever possible, yet there are a number of reasons why samples are not only adequate, but necessary (Wallis and Roberts, 1956).

For one thing, counts of an entire population may sometimes be so costly that the gain in accuracy they provide over a sample may not be worth it. During Presidential elections, polls based upon less than one percent of the population typically produce estimates that are within one or two percent of the actual vote. Secondly, there are situations where the measuring process requires the destruction of the items of the population which are tested. If we want to find out how long radio tubes will last, a certain number of tubes will have to be used up. If we want to find out how long reptiles can live without water, a certain number have to be allowed to die.

There are also many situations where the population is essentially infinite so that all the members cannot be counted. This is the case, for example, where we might wish to describe the laws of learning which are true for *all* species. In such a situation samples must be used. Similarly, in studies of personality, we cannot record every possible manifestation of a given trait, but must rely on samples of behavior.

Finally, there are many situations where the data collected from a sample are more accurate than those based upon a complete survey. This is simply due to the fact that attempts to measure large populations may produce errors due to inadequately trained personnel, omitted data, and misrecorded information, whereas small samples may be thoroughly studied by highly trained people.

It is thus evident that samples are not only useful but also often necessary. The question arises, however, of how samples should be selected in order to allow generalizations to be made about the population. The answer given by the statisticians is simply that the samples must be *random*. This means that every member of the actual or hypothetical population must have an equal chance of being included within the sample.

In the remaining sections of this chapter a number of different kinds of sampling issues in research will be described.

SAMPLING OF SUBJECTS

The criticism is sometimes made that a good deal of what passes as psychological fact is based upon either the white rat or the college sophomore. This criticism, unfortunately, has a good deal of truth because much research by psychologists is done using subjects who are convenient and accessible rather than subjects who are samples of defined populations.

In 1950, the comparative psychologist Frank Beach gave a paper in which he showed that in one of the leading journals there had been a year by year decline in the number of species studied and in the types of problems investigated. Most research was being done with rats, and more and more experiments dealt with learning. Based on this and other considerations, Beach (1960) concluded that "nearly all so-called 'animal psychologists' are primarily interested in, and draw their problems from, the area of *human* behavior. They use members of lower species as substitutes for human subjects."

If this is true, the question arises of how similar the behavior of the rat is to the human being. Although there are psychologists who will argue for one or the other side of this question, the fact remains that at present there is very little of a comparative psychology of behavior that is in any way like the comparative physiology or comparative anatomy of the biologists. For example, before diphtheria antitoxin is used on humans it is standardized on mice, guinea pigs, rabbits, and horses. Typhoid vaccine is first tested on mice, guinea pigs, and rabbits. For much research the dog is used because its anatomy and physiology closely resemble those of man and it also suffers from a number of diseases known to affect humans. Chimpanzees, although more like humans in certain aspects of their behavior, are vegetarians, and their digestive processes are less similar to man's than those of dogs.

Verplanck (1955) has reported that some of the "laws" of learning for the guinea pig are quite different than for the rat, and that we have tended to unduly restrict the behavior of our experimental animals in order to obtain reproducible findings. To the extent that these things are true, it becomes difficult to use samples of animal behavior to make generalizations about human behavior. Only by working with many species of animals in comparable situations will the limits of our ability to generalize become evident.

The problem of generalizing from one group of humans to another is also a difficult one. Most academic research is done either with students in introductory psychology classes who are requested to participate, and sometimes given rewards, or with volunteers who may or may not be paid. The kind of problem that may arise in the former situation is that the students may be reluctant to express their true feelings because of a fear of offending the teacher or losing the proffered reward. In one study, for example, dealing with emotional reactions of students while under the influence of adrenalin, the students were told they would receive two extra points on their final exam for every hour they served as experimental subjects. In one part of the experiment they were placed in an unpleasant situation designed to make them angry. Their self-reports, however, indicated that they were not angry at all. The experimenter discovered subsequently that

The subjects, who had volunteered for the experiment for extra points on their final exam, simply refused to endanger these points by publicly blowing up, admitting their irritation to the experimenter's face or spoiling the questionnaire . . . only after the purposes of the experiment had been revealed were many of these subjects willing to admit to the experimenter that they had been irked or irritated (Schachter and Singer, 1962).

The other difficulty with college student volunteers is that they have been found, in several studies, to be different from nonvolunteers both in personality characteristics and in ways of reacting. In one study of the effects of drugs on healthy, young male volunteers, routine psychological interviews and Rorschach tests were given to all subjects. It turned out that 25 out of 56 of the subjects were considered to be maladjusted: three were psychotic, seven were in treatment or seeking treatment for psychoneurosis, six admitted they were overt homosexuals, etc. The incidence of "serious maladjustment" was estimated to be twice that found in a general college population (Lasagna and von Felsinger, 1954). These same authors briefly report a study in which it was found that a group of medical students were five times as sensitive to the toxic effects of a certain quinine-like drug than were prisoners at Sing Sing. These findings cited above suggest the need for a great deal of caution in generalizing from samples of college student volunteers to other populations, or even to a general college population.

The use of volunteers presents another kind of problem in certain situations. Sometimes subjects have to be tested twice; sometimes children or adolescents are studied and an attempt is made to interview their parents or to obtain information from the parents by mail. In many such cases only a part of the original group returns for retesting and mail responses are typically quite small. For example, in a study designed to measure the effectiveness of certain psychological tests for predicting sales effectiveness, 862 salesmen working for a large, national corporation indicated a willingness to participate in the research. When it came to actually taking the battery of tests, only two-thirds of the salesmen completed it. In order to hold age and experience constant, the sample size had to be reduced to 248, so that conclusions were based on only 29 percent of the original volunteer group (Kirchner and Dunnette, 1959).

In another experiment, the attitudes of 1200 adolescents were measured by a questionnaire and an attitude test was then sent to their parents by mail. Only 16 percent of the parents responded, a result which is more or less typical of mail questionnaires and one which raises the question of the extent to which the parents who responded are typical of the whole group (Stott, 1940).

Relatively few studies have used random samples of large populations for psychological research. One interesting exception is a study of a midwestern semirural community of 2500 people in which every member had already been classified for social class level. From those families having at least one child between the ages of 10 and 13, three families each were randomly selected from the lower, middle, and upper classes. In each family, the mother and one child were tested with a short version of the Thematic Apperception Test, a projective test requiring the subjects to make up stories based on certain pictures. Results showed marked class differences in the stories that were told, implying an important variable to be considered in clinical diagnosis (Mason and Ammons, 1956).

Another illustration of random sampling of subjects from a large population is a survey of the incidence of symptoms of mental illness in New York City; the Midtown Manhattan Study (Srole *et al.*, 1962). Some of the methods and problems of this kind of research are worth describing.

A part of Manhattan containing about 110,000 people was selected as the area of study. A map of the area was then consulted and a number of blocks were selected at random, and then a number of buildings on these blocks were randomly selected, and finally a number of occupants. This produced a sample of 1911 people ranging in age from 20 to 59 years. The method used excluded people who were living away at the time of the survey, for example, people in nursing homes, in military service, or at college.

Trained interviewers were then sent to contact each of the subjects and to get information on a standard questionnaire. Eighty-seven percent of the people contacted completed it. The data were then examined separately by two psychiatrists who rated the respondents on the severity of their reported symptoms and on their degree of incapacitation. These measures were then related to social class level, age, sex, and other general variables.

Several problems arise in this kind of research (Gruenberg, 1962). One concerns the variability (or the reliability) of the questionnaire responses themselves; a second relates to the variability in response due to different interviewers; and a third relates to the variability due to differences of judgment of the psychiatrists rating the records.

In order to evaluate the consistency of a person's answers, one method that might be used would have some of the interviewers reinterview a subsample of the group originally studied. The variability between interviewers might be checked by having several different interviewers contact some of the same subjects. None of these procedures were used, although an attempt was made to use interviewers with the same ethnic or racial backgrounds as the subjects they contacted. The correlations between the psychiatrists' judgments were determined, and it was found that their degree of agreement was highest for those subjects having no symptoms or serious symptoms and lowest for the intermediate groups.

One other interesting methodological issue concerned the nature of the questions themselves. Some referred to the respondents' current activities and feelings and others to childhood events. In the analysis these responses were combined to provide estimates of symptoms that might have existed in the past or currently. Unfortunately, since retrospective reports of childhood are more unreliable than reports of present symptoms, the generalizations are perhaps somewhat questionable.

The preceding points have been made mainly to illustrate how difficult it is to obtain adequate random samples from large defined populations.

SOME SAMPLE SURVEY METHODS

A number of techniques have been developed by polling experts designed to obtain random samples from larger populations. Some of the more important ones will be briefly described here.

A SYSTEMATIC SAMPLE

In 1953, a survey was conducted in a Maryland city of 36,000 people designed to estimate the number of people over 45 years of age, their amount of illness, and their availability for work (Woolsey, 1956). The decisions that had to be made were approximately as follows:

1. An interview questionnaire was constructed and pretested. It included questions on work attitudes as well as work experience, family background, and recent illnesses.

2. Since no list of persons over 45 years of age was available, a list of all street addresses in the city was obtained from the city directory. (A supplementary list of new construction had to be added.) All designated apartments were treated as if they were separate street addresses.

3. Since no information was available on the number of households containing a person over 45, an educated guess was made so that a sample size could be decided on. On the basis of census data it seemed that 1000 households should be interviewed out of the 11,000 known households in the city.

4. Only one interview per household was to be made.

5. Using a table of random numbers, about 1500 addresses were randomly selected from the city directory. The last 500 were to be used only if the first 1000 did not yield a sufficiently large number of respondents.

6. A random sample of city blocks was selected on the basis of a detailed city map, and each address was checked. This was done to determine the accuracy of the listings in the city directory.

7. If a respondent in a household was not home at the time of the interviewer's visit, repeated calls were made until he was interviewed. Only eight respondents refused to be interviewed in over 1000 households contacted.

8. On the basis of the obtained sample data, estimates were made of the variability of sample responses, and an esti-

mate (with an associated confidence interval) was made of the number of people over 45 in the total population.

To oversimplify, the essence of random sampling is to assign each member of the population a unique number and then to select a subgroup of the population using random numbers. This method has the advantage of requiring a minimum knowledge of the population in advance, but it has the limitation of producing larger errors of estimate for a given sample size than does stratified sampling (to be described in the next section). When there is some kind of order to the members of the population (such as an alphabetical list of names, or the consecutive numbers of streets), the selection of members at a fixed interval after a random starting point is called systematic sampling. This is a simple and useful method unless there happens to be some unsuspected regularity in the list of names or addresses. Table C in Appendix III provides a list of random numbers and indicates how it may be used.

STRATIFIED SAMPLING

In many situations, the experimenter has some knowledge of the population which he can put to use. He may know the distribution of men and women in a given community, and he may know something about the racial distribution. These sex, age, and racial factors, among others, are considered strata of the overall population, and, if a random sample is taken from each strata in accord with its proportion in the total population, the resulting sample is called a stratified random sample.

If in a university there are twice as many freshmen as seniors and a sample of the entire student body is desired, the eventual sample will include twice as many freshmen as seniors, all randomly selected.

The advantage of stratifying a population before taking the sample is that the chances of picking a very deviant sample are less and estimates of population values are therefore more precise than would be the case with a simple random sample of the whole population. The major limitation of stratified sampling is that it requires advance knowledge of the strata within the population.

CLUSTER SAMPLING

Another sampling technique in common use is called cluster sampling. It relies on the existence of natural groups such as houses on a block, people in a family, or children in a classroom. If a large university wanted to obtain a sample of 100 students for a survey of attitudes, it could do this by at least two methods. Simple random sampling would require that each student on the enrollment list be assigned a number, and then 100 students would be selected on the basis of a table of random numbers.

The other method would rely on the existence of natural clusters, in this case it would be classes. Each class would be numbered, and then a random sample of (say) 10 classes would be selected. From each of the 10 classes, 10 students would be randomly selected. (For this example to be similar to typical cluster surveys, we would have to assume no overlap of students in the different classes.) Although the use of clusters to form the samples may lead to larger errors than equal-sized simple random samples, it often is cheaper from the point of view of costs. The random selection of city blocks, as in the Midtown Manhattan Study, is an example of the use of cluster sampling. From each block, of course, a random sample of families is then taken.

It should be clear from these examples, which do not include all the different sampling methods, that (a) they are all based on the principle of random selection of units, (b) that they are necessary for generalizations about populations, and (c) that they may be combined in various ways to achieve an optimum balance between precision and cost.

EXPERIMENTERS AS SAMPLES

A number of observations over the years have hinted at the idea that the sex, race, and physical characteristics of the experimenter may affect the kinds of results he obtains. One may consider this as a source of bias to be controlled or an important variable to be studied. Most of the studies of this problem, however, have been greatly limited by a lack of recognition of the sampling problem.

In one experiment, an attempt was made to determine whether the race of the examiner affected the kinds of stories told to the Negro version of the Thematic Apperception Test (TAT) (Reiss, Schwartz, and Cottingham, 1950). Both Negro and white students were tested by either one white or one Negro examiner.

It should be obvious that any conclusions of the experiment, about the general effects of racial differences in examiners, cannot be justified simply because it is impossible to adequately sample Negro or white examiners by using only one person in the sample. The one Negro or white examiner might have some special characteristics that are quite irrelevant to his race and which had an effect on the student taking the test.

Another illustration of the same sort of problem is a study in verbal conditioning in which the experimenter said "good" to the subject every time the subject used a sentence with a hostile word in it. However, two experimenters were used; one was a five-foot, 90-pound, soft-spoken young lady and the other was a 6-foot 5-inch tall, 220-pound former Marine. Results showed that the number of hostile words used was greater for the female experimenter than the male experimenter (Binder, McConnell, and Sjoholm, 1957).

In this case, also, it is impossible to make any generalizations about sex, size, or personality of the experimenter on the basis of a sample of one.

The opposite kind of study has been reported by Rosenthal (1963), that is, one in which 28 experimenters interacted with a few subjects. Motion pictures and recordings were taken in an effort to determine some of the kinds of implicit cues people use to communicate their expectations. It has been found, among other things, that male experimenters look at female subjects more than they look at male subjects.

All of these findings suggest the need to control the factor of experimenter characteristics as carefully as possible and to be aware of it as a possible limit on generalizations to be made from the data.

STIMULUS SAMPLING

A number of years ago, Brunswik (1956) brought to the attention of psychologists the idea that sampling procedures should apply not only to the selection of subjects, but also to the selection of the stimuli to be presented to these subjects. He pointed out that in studies of the judgment of personality from photographs, it was necessary not only to use adequate samples of judges, but an adequate sample of photographs as well. He also suggested that the stimuli used should, in general, be as much like the "natural" environment as possible to maximize the possibility of generalizing. He called this way of thinking *representative design.*

During and after World War II, a number of experiments were done, dealing with form perception, which used some of these ideas. One of the aims of this research was to develop stimuli which could be considered to be representative of larger populations of stimuli. With ordinary geometric figures such as triangles and squares, there are no obvious populations which they represent except other triangles and squares. How then can different shapes be constructed which can be considered samples of a population of shapes?

The basic method used is to establish a stimulus domain defined by a set of explicit rules. These rules, when followed, will produce an infinite population of shapes. Any set of shapes formed by the rules may be considered a sample of the entire population.

A simple example of a set of rules for generating shapes may be taken from the paper by Attneave and Arnoult (1956).

1. Start with a sheet of graph paper, with 100 by 100 lines.
2. Use a table of random numbers and select successive pairs of numbers between 01 and 99. Each pair will determine a point which can be plotted on the graph paper.
3. Pick a two-digit number randomly to determine how many points to plot.
4. Use a straightedge to connect the most peripheral points to form a convex polygon. This will leave a few points inside the polygon.
5. Number the sides of the polygon and assign letters to the points inside it.
6. Use a table of random numbers to decide which central points are to be connected to which sides.

Using this method, "random figures" of the type shown in Fig. 5-1 may be constructed.

Many other sets of rules may be used to produce different populations of shapes, some of which may have contours and

Fig. 5-1. A random figure constructed by use of the rules given in the text.

look more "realistic" (Wulfeck and Taylor, 1957). The value of this kind of approach is that the stimuli used in the research are random samples from defined populations and thus enable generalizations of known accuracy to be made.

DEFINING A POPULATION OF COLORS

There are some situations where the stimulus domain is not an infinite one, but it is not clearly or completely specifiable. One example of such a case is color. The question to be considered is: How many color names do people need to describe all the colors they can see? Another way of saying this is: What is the total population of color names needed to describe color "space" or color experience? If we could determine this, we could then sample this population for any research involving color.

An interesting attempt to answer this question was made by Chapanis (1965), and the following discussion will be based on his study.

The English language contains thousands of color names, and new ones are constantly being added for the purposes of advertising. A survey of the language of some best-selling novels, on the other hand, revealed only about a dozen different color names in use. Somewhere between these two extremes there should exist a set of color names that are rarely confused and which cover all the important distinctions that humans make about color.

Chapanis approached this problem by selecting a large list of color names based on the National Bureau of Standards' dictionary of color terms and added a number of modifiers such as "strong," "pure," "dark," and "pale." All basic color names were paired with all modifiers to produce a total of 233 color names. Then, a large number of colored papers taken from the Munsell Book of Color were put out on a table. These 1359 color samples were designed to represent every variation of hue, brightness, and saturation. The subject was then given a color name such as "light purple" and asked to find the colored paper on the table which best matched the name. Forty judges were used, 20 males and 20 females.

The analysis was designed to determine the degree of consistency between judges for all the color selections. It was found, for example, that purple and violet showed considerable overlap, and that compound colors such as greenish-yellow and yellowish-green could not be distinguished.

For all practical purposes, the modifiers pure, strong, and vivid turned out to be synonymous as did the terms deep and dark, and the terms pale and light. Finally, when an estimate was made of the total number of color names needed to represent all the 1359 colored pieces of paper of the Munsell system, the figure turned out to be about 55. Thus one kind of stimulus domain has been established from which samples may be taken for any research on color perception. The basic ideas involved in setting up such a population can be applied to other problems as well.

THE SAMPLING OF CONDITIONS

This is an issue which has already been discussed in some detail in Chapter 4, so that only a brief recapitulation will be presented here. When an experimenter chooses particular values for his independent variable, he is, in essence, taking a sample. If he wishes to compare a group of subjects given massed practice on a motor task with one given distributed practice, he must select two intertrial rest times to represent his two conditions out of a very large number of potential rest intervals. The massed practice group might use a 5-second interval between trials while the distributed practice groups might use a 60-second interval. Theoretically, rest intervals might be chosen ranging anywhere from zero to infinity. From this perspective, it becomes obvious that a sample of two conditions out of an infinite number of possible ones is a very poor sample indeed and little generalization is possible.

It thus becomes obvious why the multivalent and parametric types of designs are much more desirable than the bivalent ones: they increase the sampling of the independent variables and thus increase the generality of the results.

THE PROBLEM OF RESPONSE SAMPLING

In this chapter we have considered the notion of sampling and shown its relevance to the selection of subjects, experimenters, stimuli, and conditions, in any study. Now we shall examine its relevance to the problem of measuring the subject's responses.

There are at least two aspects to this problem: (1) what responses to measure and (2) under what conditions to measure them.

For a long time there has been a tendency among psychologists to choose a single measure of a phenomenon as a basis for generalizations about it. Thus learning might be measured by the number of trials to reach a criterion, arousal might be measured by heart rate changes, or motivation might be measured by the rate at which an animal stimulates his own brain with small electrical currents. However, as information accumulates in each of these areas it usually becomes evident that there are many possible ways in which a phenomenon can be measured. Very often, as new measurement methods are tried, unexpected results are obtained and new insights gained. This is related to the fact that any theoretical term such as *learning*, *arousal*, or *motivation* will have many indices which do not correlate in any simple way because they measure different aspects of the theoretical state. A few examples will make this point clear.

In psychophysiological research the measures most often

used are the galvanic skin response (GSR) and the heart rate, although, occasionally, skin temperature, blood pressure, or brain waves (EEG) are also recorded. It has been gradually discovered that the correlations between most physiological indices are quite low and that different organ systems react in essentially independent ways to imposed stimuli. Therefore, any one measure is generally a poor sample of the states of the various physiological systems of the body. Lacey and Lacey (1958) have pointed out that ". . . . no single measure can serve as an index to the state of other measures or to the total 'arousal' of the organism."

In an attempt to measure the strength of the thirst drive in rats, Miller (1961) used three different measures, each of which had obvious face validity or relevance. One measure was the amount of water the animal drank; a second was the amount of quinine that had to be added to the water to prevent the thirsty animal from drinking; and a third was the rate at which the animal would press a bar in order to obtain licks of water. Miller found that this last measure did not correlate very highly with the others and that conclusions based on it alone were at variance with those based on the first two.

In studies of the effects of electrical brain stimulation the same sort of problem arises. It had been assumed that the rate at which an animal presses a bar to deliver electric shocks to his own brain was a direct measure of the degree of "pleasure" it felt. To test this assumption, Hodos and Valenstein (1962) set up a situation in which a rat was given a choice between two bars, one of which provided a low intensity shock to the brain and the other, a high intensity shock. They found that the rats chose the bar providing the high intensity shock, even though their rate of response on it was much lower than on the other bar. Thus, rate of self-stimulation did not appear to be an unambiguous measure of strength of reward.

A somewhat related finding was obtained by Plutchik, McFarland, and Robinson (1966) when several different measures of reward strength were compared. The rate of self-stimulation for electrodes implanted at various locations in the brain was compared with the escape-from-stimulation latency at the same sites. In the latter situation the experimenter turned the current on and the monkey turned it off whenever he wanted to and the time to do this was measured. It was discovered that for most electrode locations, the monkey turned off the current relatively quickly, even though he would self-stimulate if given an opportunity.

Since it had been assumed that animals that would self-stimulate a part of their brain would also not turn off (escape from) current introduced by the experimenter at the same location, the results appeared inconsistent. These findings further supported the notion that different measures of motivation do not necessarily measure the same thing.

These examples have been given to emphasize the fact that single measures of complex states such as motivation, neurosis, or learning will be so limited as to produce conclusions of doubtful generality. Another way of saying this is that a single measure of a complex state provides a poor sample. To the extent that it is possible, multiple measures should always be used and compared. Sometimes the inconsistencies of different measures create problems that eventually lead to new insights.

RESPONSE SAMPLING METHODS

Once the decision has been made of what responses to measure in any given case, other issues arise. If a rat is learning a maze, how many trials should he be given? Each run through the maze may be considered a sample of the animal's behavior and the obvious question arises of how large a sample should be chosen.

Unfortunately, no general answer can be given because the size of the sample of responses depends upon the purposes of the experimenter and the consistency of the responses. There are some situations where certain rules of thumb can be given with regard to sample size (Chapter 10) so that only a few general considerations are mentioned here.

One of the factors determining the number of responses to record is the anticipated statistical analysis which will be applied to the data. For various arbitrary levels of desired reliability, sample sizes can be estimated. Secondly, there will usually be a point of diminishing returns beyond which new data that are recorded contribute very little to the stability of the responses. Thirdly, certain design methods require the subject to reach a stable level of response before the independent variable is introduced. Such stable levels are reached after different numbers of responses on different tasks. Finally, some design methods require the subject to begin the experiment at a very low (or poor) level of performance so that very few responses need be recorded. Thus many considerations are involved in a decision about the number of responses to record.

One further issue will be considered under the heading of response sampling methods, and that is, the observational techniques used for collecting information on complex sequences of behavior. In a situation where it might be desired to record some of the social behavior of a monkey or a child, it would obviously be impossible to try to record everything the subject does. A decision has to be made in advance about the categories of behavior the experimenter considers worth recording. This may range from something as simple as the number of times a monkey eats a pellet of food, to the number of aggressive attacks he makes on other animals. Once this is decided, a *time-sampling* plan can be instituted. This means that one or more observers make observations on the subject after either fixed or randomly selected intervals of time, and record the behavior being studied.

An example of time sampling can be taken from a report by Rheingold (1960) dealing with maternal care of human infants in institutions or at home. Observations were made on the babies for the first 10 minutes of each quarter hour for four consecutive hours. During each 10-minute period, four observations were made per minute in the following fashion:

O looked at S for a full second and then recorded on the checklist what he was doing, if someone was caring for him, the nature of the care-taking act, where he was, and how many other people were in his environment. O could take as long as 14 seconds to complete the record, but in any case she did not look up again until the 15th second when she again observed S for a full second.

The results showed some interesting differences in child care procedures in the two types of settings.

One other illustration of time-sampling methods will be given based on work in the field of human engineering. The study was concerned with the activities and distribution of the work load of bus drivers. It was undertaken so that estimates could be made of the time the operator devotes to his various tasks, their order of performance, and possible and actual errors (McFarland and Moseley, 1954).

The drivers were observed during a 7-hour trip between Boston and New York and over 1500 observations were made, some of which required motion pictures taken at intervals. Such behaviors as head, eye, hand, and leg movements were noted and related to specific vehicle traffic conditions. The percent of occurrence of a number of activities could then be tabulated (e.g., the right foot is kept on the brake during 13 percent of the observations). Knowledge gained in such studies has led to the introduction of automatic transmissions and improvement in the design and location of various controls.

These examples should indicate that time-sampling methods are quite general and can be used in a large variety of situations with either animal or human subjects (Plutchik, 1963).

SUMMARY

In this chapter, an attempt was made to show the importance of sampling concepts in experimental research. If generalizations are to be made about various populations, research must deal with adequate samples of those populations.

The notion of sampling applies not only to the sampling of subjects, but also to the sampling of experimenters. In addition, it has relevance to the question of the stimulus objects used in research, since stimuli can also be considered to be samples selected from larger populations of stimuli. The concept of sampling applies also to the conditions of the experiment, that is, the values of the independent variable which are selected. If only two values are used, a high one and a low one, this is generally a poor sample of an entire dimension and multivalent studies are needed to enable generalizations to be made. Finally, the sampling notion is relevant to the responses of the subject. Complex states, such as motivations, cannot be unambiguously measured by single measures alone, and multiple indices are needed to sample the system. Various survey sampling procedures are described as well as time sampling as a method for sampling responses.

BASIC STATISTICAL CONCEPTS

Acceptance of error and bias as unavoidable implies that we cannot rely upon a single experiment for the demonstration of a natural phenomenon, that we can never interpret the results of research, even when it is repeated, with absolute certainty, and that a knowledge of any phenomenon is always tentative and partial, never final and complete.

—WILLIAM S. RAY

Statistics is a branch of mathematics which has great practical value as a tool in experimental research. Statistical methods are essentially ways of handling information obtained by repeated measurements. Probability theory provides the basic framework for statistical thinking, and its aim, generally, is to make predictions about the frequency with which certain results are likely to occur in the long run. Statistics helps make experimental conclusions seem plausible, not inevitable. It presents methods for making intelligent decisions in uncertain situations. Some statisticians have suggested that statistical analysis is like gambling or getting married since it involves making important decisions on the basis of incomplete information.

Historically, statistics had its roots in some very practical activities, the two major influences being the gathering of vital statistics or census data and gambling. The desire to compute correct odds on gambling games led to the initial development of the theory of probability in France in the seventeenth century. Extensive development of this theory occurred in the nineteenth century, and it was applied to problems in astronomy, insurance, crime rates, and heredity. In the twentieth century there has been a huge increase in the collection of information for purposes of prediction and in the development of sophisticated mathematical procedures used to analyze such data.

During World War II a branch of applied statistics was developed called *operations research*. It helped solve such problems as optimum size of transatlantic convoys, optimum flight patterns used in hunting submarines, relative importance of different factors in the effectiveness of bombing missions, and other problems related to the war. Some of these same techniques are used today in connection with trucking operations, inventory decisions, and strategies in competitive games. Unusual current uses of statistics relate to the approximate dating of fragments of pottery or bones found in archeological research and to the study of literary styles in the Bible. There is no doubt that the use of statistical thinking in contemporary research will continue to increase.

DESCRIPTIVE AND INFERENTIAL STATISTICS

When the government collects census data every 10 years, an attempt is made to obtain information about every citizen living in the United States at that time. All members of the total *population* are to provide information. This kind of situation is to be distinguished from the more common one in which some part, or *sample*, of the total population is examined in order to be able to make estimates or inferences about what the total population is like. For example in presidential voting polls some 5 to 10,000 people are interviewed throughout the country, and an estimate is then made of how 50 or 60 million voters will act.

A population includes all members of a defined group, but it is important to recognize that what is called a population depends on the purposes of the experimenter. Examples of populations are (a) all white rats of the Wistar Institute strain, (b) all students attending a particular university, (c) all elementary school children in a certain school district, (d) all people living in America in 1960, (e) all clinical psychologists in Indiana, (f) all scientists in government service in 1960, etc. In some cases the population is a finite one with a single clearly specifiable number of people, e.g., all persons who got married in 1965. In other cases, the population is an infinite or very large one, which does not have a single number to specify the total number of individuals. For example, the number of mice used each year in research is a very large number, with over 2 million being distributed from one major center alone. Even if we could conceivably test this huge population at any one time, within a few days there would be a large addition to the population. Since we are interested in the characteristics of all mice, those born next year as well as last, the population is essentially unlimited.

Many populations studied by psychologists are of this type. This means that it is essentially impossible to count every individual in the population, and therefore we must study representative samples. These samples are used to make *inferences* or *estimates* about the characteristics of the total population.

Because of the distinctions between a population and a sample, statistics is usually divided into two general branches. *Descriptive statistics* is concerned with ways of efficiently describing populations. This includes ways of summarizing census-type data for clarity of communication. *Sampling* or *inferential statistics* is concerned with the use of samples to make estimates and inferences about larger populations. Most psychological research is of this type.

SOME BASIC STATISTICAL CONCEPTS

This chapter will not attempt to describe all the procedures that are used in statistical analysis since there are many good textbooks which provide such information (e.g., Wallis and Roberts, 1956; Guilford, 1965). There are, however, a few statistical concepts which are basic to an understanding of many of the procedures used in research; these will be described and illustrated here. These basic notions are (a) the frequency distribution and its measures, (b) the z-statistic, and (c) sampling distributions.

THE FREQUENCY DISTRIBUTION

Since statistics is fundamentally concerned with information obtained by repeated measurements, it is obviously necessary that such information be adequately described. This is usually done by means of a frequency distribution, where the frequency with which an event occurs is plotted against the type or magnitude of the event. Figure 6–1 shows such a frequency distribution. It is based upon census data relating to the age at which males first marry. The distribution is not symmetrical, but skewed to the

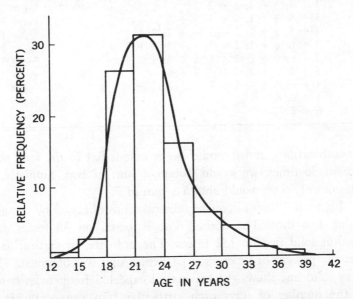

Fig. 6-1. A frequency distribution showing the percent of the male population married at different ages.

right with most marriages occurring between 21 and 24 years of age. A frequency distribution of this sort contains all the basic information obtained in any survey or experiment.

In many situations, the shape of the distribution changes somewhat as the number of cases is increased. Suppose, for example, that two dice are tossed a number of times and that a record is kept of the sum on each toss. This sum may range from 2 to 12. There is only one combination that can produce a 2 and only one combination that can produce a 12. There are two combinations that can produce a sum of either 3 or 11. The various possibilities are listed in Table 6–1. There is a total of

Table 6-1. Various combinations of two dice

Sum	Produced By	Expected Frequency (%)
2	1 + 1	$\frac{1}{36}$ = 2.8
3	1 + 2; 2 + 1	$\frac{2}{36}$ = 5.6
4	1 + 3; 3 + 1; 2 + 2	$\frac{3}{36}$ = 8.3
5	1 + 4; 4 + 1; 2 + 3; 3 + 2	$\frac{4}{36}$ = 11.1
6	1 + 5; 5 + 1; 2 + 4; 4 + 2; 3 + 3	$\frac{5}{36}$ = 13.9
7	1 + 6; 6 + 1; 2 + 5; 5 + 2; 3 + 4; 4 + 3	$\frac{6}{36}$ = 16.7
8	2 + 6; 6 + 2; 3 + 5; 5 + 3; 4 + 4	$\frac{5}{36}$ = 13.9
9	3 + 6; 6 + 3; 4 + 5; 5 + 4	$\frac{4}{36}$ = 11.1
10	4 + 6; 6 + 4; 5 + 5	$\frac{3}{36}$ = 8.3
11	5 + 6; 6 + 5	$\frac{2}{36}$ = 5.6
12	6 + 6	$\frac{1}{36}$ = 2.8

36 combinations, and it would be expected that *in the long run*, once in 36 times, we would obtain a sum of two. Similarly, 6 times out of 36 we would obtain a sum of 7.

Figure 6–2 shows frequency distributions obtained by actually tossing two dice. The dashed line is based on 38 tosses and the thin solid line on 152 tosses. The ordinate, or vertical axis, gives the percent of times each particular sum was obtained. The heavy solid line shows the theoretical expected frequencies based on the number of ways each particular sum can occur. It is evident that as the number of tosses (cases) increases, the distribution becomes smoother and, at the same time, begins to approximate the theoretical curve, i.e., the one implied by Table 6–1. This process frequently occurs in experimental research as the number of cases or the number of measurements increases.

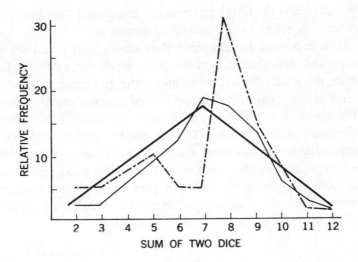

Fig. 6-2. The dashed line is a frequency distribution based upon 38 tosses; the thin solid line is based upon 152 tosses. The heavy solid line shows the theoretical expectation.

CENTRAL TENDENCY

In order to use the information presented in a frequency distribution for purposes of description or inference, it is necessary to summarize certain properties of the distribution. The two most important of these are the mean and the standard deviation.

It is very useful to find a single number to represent what is typical of a group of scores. Ideally, such a number should (a) be near the center of the distribution, (b) not weight extreme scores too much, (c) be computable by simple algebraic operations, and (d) be fairly stable from sample to sample. On the whole, the value that meets these criteria most adequately is the arithmetic mean, M or $\overline{X}$, defined simply as the sum of all the measurements, ΣX, divided by the number of cases, N, or in symbols

$$\overline{X} = \frac{\Sigma X}{N} \tag{1}$$

The symbol Σ is the Greek letter sigma and means "the sum of." The letter X refers to the individual scores.

It is important to remember that this is only one kind of average and that there are many other types, for example, the median, the mode, the harmonic mean, the geometric mean, and the root mean square. Which one is used depends on the nature of the problem, but the one used most frequently is the arithmetic mean defined above. This is partly because it is very easy to combine means from different groups, and because the mean multiplied by the number of cases immediately gives the total score, something which is not true for the other averages. In connection with sampling problems, the mean of a sample is the best estimate of the mean of a population.

VARIABILITY

Two frequency distributions may have the same mean yet differ greatly in the range of scores and in the shape of the distribution. Such differences may be revealed by measures of variability. As is the case with averages, there are many measures of variability, but the most useful is called the standard deviation. This measure is also a kind of mean, but it is a mean based on the deviations of each score from the arithmetic mean of the whole distribution.

For example, if four IQ scores, 102, 103, 107, and 112, are determined in a given sample, then the mean IQ is 106. The deviation d of the first score from the mean is -4, of the second score is -3, of the third score is $+1$, and of the fourth score is $+6$. The average of these four deviations, -4, -3, $+1$, and $+6$, is equal to zero. However, if each of the deviations is squared, then all negative signs are eliminated as follows: 16, 9, 1, 36. The mean of all these deviations (16 + 9 + 1 + 36 divided by 4 = 15.5) is called the variance. The standard deviation is the square root of the variance, or 3.9. The general equation used to compute the standard deviation s is

$$s = \sqrt{\frac{\Sigma d^2}{N}} \tag{2}$$

where Σd^2 is the sum of the squares of each of the individual deviations from the mean and N is the number of deviations, which is the same as the number of cases. Notice that this figure representing the standard deviation is roughly the same size as most of the deviations recorded in the first place. A second important point to notice is that, since the deviations are originally given in terms of IQ units, the mean of the deviations is still in IQ units. It is important to remember that the standard deviation is always given in the same units as the original scores. If we recorded the speed of a person's reactions in fractions of a second, the standard deviation of his scores would also be a value recorded in terms of fractions of a second.

There is a third important point that stems from those already mentioned. Since, in a frequency distribution, the score values are plotted on the horizontal axis, or abscissa, the standard deviation represents a certain kind of average distance along this abscissa. In fact, the standard deviation is often used as a kind of yardstick for comparing different distributions. It is especially useful if the different distributions are *normal* or approximately so. A normal distribution, roughly speaking, is one which is symmetrical around the mean, and bell-shaped. Many distributions obtained in research look this way and in addition many actual distributions seem to become increasingly normal as the number of cases increases. We must recognize, however, that the normal distribution defined by a mathematical equation is only a useful approximation to the kinds of distributions actually obtained in empirical research.

In computing the standard deviation it is sometimes very tedious to apply equation (2), particularly if the mean includes some decimal places and there are many deviations to square. As an alternative, it is possible to compute the standard deviation by using the original scores obtained in the experiment. Equation (3), although it looks longer, is actually simpler to apply in practice because there are usually tables available giving the squares of all numbers up to 1000. The equivalent computational formula for the standard deviation is

$$s = \sqrt{\frac{N\Sigma X^2 - (\Sigma X)^2}{N^2}} \tag{3}$$

where N refers to the number of scores, ΣX refers to the sum of all of the scores, and ΣX^2 refers to the sum of the squares of all the scores.

One of the important values of the standard deviation is that it can be used as a yardstick for locating the relative position of any score in a frequency distribution. This notion is fundamental to most applications of statistics, and it will be described in the following section.

THE z-STATISTIC

Suppose two boys in two different classes have each received an 80 on a mathematics exam. Does the same score necessarily mean that both boys did equally well? A moment's reflection will show that the meaning of a given test score depends upon how easy or difficult the test was. If the average score in the first class was 70 on the test, then the 80 is a fair grade, whereas if the average score in the second class was 85, the 80 is a poor grade.

The z-statistic attempts to take into consideration both an individual's score (i.e., his position in the distribution) and the average performance of the group (i.e., the mean of the distribution). It does this by finding the difference between any given score (X) and the mean (M) of the distribution and then divides this distance by the yardstick, that is, the standard deviation (s). In mathematical notation it looks like this

$$z = \frac{X - M}{s} \tag{4}$$

To take a simple example, if a student has an 80 on an exam in a class where the mean grade is 72 and the standard deviation is 8, then his z-value is $(80 - 72)/8 = 8/8 = 1.00$. This means that his grade is exactly one standard deviation above the mean of the class. If his score was an 88, he would be two standard deviations above the mean of the class. If his score was 84, he would be 1.5 standard deviations above the mean of the class, and if his score was 72, he would have a z-value of 0 and be zero standard deviations above the mean of the class.

A z can also be negative. Thus in the second class mentioned above, having a mean of 85 and a standard deviation of 5, the student receiving a grade of 80 would have a z of $(80 - 85)/5 = -(5/5) = -1.00$. If his test score had been a 78, then his z would have been $(78 - 85)/5 = -(7/5) = -1.40$. Therefore, knowing a person's z locates him within a frequency distribution. When measurements are changed into zs, every distribution has a mean of 0 and a standard deviation of 1. In a sense, this converts all distributions into the same standard form and makes comparisons easier.

There is a second important idea connected with the use of a z—it also provides an estimate of the relative position of a score in terms of the percent of scores it exceeds in the distribution. Since the mean is exactly at the middle of a distribution, any score (i.e., a z of 0) which falls at the mean exceeds 50% of the scores of the distribution. Similarly a z of 1.0 exceeds approximately 84% of the distribution and a z of 2.0 exceeds about 97.5% of the distribution. Figure 6–3 shows the relative percents of the distribution which are cut off by standard deviation units above and below the mean. It is possible to construct a detailed table showing what percent of a normal distribution is exceeded by every possible *z*. An abbreviated version of such a table is given in Appendix III (Table A).

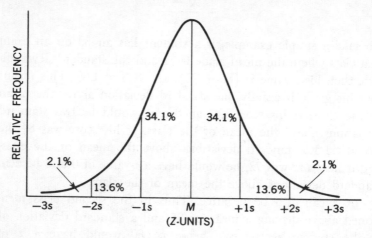

Fig.6-3. An example of a normal distribution. M represents the mean and s the standard deviation. The numbers inside the distribution represent the percent of cases cut off by successively placing a length equal to a standard deviation along the abscissa.

SAMPLING DISTRIBUTIONS

Another fundamental idea in statistical theory is the notion of a sampling distribution. This may be illustrated by the following example. Suppose we want to determine whether girls or boys are brighter in a large public school system containing several thousand children. One way in which we might proceed is to get two alphabetical lists of names, one for all the boys and one for all the girls, and take every 100th name on each list. Assuming that there are 5000 boys and 5000 girls in the school system, this would give us a random sample of 50 boys and 50 girls. If we then determine the IQs of these children, it may turn out that the mean IQ for the girls is 3 points higher than the mean IQ for the boys. How shall we interpret this difference? Does it prove that the girls are brighter than the boys?

The obvious answer is that we really do not know. It is quite possible that some other random sample of 50 boys and 50 girls could have given us a slightly different result. It is, in fact, possible to imagine repeating the experiment over and over again, each time selecting a different random sample of 50 boys and 50 girls. In some experiments (i.e., samples) the mean for the girls might be higher, while in others the mean for the boys might be higher.

These mean differences may be plotted in the form of a frequency distribution as shown in Fig. 6-4. Such a distribu-

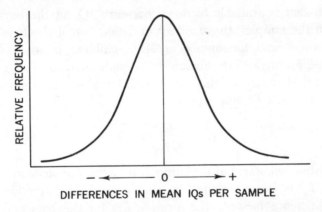

Fig. 6-4. A theoretical sampling distribution of differences in mean IQ between girls and boys for a large number of samples. This illustrates the case where the average difference between boys and girls is zero.

tion, based upon a very large number of samples, is called a *theoretical sampling distribution*. It is called theoretical because rarely, if ever, are enough samples actually taken to determine such a distribution. In fact, quite typically, *only one sample is taken, and it is used to make an inference about the total population.*

Fortunately, it is still possible to say a good deal about the theoretical sampling distribution on the basis of the one sample, *if certain requirements are met.* For example, the one sample used must be selected randomly, i.e., every student in the school system must have had an equal chance of being chosen. Secondly, we assume that all samples are of equal size, and, thirdly, we assume that the standard deviations (or variances) for the IQs of boys and girls in all samples are approximately the same. This last assumption is called the assumption of *homogeneity of variance*.

If these various requirements are met, it becomes possible to apply some simple equations to try to answer the question of whether the girls or the boys are brighter in this population of children. The first step requires *estimating* the standard deviation of the theoretical sampling distribution. The only information that is available to us is the mean IQs of the boys and girls in the samples, the standard deviation (s) of the boys' and girls' scores, and the number (N) of children in each of the samples. From this information an estimate may be made of the standard deviation of the theoretical sampling distribution by means of the following equation:

$$s_t = \sqrt{\frac{s_1^2}{N_1} + \frac{s_2^2}{N_2}} \tag{5}$$

This estimated standard deviation s_t is called the *standard error*. Once it has been obtained it can be used to determine a z. The difference between the mean scores for the boys and girls is divided by the standard error, as follows:

$$\tilde{z} = \frac{M_1 - M_2}{s_t} \tag{6}$$

The symbol $\sim$ over the z is used to indicate that this is an *estimated* z based on samples.

However, there is one important addition that is necessary to make this estimated z strictly analogous to an ordinary z. To determine a z, the mean of a distribution is subtracted from a particular score and then divided by the standard deviation yardstick. This means that in the comparison of the IQs of boys and girls, we need to know what the mean of the theoretical sampling distribution is so that we can compare it to the actual obtained difference in the sample. But here a problem arises. We do not know what the mean of the theoretical sampling distribution is. Therefore, the only way the statistician can proceed is to *assume* a particular mean for the theoretical distribution. For example, he can assume that the "true" difference in the mean IQs is 4 points in favor of the girls. Or he can assume that the "true" difference is 7 points in favor of the boys. These assumptions, while possible, seem so arbitrary that the statistician usually makes the assumption that there is *no difference* in the true mean IQs of boys and girls in this population. This is at least reasonable if he has no other information available to him. This assumption of no real difference between the two groups in the total population is called the *null hypothesis*. It implies that the mean of the theoretical sampling distribution is zero. In equation form, therefore, the z is then

$$z = \frac{(M_1 - M_2) - 0}{s_t} \qquad (7)$$

The importance of this way of writing the z is that it always implies a null hypothesis. It reminds us that when we compare the mean scores of two samples, we are using as a convenient reference point the *assumption that the two groups are really the same in the total population.*

Another way of saying this is that the theoretical sampling distribution with a mean of zero (the null hypothesis) is what would be obtained if there was no difference between boys and girls in mean IQ and many hundreds of samples were taken. In some of them the difference would favor the boys and in some it would favor the girls, but in the long run most would be very close to zero. This sampling distribution would result if no real difference existed and only chance factors caused our samples to vary from experiment to experiment.

The basic strategy is to use this sampling distribution as our reference curve and then try to *determine whether an actual obtained difference was likely or unlikely* to have occurred on the basis of chance factors, i.e., on the basis of variations in our random samples.

Let us explore these ideas using some actual figures. Suppose the girls had a mean IQ of 104 and the boys had a mean IQ of 101. Assume the standard deviation (s_1) for the sample of girls is 14 and the standard deviation (s_2) for the sample of boys is 15. We then estimate the standard error (i.e., standard deviation) of the theoretical sampling distribution by Eq. (5).

$$s_t = \sqrt{\frac{s_1{}^2}{N_1} + \frac{s_2{}^2}{N_2}}$$

$$s_t = \sqrt{\frac{14^2}{50} + \frac{15^2}{50}}$$

$$s_t = \sqrt{3.92 + 4.50}$$

$$s_t = \sqrt{8.42} = 2.90$$

We then use Eq. (7) to estimate a z for the difference of $104 - 101$.

$$\bar{z} = \frac{(M_1 - M_2) - 0}{s_t} = \frac{(104 - 101) - 0}{2.9}$$

$$\bar{z} = \frac{3}{2.9} = 1.03$$

What these computations have shown is that the difference of 3 IQ points in favor of the girls falls 1.03 z units (i.e., 1.03 standard deviation units) from the mean of the distribution. We can then look in Table A of Appendix III and discover that this score corresponds to a difference in means that is greater than approximately 85% of the differences found in the theoretical sampling distribution of differences. Therefore, about 15% of the theoretical differences are larger than the obtained one. These facts are shown graphically in Fig. 6–5.

Now, we should recall that the distribution shown in Fig.

6–5 is what we would get if (a) there was really *no* difference between the boys and the girls (null hypothesis), (b) we took many samples of boys and girls, and (c) only chance factors were operating to cause differences. This means that a difference in favor of the girls of three IQ points could occur about 15% of the time in random samples *even if there was no real difference*

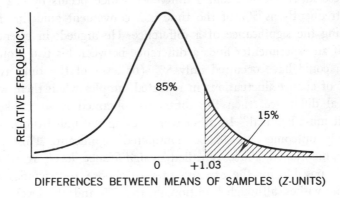

Fig. 6-5. The right-hand tail of the distribution shows the percent of cases which exceed a **z** of +1.03 in a normal distribution.

between the boys and the girls in IQ. Therefore, it is quite possible that this particular difference of three IQ points which was actually obtained in the experiment could have been a result of chance variations due to random sampling. We therefore conclude that the difference in IQ we actually obtained is a relatively frequent occurrence even when there is no real difference in IQ, and so we say that the difference is not real or *not significant*. To say this still another way, we have found that the sample difference of three IQ points is consistent with the null hypothesis that there is really no difference between the boys and girls in IQ.

A new question should have occurred to the reader. If this difference of three IQ points is not considered "real" or "significant," how large does a difference have to be before it is considered significant? Unfortunately, there is no single or simple answer to this question. Many factors go into this decision, and they relate to such matters as the implications of a wrong judgment, the cost of doing the experiment, and the adequacy of the sampling procedure in the first place. However, a tradition has developed over the past 30 years stemming from the work of the British statistician Ronald Fisher, who first introduced many of these ideas. He felt that a difference which occurs by chance as infrequently as 5% of the time is a convenient guideline for deciding the significance of a difference. He argued, in essence, that if an experimenter finds a difference between his two groups which could have occurred only 5% (or less) of the time as a result of chance fluctuations in repeated samples when there was no real difference, then the difference obtained is so unlikely that it must be "real." In other words, using the null hypothesis, unlikely outcomes are to be considered significant. This 5% figure mentioned above is called a *significance level*. It is, of course, possible for the experimenter to choose any significance level he wishes, although traditionally the 5% and 1% levels are most frequently used. This point will be discussed more fully in a later section.

ONE- AND TWO-TAILED TESTS

The previous example actually represented an oversimplification. It is now necessary to qualify the conclusions. In our hypothetical example we assumed that the girls had a mean IQ three points higher than the boys. When we estimated the z, we took $M_1 - M_2$ and divided by the standard error. Now it is just as reasonable to take $M_2 - M_1$ and divide by the standard error. This would, of course, give us exactly the same z except that it would be negative, that is, -1.03 instead of $+1.03$. Graphically it would appear as in Fig. 6–6. What Fig. 6–6 shows is the percent of time a difference as large as three IQ points would occur if we took many samples and if there was really no mean difference between the boys and girls in IQ. This difference of three IQ points could be either in favor of the girls or of the boys. It appears that in 30% of the samples a difference as large as three IQ points could occur as a result of random variations in the samples. Therefore, the actual finding of this slight difference in favor of the girls is not significant.

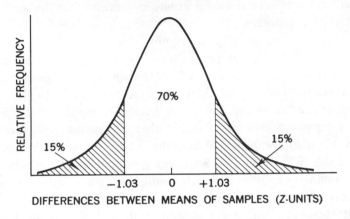

DIFFERENCES BETWEEN MEANS OF SAMPLES (Z-UNITS)

Fig. 6-6. The two tails of the distribution show the percent of cases which exceed a **z** of ±1.03 in a normal distribution.

When we consider both ends of the sampling distribution, as we did here, we are dealing with a *two-tailed test* of significance. This implies that for a 5% significance level we need $2\frac{1}{2}$% of the cases in one tail of the distribution and $2\frac{1}{2}$% of the cases in the other tail. Similarly, if we were interested in a 1% significance level, we would find an estimated z that corresponded to $\frac{1}{2}$% of the cases in one tail and $\frac{1}{2}$% of the cases in the other tail of the distribution. In general, *with large samples* the estimated z must be 1.96 or greater for a difference to be significant at the 5% level or better, and it must be 2.58 or more to be significant at the 1% level or better.

SIGNIFICANCE TESTS WITH SMALL SAMPLES

The method described above for testing the significance of a difference between two samples is suitable if the samples are large in size, but it becomes less suitable as the sample size decreases. Although there is no sharp line of distinction between what is considered a large sample and what is considered a small sample, the usual rule of thumb is to consider small those samples whose combined N is less than 40 or 50. When such a situation exists, several modifications are necessary in the method of testing hypotheses.

The first change is in the method for computing the standard deviation of the sampling distribution. A "pooled" estimate of the standard error is used which is slightly more complicated than before. The second change is in connection with the use of a z-table. A special table has been developed which gives the estimated values of z, except that the zs are now usually referred to as t-statistics. When this t-table is used (Appendix III, Table B), we find that the interpretation of t depends on the number of subjects in the sample. This number, called *degrees of freedom*, is actually computed by treating the samples as if they each had one less subject than they actually have. Thus, if one group has eight subjects and the other six subjects, the degrees of freedom looked up in the t-table are $7 + 5 = 12$.

The actual equation used in computing a t-value for small samples is

$$t = \frac{(M_1 - M_2) - 0}{\sqrt{\dfrac{\Sigma X_1^2 - N_1 M_1^2 + \Sigma X_2^2 - N_2 M_2^2}{N_1 + N_2 - 2} \left(\dfrac{1}{N_1} + \dfrac{1}{N_2}\right)}} \tag{8}$$

N_1 and N_2 refer to the sizes of the two samples, M_1 and M_2 are the means for the samples, and ΣX_1^2 and ΣX_2^2 refer to the sum of the squares of the individual scores in each of the samples. The zero, of course, implies the testing of a null hypothesis.

Let us now take a specific example and work a problem through. Suppose we selected randomly five boys and five girls from a large school system and determined the mean IQ of each group, and let us assume that the mean for the girls is 7 points higher than for the boys. The actual scores for the individuals are given in Table 6–2.

Table 6-2. A set of hypothetical IQ scores for randomly selected samples of five girls and five boys

	Girls			Boys	
Subject	IQ (X_1)	$X_1{}^2$	Subject	IQ (X_2)	$X_2{}^2$
1	114	12996	1	103	10609
2	106	11236	2	101	10201
3	103	10609	3	111	12321
4	107	11449	4	100	10000
5	115	13225	5	95	9025
$\Sigma X_1 =$	545	$59515 = \Sigma X_1{}^2$	$\Sigma X_2 =$	510	$52156 = \Sigma X_2{}^2$
$M_1 = 109$			$M_2 = 102$		

If we substitute the appropriate values from Table 6-2 into Eq. (8), we get

$$t = \frac{109 - 102}{\sqrt{\dfrac{59515 - (5)(109)^2 + 52156 - (5)(102)^2}{5 + 5 - 2}\left(\dfrac{1}{5} + \dfrac{1}{5}\right)}}$$

$$t = \frac{5}{\sqrt{12.30}} = \frac{5}{3.50} = 1.43$$

This value of t of 1.43 may be looked up in Table B of Appendix III with an N (or degree of freedom) of $5 + 5 - 2 = 8$. The table indicates that t would have to be 2.3 to be significant at the 5% level, and we can therefore conclude that the girls are not significantly different from the boys in IQ. The difference between the means obtained in the samples can reasonably be attributed to a chance difference related to the random sampling.

The correct use of the t-test, like all other statistical tests, depends upon certain requirements being fulfilled. The first and most important requirement is that the members of the sample be selected randomly from some defined population. The second requirement is that the standard deviations of the two groups be equal. This is the requirement of homogeneity of variance. The third requirement is that the populations from which the samples have been drawn be normal.

These may seem like very stringent requirements, and they

are. Fortunately, however, it has been demonstrated that even where these requirements are not met very well, the t-test provides an accurate answer to the question of the significance of the difference between two means. For example, one psychologist (Boneau, 1960) deliberately established three very different distributions, one normal, one rectangular, and one J-shaped, and then drew samples of size 5 or size 15 from them to be compared by means of a t-test. (This, of course, was done with a computer since thousands of samples were drawn.) Boneau also arranged that some of the samples have variances (i.e., the square of the standard deviation) four times the others, thus violating the requirement of equal variability in the samples.

After analyzing his results, he concluded that *so long as the sampling is random,* lack of normality of the populations has little influence on the t-test. Secondly, he found that the large differences in the size of the variances had little effect on the conclusions of the t-test, *so long as the sizes of the samples were the same.* In fact, he concluded that "samples of sizes of 15 are generally sufficient to undo most of the damage inflicted by violation of assumptions," so long as sampling is random. These findings are well worth remembering.

ANALYSIS OF VARIANCE: SOME BASIC CONCEPTS

The $\bar{z}$-test and the t-test described above are used when the experimenter wishes to determine if the means of two groups are significantly different, but in many situations the experimenter is interested in the differences between three or more groups. He might wish, for example, to study differences between three breeds of dogs, or between three methods of teaching mathematics, or between avoidance produced by four levels of electric shock.

At first glance, one might think that we could simply compare all possible pairs using the $\bar{z}$- or t-test. Thus, breed 1 might be compared with breeds 2 and 3, and then breed 2 could be compared with breed 3, making three t-tests. If four levels of shock were used, then level 1 could be compared with levels 2, 3, and 4, level 2 could be compared with levels 3 and 4, and level 3 could be compared with level 4, making six t-tests in all. If there were 12 different groups or conditions, 66 t-tests would be possible.

If a 5% level of significance is chosen, then, because of random fluctuations, in five comparisons out of a hundred an obtained difference between two groups would be judged to be significant even if it was not; i.e., we could be in error five times out of a hundred if we repeated our experiment indefinitely. As the number of t-test comparisons increases, the chances of finding a significant difference by mistake also increases.

It might seem that one way of overcoming this problem is to simply pick the largest observed difference among the comparisons and apply the t-tests only to that. However, this approach is not valid since the chances that a single randomly selected difference will exceed a certain value is not the same as the chances that the *largest* of a number of randomly selected differences will exceed this value. In other words, the chances that one of the comparisons will be significant when four groups are compared are much greater than the chances that a difference will be significant when only two groups are compared.

There is, however, another solution to the problem of comparing several different groups or conditions, and it involves the use of a technique known as *analysis of variance*. Since the actual computational details become rather complicated, only a general survey of the ideas involved will be presented here.

Suppose groups of 50 boys and 50 girls are randomly selected from a school district and their mean IQs and the standard deviation of their IQs calculated. Suppose also that there is no real difference in IQ between boys and girls. If this is true, then the mean IQ of the boys and girls should be approximately the same. If we now combine both samples into one and compute a new standard deviation based on 100 students rather than 50, the standard deviation of the combined group should be approximately equal to that of either group alone, since the range of IQs has remained unchanged.

Suppose that we now add another group of 50 children, all of whom are known to be feebleminded, that is, each child has an IQ below 70. If we now compute the standard deviation of IQs for all 150 children, we will obviously find an increase in variability since we have added a set of extreme scores. Thus, the variability of a set of scores may reflect the existence of different kinds of groups; the more different the groups, the greater the variability of their combined scores.

This basic idea has been formalized in the analysis of variance. For example, if we randomly select three groups of children from a given population, we would expect them to be nearly the same. If one group is now praised for success in solving arithmetic problems, and one group is punished (by misinforming them of their results), and one group is ignored, then we might expect differences in problem-solving achievement to appear. In this situation we have two major sources of variability: one concerns the differences between the groups who are treated differently, and the second concerns the differences between the subjects who are treated alike.

If praising or punishing the children had no effect, then the variability between the three groups would be nearly the same as the variability between the subjects in the experiment. Analysis of variance involves making a formal comparison between the variability due to different treatment of groups and the variability due to random differences between subjects. The test used is called an F-test and requires a comparison of variances. When one kind of variability is much larger than the other kind, the treatments are said to exert a significant effect on performance. Although the analysis of variance has many complex ramifications, most of them are "reducible to the single problem of testing whether one estimate of variance is significantly greater than a second such estimate" (Fisher, 1954).

Conventional 5 and 1% levels of significance are usually used.

If the F-test shows that the experimental treatments imposed on the subjects produce a significant effect, it is often still necessary to do further t-tests to determine which of the particular groups exerts the largest effect.

As is the case in using the $\bar{z}$- or t-test, the analysis of variance also requires that certain assumptions be met. These are (1) the subjects should be randomly and independently selected from the populations involved; (2) the standard deviations (or variances) of the different groups should be equal; and (3) the populations from which the samples are drawn should have normal distributions. If these requirements are not met, conclusions based upon the use of analysis of variance will be in error, although it has been found that some variation in these requirements is possible without much effect on the accuracy of statistical tests. A mathematician has pointed out that "since an experimenter could rarely, if ever, convince himself that all the assumptions were exactly satisfied in his data, the technique must be regarded as approximate rather than exact" (Cochran, 1947). In fact, all statistical tests are useful but limited tools for helping to make difficult decisions.

SOME STATISTICAL ISSUES

The statistical ideas and techniques that have been described are part of the "classical" tradition; they represent the more commonly used notions in experimental research. In recent years, however, there have been various criticisms made of these ideas, and some tentative alternatives have been proposed. Although some of these alternatives require considerable mathematical sophistication for a full understanding, it is possible to present the issues in a general way.

LEVELS OF SIGNIFICANCE

In the early part of this century the British mathematician R. A. Fisher mentioned earlier developed the concept of tests of significance and showed how they could be applied to practical problems. The particular problems he was concerned with were biological—for example, whether the use of a certain type of fertilizer would increase the yield of corn. With variability in rain, soil characteristics, and seed properties, it was obvious that results were seldom clear-cut. Therefore Fisher proposed a rule of thumb that seemed reasonable to him. He assumed that if a certain outcome could have occurred by random sampling from a single population five times out of a hundred, and that if in the one sample he took it had actually been found to occur, then it was a rare enough event to consider significant. The concept of significance was thus closely tied up with the notion of rarity of occurrence of a phenomenon. Fisher pointed out that there is always a risk of error in making a decision. He decided that 5 mistakes in 100 repetitions was a reasonable risk to take, and therefore proposed the 5% level of significance as a dividing line.

When the psychologists began to use these statistical ideas, this rule of thumb gradually began to dominate their thinking too, and it has almost become elevated to the status of a principle at the present time. Textbooks of statistics usually caution the researcher to establish a level of significance in advance and to stick to it, but seldom do they question the general reasonableness of a 5% level for establishing significance of a difference between two groups.

There are, however, many factors which should affect the choice of a signficance level as a basis for making a decision. If the experimenter is lenient in his selection of a significance level, he is more likely to identify variables that should be studied more intensively, but at the same time, he will also discover more effects due simply to the operation of chance factors. If the experimenter establishes a very stringent criterion for significance, he will be reasonably certain of the reality of any difference he has obtained, but he may then miss some promising leads.

At one time or another, statisticians have suggested possible considerations for selecting significance levels. For example, in 1959 a statistician made a survey of all articles appearing in all issues of four well-known psychological journals in a one-year period (Sterling, 1959). He found that of the 362 articles which were published, 294, or 81%, used tests of significance in evaluating the results. Of these articles, over 97% concluded that the differences they found were significant at the 5% level. Another way of saying this is that almost all the 294 articles using tests of significance rejected the null hypothesis at the 5% level. Only about 3% of the articles did not reject the null hypothesis and concluded that the experimental conditions they imposed had no effect. None of the reports were found to be replications of previously published experiments.

When an investigator rejects the null hypothesis at the 5% level, it means he is willing to risk being wrong 5 times in 100 replications. In the light of this survey it appears that investigators do not generally publish experiments if they do not show significant differences at the 5% level or better. This means that the readers of experimental journals have no idea of how many times an experiment may have been replicated by some other investigators without their being able to reject the null hypothesis, since it is likely that many more experiments are performed than are actually published. Let us illustrate this point with an hypothetical example. Suppose ten investigators at different times and places perform experiments to determine if praising children tends to increase their proficiency in arithmetic; assume that no clear-cut effects are found. No reports of this work are published. If another investigator then repeats these experiments and finds a significant effect and publishes a report of his research, how shall we interpret this?

It is obvious that even if there is no real difference between two groups or two conditions, if we take enough samples we will occasionally find what appears to be a real difference but which is due, in fact, to random sampling fluctuations. This means, most likely, that a certain number of the published articles describing a significant difference between groups are actually in error, and that the observed differences are chance effects of sampling. These people are making what is called a Type I error, i.e., they are rejecting the null hypothesis when it is true. (A Type II error accepts the null hypothesis when it is false.) What this all means is that a Type I error has a good chance of ending up in print, whereas a Type II error does not. Since the reader does not know how many other related experiments have been performed with negative results (i.e., where no significant differences were found), he cannot accept at face value the risk stated by the author.

Some statisticians have suggested the need for conservatism in judging the significance of results. The statistician Cochran (1947) points out that when distributions are not normal, the use of the t-test, although fairly accurate, tends to err slightly in the direction of announcing too many significant results. In a similar vein, Lindquist (1953) points out that a good deal of research is concerned not so much with whether some condition affects some result (e.g., whether praise affects arithmetic performance), but rather with whether or not it is a relatively important factor. He writes:

Having performed exploratory experiments with a number of possible factors, all of which may be real but not equally important, we would like to give priority in subsequent experimentation to the factors which are most important. If we always set a high level of significance for our tests at the exploratory level, we may be quite sure that we will not follow many completely false leads, and at the same time we will have some assurance that the true leads which we ignore (because of Type II errors) are probably among the less promising ones.

Another proposed reason for applying more stringent levels in evaluating the significance of differences relates to a recent development in mathematical statistics called *Bayesian Statistical Inference*. Although the details of the theory are quite technical, a few of the ideas and their implications may be summarized here. Bayesian statistics may be thought of as a set of methods for describing the opinions of ideally consistent people. Each person approaches a new situation with an expectation or "prior probability" estimate. This becomes modified by exposure to new data, but the new data are meaningful only in the context of the prior expectations. If, for example, a person who does not feel well takes his temperature and gets a reading of 110 degrees, he will most likely not rush off to the hospital but will assume that the thermometer is broken. A finding too inconsistent with prior opinions will normally lead to a reevaluation of the observed facts.

In most experimental situations, the investigator imposes conditions on his subjects which he has some reason to believe will have an effect on them. He may inject them with a drug or change their motivation or impose a stress. In such cases the use of a null hypothesis which assumes no effect is really considered to be rather unlikely by the experimenter, and his prior expectation is that it has small chance of being correct. On the other hand, his prior expectation of an effect of some sort is quite high. In making a null hypothesis test, he is therefore typically comparing an unlikely, fairly precise, null hypothesis, against a likely, rather diffuse, expectation of some effect. When this idea is formalized mathematically, it turns out that many situations may arise where the usual t-test would imply rejection of the null hypothesis, whereas the Bayesian approach in the same situation would imply *acceptance* of the null hypothesis. This is partly related to the fact that most rejections of the null hypothesis are based on test statistics close to the borderline (i.e., 5% level). As the level used for the evaluation of significance becomes higher (e.g., 1 or $\frac{1}{10}\%$, etc.) the usual t-test and the Bayesian approach tend to agree more and more. This therefore argues for greater conservatism in evaluating null hypotheses. For a detailed discussion of Bayesian inference, the interested student should see the paper by Edwards, Lindman, and Savage (1963).

Another statistical issue that has arisen in the evaluation of experimental data concerns the question of whether to use one or two tails of the theoretical sampling distribution. Suppose, for example, that two groups of randomly selected schizophrenic patients are picked for a study designed to determine if a new drug is an effective tranquilizer. An experimental group takes pills containing the drug, the control group takes pills containing a placebo (e.g., sugar). The general behavior (on the ward) of members of both groups is then rated and compared. The null hypothesis is that there is no real difference between the groups.

Now it is at this point in the analysis that some investigators have argued that the only difference of interest to them is a difference in favor of the experimental group, e.g., an increase in cooperativeness on the ward. In such a case, they say, it is possible to use only one tail of the sampling distribution (as shown in Fig. 6–5) to evaluate the significance of any difference that might occur. They would, in essence, be asking the question, "What are the chances of finding an increase in cooperativeness of a given amount in favor of the experimental group as a result of chance fluctuations alone?" They ignore the possibility that the experimental group might actually get worse as a result of the drug.

The advantage of such an approach is that it makes it easier for the experimenter to find a significant difference. This is because the z or t necessary to indicate where 5% of the cases in one tail of a normal distribution falls is smaller than the z or t needed for $2\frac{1}{2}$% of the cases in each tail (see Fig. 6–6). Using a one-tailed test, a z of 1.64 is significant at the 5% level, while in the two-tailed distribution a z of 1.96 is necessary for significance at this level. Therefore, experimenters who use a one-tailed test find it easier to get a significant difference between their groups and thus to reject the null hypothesis.

A number of articles have appeared criticizing the use of

the one-tailed test. Burke (1953) has objected to it on the grounds that the discovery of new phenomena will be impeded if we tend to neglect differences in the unexpected direction. Second, by making it easier to find significant differences, relatively unreliable effects will be accepted as important. Third, it becomes easier to abuse the statistical tools we have, since an investigator who does not find a significant difference using a two-tailed test might then think up a reason for switching to a one-tailed test in order to reject the null hypothesis. Cochran (1947) has also pointed out that if a distribution is not normal, the one-tailed test is more vulnerable to error. These are all strong reasons against the use of one-tailed tests in psychology.

Eysenck (1960) presents his objections to the one-tailed test in a different way. He points out that the results of statistical evaluations are generally stated in terms of the probability of rejecting the null hypothesis. It is usual to pick a certain probability value such as 0.05 (i.e., 5% significance level) and use this to divide the range of probabilities into two parts, a significant and an insignificant part. Although this is customary, it has little advantage, since it divides a continuum into a dichotomy, losing information, and determining in an arbitrary way which research is to be considered successful and which unsuccessful. On the contrary, the results of a particular experiment achieve meaning only in a broad context and depend upon such things as their relation to previous research, their predictability from theory, and the number of cases involved. If, for example, a study of extrasensory perception produced a result significant at the 5% level, it would be of questionable meaning in view of the many previous failures to find significant effects. Two similar experiments finding significant differences at the 4 and 6% level respectively are actually in good agreement even though one is arbitrarily called significant and the other is not. Eysenck goes so far as to suggest that the concepts of significant and nonsignificant as determined by an arbitrary rule of thumb be dropped entirely and that each experiment must be interpreted in the light of all available background information. There should be a clear separation of the objective statement of the probability of disproving the null hypothesis by means of a two-tailed test and the subjective evaluation and interpretation of the results.

The comments by all these authors show again the need for careful evaluation of experiments, not only in terms of simple statistical rules, but also in terms of other kinds of information. Statistics is a tool of research and not an end in itself, and it cannot guarantee meaningful conclusions simply by virtue of its application to experimental findings.

One vivid illustration of this point occurred in a Canadian hospital many years ago when diphtheria vaccine was first introduced. Over a period of several years the diphtheria vaccine was administered to several hundred people admitted to the hospital with diphtheria, while a control group of patients in the same hospital were treated in the fashion that had been in common use up to that time. It was found that 16% of the patients given the diphtheria vaccine died, while only 8% of the patients who were treated in the usual way died. The difference turned out to be statistically significant at better than the 5% level. The vaccine was apparently a menace to health, yet today this same vaccine is used routinely as a preventive measure. Why?

The answer is simply that the hospital authorities had been administering the vaccine only to patients who were very seriously ill (like trying a new drug on a terminal cancer patient), while they gave their usual treatment to those patients with milder symptoms. The groups were not comparable, and this resulted in a higher recovery rate for the older method. The moral of the story is that a significant difference does not prove anything unless the experiment is well designed. Even under ideal conditions there are limitations to what can be discovered from a single experiment.

There is an important implication that follows from the preceding discussions. One of the fundamental characteristics of scientific data is that the results of experiments are reproducible by any competent investigator in another laboratory, or by the same investigator on subsequent occasions. Rather than rely exclusively on statistical tests to confirm the reality of an obtained effect, researchers should rely more on independent replication of results. This is particularly important when differences appear significant at some borderline significance level, regardless of what that level is. To paraphrase an old Chinese proverb, "One replication is worth a thousand t-tests."

NONPARAMETRIC METHODS

In the last few years, a number of statisticians have provided tests of significance which do not require as many assumptions as the t-test and the F-test already described. The major characteristic of these so-called "nonparametric" tests is that they do not generally make any assumptions about the shape of the distributions from which the samples have been selected. They do not assume, for example, that the distributions are normal.

This characteristic, which makes such tests more generally applicable, is only one advantage among several. In addition, they may be used with scores which are only rankings as well as with more sophisticated forms of measurement. Rankings of two groups of officers on leadership ability may be compared using nonparametric tests, whereas the use of a z- or t-test with the same data may introduce an unknown degree of bias. Another advantage of these techniques is that the use of ranking systems greatly simplifies the computational detail.

These are all important advantages, and they justify the increasing frequency with which such tests are being used in research. They do have some disadvantages, however, which limit their value. The major limitation is that they are usually less sensitive to differences than the usual t-test would be. In other words, these tests are less likely to detect a significant difference between groups, if it is present, than the classical tests. This is simply due to the fact that the nonparametric tests usually reduce a set of measurements to ranks and manipulate only the ranks. This actually causes a loss of information concerning the absolute differences between the measurements.

To take an example, suppose eight dogs, representing two different breeds, are tested to determine the number of trials each animal takes to learn a signal necessary to avoid an electric shock. Assume that four beagles take 5, 8, 20, and 35 trials, and that four terriers take 3, 6, 14, and 21 trials. The mean number of trials for the beagles is 17 and for the terriers 11; therefore, a breed difference is suggested. However, if these values are reduced to rankings and all 8 measures are ranked, we get rankings of 2, 4, 6, and 8 for the beagles and rankings of 1, 3, 5, and 7 for the terriers. The mean ranks are 5 and 4 respectively, thus making the possibility of a significant breed difference less likely. In the language of the statistician, the nonparametric tests have less *power efficiency* than the classical tests. They are more likely to accept the null hypothesis, even when it is false, than the classical tests would.

Another limitation of nonparametric tests when used for the analysis of variance is that they are generally unable to test for certain aspects of the relationships between two or more variables (namely, interactions) without making some of the same kinds of assumptions that parametric tests, such as F, make.

It is important to emphasize that *both* the classical and nonparametric tests assume that the members of the sample are drawn randomly and independently from whatever populations are being studied. If the sample is biased and the selections are not independent, there are no tests which give valid conclusions.

AN EXAMPLE OF A NONPARAMETRIC TEST:
THE MANN-WHITNEY U-TEST

This is one of the better known of the nonparametric tests and is useful when two groups are to be compared and when the populations are believed to be markedly non-normal.

Suppose two strains of mice are to be evaluated for exploratory activity. Five mice of each strain are randomly selected and allowed to wander through an enclosure marked with grid lines. The number of lines crossed in a 10-minute period is the index of exploratory drive. The scores for the mice, recorded as the number of grids crossed in a 10-minute period, are as follows:

Strain A	210	282	256	270	234
Strain B	190	203	220	252	242

It is now necessary to arrange the scores in order of size, but in doing this the sample from which each score comes should be identified.

190	203	210	220	234	242	252	256	270	282
B	B	A	B	A	B	B	A	A	A

The statistic U is obtained by counting the number of A-scores preceding each B-score, as follows:

$$U = 1 + 2 + 2 = 5$$

This value of U may be looked up in a special table, found in Siegel (1956), and it will be seen that a sequence of this sort is significant at approximately the 7% level, i.e., it is not significant by the usual 5% criterion. Another way of saying this is that on the assumption of the null hypothesis of no difference between these two strains of mice, a sequence of the kind obtained will be found 7 times in 100 on the basis of random sampling fluctuations using sample sizes of 5.

Those interested in a comprehensive discussion of nonparametric tests with detailed illustrations of their use in psychology might examine the book by Siegel (1956). It should be evident that in order to utilize any kind of statistical test intelligently, we must consider the reasonableness of the assumptions which underlie its use. Nonparametric tests are helpful in certain situations where there is marked non-normality and where the data are essentially rank-order type information, but they are no substitute for careful planning of experiments and random selection of subjects.

THE TREATMENT OF

FUNCTIONAL DATA

> Although all science is fundamentally empirical, it is easy to put too much confidence in a curve or formula fitted to some observed points but unsupported by any conceptual scheme. . . . Purely empirical formulas should not be trusted too far from the data on which they are based. A good theory can help considerably.
>
> —E. BRIGHT WILSON, JR.

The previous chapter has described some fundamental concepts, as well as some cautions, connected with the use of statistical procedures. Most of the techniques presented tend to be used in the context of exploratory research; they are generally concerned simply with determining whether a variable manipulated by the experimenter can produce a reliable effect. Such research is designed to determine, for example, whether time between trials is a factor influencing learning, or whether stress is likely to influence memory. The answer is typically given in yes-no or dichotomous terms. Yet it is a fact that most variables of interest to psychologists—intelligence, stress, learning, anxiety, motivation—are not dichotomies but are continuous functions which vary or can be made to vary over a range of values. Once we go beyond the simple exploratory study concerned only with identifying variables, we become interested in finding out how a systematic change in one variable affects another. In other words, we become interested in the precise relationships between two or more variables. Unfortunately, much of classical statistics, using methods such as t-tests, is concerned primarily with exploratory research and is not particularly applicable to the study of functional relationships. In view of this, what kinds of mathematical or statistical devices can be used in dealing with the resulting functional data? The purpose of the present chapter is to describe a few of the simpler mathematical concepts used in the analysis of such information.

THE SEARCH FOR LAWS

Scientists typically seek generalizations. They are rarely interested in the results of single experiments except insofar as they relate to other studies and other sources of information. Although at an early stage of investigation of a problem they may use a qualitative statement of a relation, they aim toward eventually making the statement more precise. They attempt to go from a tentative generalization to a precise law.

Let us look at one classic illustration of this process. Well over 100 years ago experiments were performed to learn how people see and hear the world. One kind of study was concerned with *differential thresholds*, that is, how sensitive our sense organs are to small changes in the intensity of stimulation.

One of the first things discovered was that the sensitivity of the eye to a change in illumination depended on what the initial level of illumination was. In a dimly lit room only a small increment in light intensity was needed before a change was noticed, whereas in a brightly lighted room a larger change in light intensity was required for the change to be noticeable. Similar findings were also observed for other sense modalities. Such research was exploratory. It identified an important variable (i.e., the intensity of the stimulus) and a crude kind of generalization was possible: the brighter the initial illumination, the greater the amount of light that was needed before a change was noticed.

It was not long before attempts were made to extend these studies in order to determine in a more precise way the relation between initial level of intensity (symbolized I) and the change necessary to be just noticed (symbolized ΔI and pronounced delta I or "change in" I). Experiments showed that over a wide range of intensities the just noticeable change was directly proportional to the initial level of intensity. This fact could be summarized by a single mathematical equation

$$\frac{\Delta I}{I} = C \tag{1}$$

This means that the ratio of the just noticeable change to the initial level is always a constant, symbolized by the letter C. This simple equation is known as Weber's law, and it summarizes in a simple way, a great many observations that have been made. In addition, it allowed *interpolations* and *extrapolations* to conditions that had never been tried before. It also provided some reliable information that needed explaining. In other words, theorists now had something to theorize about. As might be expected, however, this simple relationship turned out to be correct only for a part of the range of intensities, and as more extreme values were used, more complicated equations became necessary.

This general pattern of (1) identifying a variable, (2) determining precise functional relations between it and some measure of response, (3) extending the range of study of the variable, and (4) expressing the relationship in mathematical terms has been followed in many areas of psychology, particularly in connection with sensory psychology and learning.

Putting a set of observations into mathematical form has several advantages. For one thing, it enables interpolations and extrapolations to be made. This is extremely important since researchers are usually interested in the *relation* between two (or more) variables and *not* in the particular values they happened to pick for study. Thus, in an experiment in which the effects of 24 hours of deprivation are compared with the effects of 12 hours of deprivation, the investigator would ideally like to know what the effects of *all* deprivation times are and not just the effects of 24 and 12 hours. If he established a functional relation between deprivation time and speed of running a maze, then he could estimate what might happen if he used 18 or 23 or 32 hours of deprivation. If the results were reliable and consistent, they could be described by a mathematical equation and called a *law*.

A second important value of the mathematical statement of a relationship is that it often provides a clear-cut basis for theory construction. Theories are generally designed to explain results, and they can do this only if the results to be explained are clearly stated and unequivocal.

Third, the mathematical statement of relations sometimes helps clarify inconsistencies in previous research. When Weber's law was stated precisely, it was immediately recognized to be only an approximation to the facts. Several other mathematical formulations have since been tried with varying degrees of success in summarizing the experimental observations. This point will be elaborated later in this chapter.

CONCEPTS OF CURVE FITTING

At the conclusion of the data collection phase of a multivalent (or parametric) experiment, the investigator usually has a set of measurements of some dependent variable at certain selected values of an independent variable. For example, the measurements may consist of the number of trials it took a group of animals to learn to jump over a partition in order to avoid getting an electric shock, the independent variable here being the intensity, in milliamperes, of the electric current. The usual first step in analyzing the data is to determine the mean values for each set of measurements and then to plot them on a graph as illustrated in the hypothetical data of Fig. 7–1. The circles represent the mean values based on five animals per group. The problem now arises of how best to summarize the relationship by means of a mathematical equation. This is the problem of fitting a curve to the data. The aim is generally to find a single expression which represents the mean values as closely as possible. Unfortunately this is a more difficult problem than one might realize, and it is "in a sense an art; it cannot be reduced to a set of inflexible rules" (Lewis, 1960).

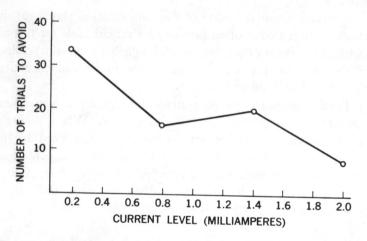

Fig. 7-1. Hypothetical data illustrating the results of a multivalent experiment.

One reason it is difficult is that it is theoretically possible to fit an infinite number of different mathematical equations to a finite set of observations. Therefore, some other criteria must be considered. The two criteria that are most important are the criteria of *continuity* and of *simplicity*.

The assumption of continuity refers to the belief that there is only *one smooth* curve that should be fitted through the obtained experimental points. The alternative would be to fit a series of straight lines from point to point as is illustrated by

Fig. 7–1. Such a series of straight lines is *discontinuous*: they imply several different mathematical relations. The assumption of continuity is made, on the other hand, for two reasons. It implies that a *single* equation is necessary for fitting the data, *and* it implies that the observed variation is partly due to the existence of errors of observation and sampling. It is assumed that if our observations were made with more precision and if the number of measurements was greatly increased, the apparent irregularities in the curve would disappear, leaving a smooth, continuous transition from point to point.

Another way of saying this is that there is an unknown amount of error associated with each measurement and that the smooth continuous curve we draw is designed to approximate the *theoretical outcome* under ideal conditions using large numbers of subjects and many precise measurements. Such a theoretical curve is usually called a *best-fitting* curve. The expression best-fitting curve is used in a general sense and can apply to straight lines as well as curved lines.

A problem still remains. There are many continuous curves that may be drawn through a set of points on a graph, and therefore, a further decision must be made. This decision is usually made on the basis of a desire for simplicity. What is simple for the layman may not necessarily be considered simple by the mathematician, and so the term is used only in the mathematical sense. Some equations are mathematically simpler than others, and the researcher usually tries to select the simplest equation that fits his data closely. For example, a straight line is considered simpler than a curved line.

MATHEMATICAL EQUATIONS: A COMMON LANGUAGE

If the investigator is interested in the simplest mathematical equation that fits closely to his data, then his range of choices is considerably narrowed. From a mathematical point of view there are only three or four types of simple equations that are frequently found to be appropriate to many types of empirical measurements. For example, the following is an *exponential* equation used in optics to estimate the intensity of light (I) transmitted through a filter, that is, a piece of dark glass.

$$I = I_o \, e^{-kd} \qquad (2)$$

I_o is the intensity of the light source, d is the depth of the absorbing material, k is a constant, and e is a constant. The difference between k and e is that k is an empirical constant whose value depends on the particular type of glass used, while the e is a universal constant, like pi ($\pi = 3.1415 \ldots$) which has the same value in all situations. The value of e is approximately $2.718 \ldots$, and it is usually referred to as the base of the natural system of logarithms.

An equation used in meteorology is

$$p = p_o \, e^{-kh} \qquad (3)$$

where p is the pressure of the atmosphere at a certain height, p_o is the pressure at sea level, and h is the height. The values k and e are again constants, k specific to the situation and e always the same.

The third example comes from the field of psychology. A well-known psychologist named Clark Hull formulated a mathematical theory of learning (1943). In the theory, he tried to relate the strength of a habit (H) to the number of trials of training (N) the subject had, and to the plateau (M) the performance would gradually approach. His equation was

$$H = M - Me^{-iN} \qquad (4)$$

Here again, i is an empirical constant and e is the same universal constant used before. Although this equation is slightly different in form than those cited above, it is of the same general exponential type.

The point of these illustrations is that the same, or very similar, mathematical types of equations can be used in a wide variety of contexts to describe very different kinds of observations. These equations may be thought of as a kind of generalized language which enables us to talk about the common characteristics of different situations. Another way of saying this is that mathematical equations are general models, or analogies, that can be fitted to many different situations. Therefore, if we learn something about a few common models (i.e., equations) then it is likely that they can be used to describe many different situations we will encounter in research.

SOME SIMPLE EQUATIONS

The simplest equation with which the mathematician deals is one which represents a straight line. In symbolic terms the equation is

$$Y = a + bX \tag{5}$$

where a and b are constants. If we take any fixed values for a and b, such as 2 and 3, we get an equation $Y = 2 + 3X$ which can be graphically represented by the line in Fig. 7–2a. Given

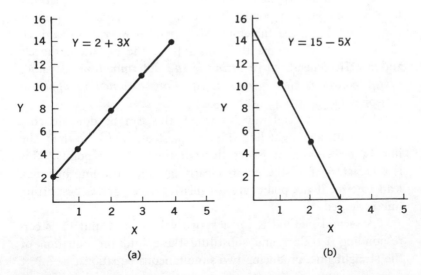

(a)

(b)

Fig. 7-2. Examples of linear equations.

the equation, the line can be plotted by substituting values for X and calculating the resulting value for Y. If X is 0, then Y is equal to 2. If X is 1, then Y is equal to 5, etc. Notice that the line crosses the Y-axis at $Y = 2$ and that the steepness or slope of the line is equal to 3. The slope is determined simply by seeing how much of an increase occurs in Y for each increase of one unit of X. In Fig. 7–2b, the line represents the equation $Y = 15 - 5X$. Here we notice that the line crosses the Y-axis at 15, but that it slopes downward to the right, i.e., it has a negative slope. For each unit increase in X there is a decrease of 5 units of Y.

It should be obvious by now that a simple generalization can be made about linear equations when they are put in the form $Y = a + bX$. It will always be the case that the constant a will determine where the line crosses the Y-axis, or to use a more formal terminology, it determines the Y-intercept. The constant b will always determine the slope.

Now we may understand what an investigator means when he says he wants to fit a straight line (i.e., a linear equation) to a set of obtained points. The data points actually represent the X and Y values; therefore, his job is to work backward, so to speak, and determine the constants of the equation, the a's and b's. In general, *curve fitting is the determination of values of the constants that belong in equations assumed to apply to sets of data.*

There are several ways in which this can be done in connection with a straight line. The simplest method is to draw the line by eye so that it passes through the observed points. This is satisfactory if all the points clearly lie along the line but may lead to error if the points are irregularly spaced and a best-fitting line is desired.

A second method is to pick two values of X and their corresponding Y values and substitute these into the equation of the straight line, producing two simultaneous equations.

Table 7-1. Hypothetical data showing the relation between the intensity (I) of a stimulus and the magnitude of the just noticeable difference ($\triangle I$)

$X(I)$	$Y(\triangle I)$
1	0.10
2	0.18
3	0.31
4	0.39
5	0.47
6	0.55

Thus, if the second and the fifth pair of points in Table 7–1 are selected the equations would be

$$0.18 = a + b(2)$$
$$0.47 = a + b(5)$$

These can be solved by simple algebraic methods to yield values for a and b. The difficulty with this procedure, however, is that the values of a and b depend on which pairs of points are selected. Therefore, the method used in practice follows this general pattern but uses all the information in the data.

This is done by dividing the data into two equal halves (odd versus even pairs would do as well) and getting the sum or means for each half. These values are then substituted into the two equations and solved. Using the data of Table 7–1, we select the first three points and determine the sums for the Xs and for the Ys. Then we do the same for the last three points. The sum of X for the upper half is $1 + 2 + 3 = 6$ and for the lower half it is $4 + 5 + 6 = 15$. The sum of Y for the upper half is $0.10 + 0.18 + 0.31 = 0.59$ and for the lower half it is $0.39 + 0.47 + 0.55 = 1.41$. For each half the as has been added three times. These values are now substituted into the equations of a straight line

$$0.59 = 3a + b(6)$$
$$1.41 = 3a + b(15)$$

These equations can be solved by subtracting the upper equation from the lower one to yield

$$1.41 - 0.59 = 3a - 3a + b(15) - b(6)$$
$$0.82 = b(9)$$
$$0.091 = b$$

By replacing this value of b in one of the above equations, we can solve for a.

$$0.59 = 3a + (0.091)\,(6)$$
$$0.59 = 3a + 0.546$$
$$0.590 - 0.546 = 3a$$
$$0.044 = 3a$$
$$0.015 = a$$

The equation of the straight line is therefore

$$Y = 0.015 + 0.091X$$

This method is called the *method of averages* and is a simple and convenient way of estimating the constants of a linear equation.

THE METHOD OF LEAST SQUARES

The technique generally considered most accurate for determining the constants of a straight line equation is called the method of least squares. It is the most frequently used method for determining the best fitting line for a set of observations.

When we draw a best fitting line by eye, we generally try to place the line in such a way that there are as many points on one side of the line as on the other. We also try to make the average distance (i.e., deviations) of the points from the line in both directions balance. These criteria, however, will not produce a unique placement of the best fitting line, and another criterion must be substituted. This criterion is that *the sum of the squares of the deviations of the observed points from the line must be a minimum*. When this criterion is met, a unique best fitting line is obtained based on all of the data of the experiment.

On the basis of this assumption it is possible to develop equations that enable us to determine the constants a and b of the best fitting line for a set of observations. The procedure again involves the establishment of a pair of simultaneous equations which are then solved for a and b. The solutions can be generalized in the following two equations.

$$a = \frac{\Sigma X^2 \, \Sigma Y - (\Sigma XY)(\Sigma X)}{N\Sigma X^2 - (\Sigma X)^2} \qquad (6)$$

$$b = \frac{N\Sigma XY - (\Sigma X)(\Sigma Y)}{N\Sigma X^2 - (\Sigma X)^2} \qquad (7)$$

In these equations a and b are the constants to be determined, N refers to the number of paired observations, ΣX is the sum of the values of the X (or independent) variable, ΣX^2 is the sum of the squares of the X values, ΣY is the sum of the values of the Y (or dependent variable), and ΣXY is the sum of the values obtained by multiplying each X value by its corresponding Y value.

The use of these equations may be illustrated by the data of Table 7–2 which is Table 7–1 rewritten and extended. To

Table 7-2. Hypothetical data showing the relation between the intensity (I) of a stimulus and the magnitude of the just noticeable difference (ΔI)

$X(I)$	$Y(\Delta I)$	XY	X^2
1	0.10	0.10	1
2	0.18	0.36	4
3	0.31	0.93	9
4	0.39	1.56	16
5	0.47	2.35	25
6	0.55	3.30	36
21	2.00	8.60	91
ΣX	ΣY	ΣXY	ΣX^2

determine the Y-intercept a, we substitute the various sums from Table 7–2 into equation (6):

$$a = \frac{(91)(2.00) - (8.60)(21)}{6(91) - (21)(21)}$$

$$a = \frac{182 - 180.6}{546 - 441}$$

$$a = \frac{1.4}{105}$$

$$a = 0.013$$

We may proceed similarly with equation (7) to determine the slope constant b:

$$b = \frac{6(8.60) - (21)(2.00)}{6(91) - (21)(21)}$$

$$b = \frac{51.60 - 42.00}{546 - 441}$$

$$b = \frac{9.60}{105}$$

$$b = 0.091$$

The resulting best fitting linear equation determined by the method of least squares is therefore

$$Y = 0.013 + 0.091X$$

If this equation is compared with the one calculated by the method of averages, we see that there is a slight discrepancy but that the two methods are in very good agreement. The differences are due largely to the arbitrary way of dividing the data into two groups in the method of averages. Whenever a precise estimate is desired, the method of least squares should be used.

USES OF LINEAR EQUATIONS

There are at least three different kinds of situations in which linear equations are used. They are used to describe experimental data and are often a good first approximation for a set of observations. This was seen, for example, in our discussion of Weber's law. The Woodworth and Schlosberg text (1954) gives a number of illustrations of linear relations observed in psychological research.

Linear equations are also used in analyzing the appropriateness of more complex curve forms for given sets of data by providing a simple *transformation*. More will be said about this point later.

Finally, linear equations are at the basis of one of the important tools of statistical analysis—the correlation technique. We shall begin by briefly examining this last point.

CORRELATION AS LINEAR COVARIATION

If two sets of measurements are collected, we may, if we wish, attempt to correlate them. The measurements may consist of such things as IQs and high school averages for a group of students, age and speed of learning scores in a group of rats, or length of reported breast feeding in infancy and frequency of cigarette smoking in a group of adults. In such cases it is not necessary to assume that one of the variables is, in any sense, the cause of the other. We look only at the covariation or the degree to which they vary together. If one of the variables increases when the other does, we speak of a positive correlation; if it decreases when the other increases, we speak of a negative correlation; and if there is no systematic relation between the two variables, we describe this as a zero correlation. The degree of correlation is indicated by a coefficient which may vary from +1.0 to −1.0. These general possibilities are illustrated in Fig. 7–3.

The method that is actually used to obtain a specific numerical value of the correlation coefficient depends upon certain assumptions. One of these assumptions is that the relationship between the two variables, X and Y, can be adequately described by a best fitting *straight line*. The way the best fitting

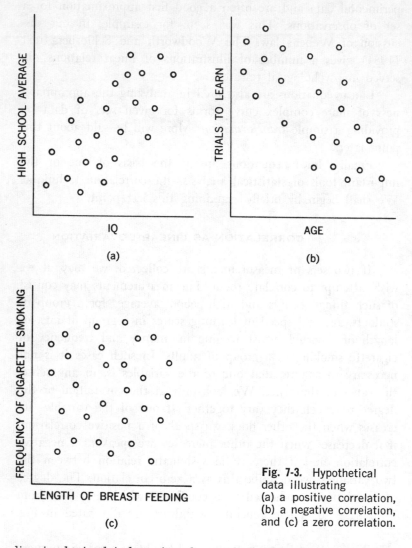

Fig. 7-3. Hypothetical data illustrating (a) a positive correlation, (b) a negative correlation, and (c) a zero correlation.

line is obtained is by using the method of least squares to determine the slope of the line. This is done after all the scores are converted to z-scores to make all distributions comparable. Then two best fitting lines are determined, one with the deviations minimized in relation to the X-axis, and the other with the deviations minimized in relation to the Y-axis. The correlation coefficient r is then simply the average of the two slopes (except that in this case, the geometric mean is used instead of the arithmetic mean).

The process described above would be quite tedious to compute, so several alternate, but equivalent formulas are used. If the data are conveniently arranged in z-score form, then

$$r = \frac{\Sigma z_x z_y}{N} \tag{8}$$

where N is the number of pairs of measurements and $\Sigma z_x z_y$ is the sum of the products of paired z-scores.

Unfortunately, data in z-score form is seldom available, so a computing formula based upon the original scores is typically used. This equation is

$$r = \frac{N\Sigma XY - (\Sigma X)(\Sigma Y)}{\sqrt{[N\Sigma X^2 - (\Sigma X)^2][N\Sigma Y^2 - (\Sigma Y)^2]}} \tag{9}$$

N is again the number of paired measurements, ΣX and ΣY refer to the sum of the X- and Y-scores, ΣX^2 and ΣY^2 refer to the sum of the squares of the X- and Y-scores, and ΣXY is the sum of the products of all XY pairs.

The correct use of this formula, as well as most other correlation methods, depends upon the appropriateness of the assumption of linearity, that is, the extent to which a straight line is a best fit for the set of observations. Thus, concepts relevant to linear equations are basic to this important tool.

LINEAR EQUATIONS AS TRANSFORMATIONS

Another and equally important use of linear functions is in connection with the testing of theories and the evaluation of goodness of fit. This last expression means, among other things, that one kind of mathematical equation is more appropriate to observations than another; it describes them better because it "fits" the points more closely. To make this idea clearer, we will examine a specific illustration.

Around the middle of the last century a German physicist named Fechner proposed that there existed a simple relationship between the strength of a person's sensations and the intensity of stimuli which impinged upon his sense organs. Fechner suggested that the relation was logarithmic and that it could be expressed by the equation

$$S = k \log I \tag{10}$$

where S was meant to represent the strength of a person's sensations, k was a constant which depended on the sense modality, and I was the intensity of the stimulus. The logarithm of a number is defined as the power to which the number 10 must be raised in order to produce that number. (The logarithm of 100 is 2 because $10^2 = 100$; the logarithm of 1000 is 3 because $10^3 = 1000$.)

If we examine Fechner's equation, we see that it implies that a person's sensations do not increase in strength in the same proportion as the external stimulus does. An increase in the external stimulus from 100 units to 1000 units would only increase the strength of the sensation from 2 to 3 units (if k had a value of 1.0). If the external stimulus increased 1 million times, the sensation might increase only 6 times.

Although there was evidence that such a relationship might be true for some cases, there were enough discrepancies to prompt psychologists to look for other equations to represent the various findings.

One of the recent attempts along these lines has been made by Stevens (1957), who has suggested that the relationship between sensation S and the intensity I of the stimulus can be represented by a *power law* of the form

$$S = kI^n \tag{11}$$

where k is an arbitrary constant and n is another constant which depends on the sense modality and the individual subject.

Given these different equations, how does one go about deciding which is more appropriate to the experimental data? One of the major methods that is used is to transform the theoretical equation into the equation of a straight line and check for linearity of the observed data. This notion will now be explained.

The word *transformation* as used in mathematics refers to any procedure which systematically modifies a number or an equation. For example, if we have a set of numbers and we double each one, this is a simple transformation. Similarly, taking the square root or the logarithm of each number is a transformation. But this idea can be applied to equations as well as to numbers. If we have an equation such as $Y = 2X$, then we can transform the equation without altering its basic equivalence by performing the same operation on both sides. Thus $2Y = 4X$ or $\sqrt{Y} = \sqrt{2X}$ or $\log Y = \log (2X)$. So long as we use the same procedure on both sides of the equation, the equality remains.

Let us illustrate this point by reference to an equation of the form

$$Y = aX^b \tag{12}$$

This type of equation is referred to as parabolic or hyperbolic, depending on the value of the exponent b; it is also called a power function. Depending on the values of the constants, the curve may increase or decrease, but in all cases the curves gradually approach a plateau or *asymptote*.

It is possible to transform this equation into another useful form by means of a logarithmic transformation, that is, by taking the logarithm of both sides. This will yield $\log Y = \log (aX^b)$. This can be reduced still further on the basis of some rules governing the manipulation of logarithms, rules which are typically covered in any high school algebra course. For example, one rule says that the logarithm of a product ab is equal to the sum of the logarithms of each term, or $\log ab = \log a + \log b$. Another rule says that the logarithm of a number raised to a power ($\log X^a$) is equal to the power times the logarithm of the number, or $\log X^a = a \log X$.

We will now use these rules to simplify equation (12).

$$\log Y = \log (aX^b)$$

But since aX^b is the product of two terms a and X^b, we may write

$$\log Y = \log a + \log X^b$$

The term $\log X^b$ may be further reduced to $b \log X$ by the second rule governing the manipulation of logarithms. Thus the equation finally becomes

$$\log Y = \log a + b \log X \qquad (13)$$

The equation $Y = aX^b$ when written in this form is actually the equation of a straight line. This will become evident if we substitute the letter Y' for $\log Y$, a' for $\log a$, and X' for $\log X$. The equation may then be written

$$Y' = a' + bX' \qquad (14)$$

This is quite obviously the equation of a straight line if we plot Y' against X'. In practice, this would mean plotting $\log Y$ against $\log X$. The slope of the line which results is the constant b and the Y-intercept is actually equal to $\log a$; from this a can be calculated.

To summarize the points made here: If we assume an equation of the form $Y = aX^b$, then we can transform this equation into a straight line form by taking the logarithms of both sides. If the experimental data actually conform to this equation, then by plotting the log of the X-values against the corresponding log of the Y-values, a straight line should result graphically. If it does not, then it means that the equation is probably inappropriate. This general procedure of transforming a complex equation into a straight line form is not limited to the one type of function described above but can be used with many different kinds of equations.

In the light of this discussion, it is evident that the equation suggested by Stevens is in a form which can be easily transformed into a straight line for testing. Given that

$$S = kI^n$$

then

$$\log S = \log k + n \log I$$

This means that if the so-called *power law* is true, when we plot the logarithm of the intensity (I) of the stimulus, against the logarithm of the subjective sensation S, we should find a straight line whose slope is n and whose Y-intercept is $\log k$.

It is easy to measure the intensity of a physical stimulus such as a light or a sound, but how can we measure the intensity of a subjective sensation? Since this point will be discussed in detail in a later chapter, we simply note at this time that a rating scale method (magnitude estimation) can be used for evaluating the intensity of subjective sensations. In one study Stevens (1957) used a scale of 0 to 100 and required subjects to rate the intensity of their sensations. The physical stimuli were tones and lights of varying intensity. When the logarithms of both these sets of measurements were plotted, the results looked like those in Fig. 7-4. The plotted values in both cases

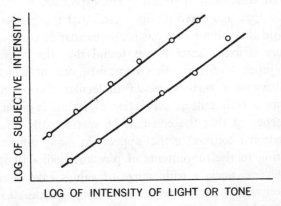

Fig. 7-4. The logarithms of varying light or sound intensities are plotted against the logarithms of magnitude estimations of subjective intensity. (Adapted from S. S. Stevens, 1957.)

fall very nicely along straight lines, implying that the equation $S = kI^n$ is a very good summary of these data. Hence, the linear function plays a role in deciding on the appropriateness of complex theoretical equations for particular sets of observations.

We have thus seen that the straight line equation is a valuable tool (1) in summarizing data, (2) in correlational analysis, and (3) in testing the appropriateness of complex, theoretical equations for specific sets of data. For more detailed discussions of some of these points, the interested reader is referred to Guilford (1954) and Lewis (1960).

A NOTE ON CONSTANTS

From a mathematical point of view it is always possible to calculate the constants that are used with a particular equation. Since the values of the constants depend upon the obtained data, they may vary from experiment to experiment. It is therefore always especially interesting when an investigator discovers the *same constant* appearing in several different situations. It suggests to him that there may be some common elements in the different situations that are worth exploring.

A long time ago chemists discovered that the product of the pressure and the volume of a gas is approximately constant if the temperature is fixed. Later it was found that the constant was itself the product of two other constants, one of which (Avogadro's) became a cornerstone of molecular theory. Similarly, the distance a body falls as a function of time t is given as $16t^2$. It was discovered that the constant 16 was actually one half of the gravitational constant g that appears in many different equations relating to the movements of physical bodies in space.

In Stevens' work, a wide range of values have been found for the constant n in the power law, ranging from 0.3 to 3.5. A study by Jones and Marcus (1961) has revealed large differences in the constants of the equation obtained from different individuals in the same test situation. They have therefore proposed that the constant n be considered as the product of two constants, one of which is to reflect the individual and the other the modality. If this program can be successfully implemented, perhaps a generalized constant will be found which is appropriate to many different situations.

A final point is that curve fitting is most useful in the context of a theory. This idea was stated in the quote introducing this chapter, and there is no better way to emphasize the point than to repeat part of it: "Purely empirical formulas should not be trusted too far from the data on which they are based. A good theory can help considerably."

CONCEPTS OF CAUSALITY

IN EXPERIMENTATION

The scientific methodologies in the various sciences undergo continual change, and the mark of a successful investigator is that he can find novel methods of solving his problems.

—ALPHONSE CHAPANIS

The fact that there exist many different experimental design methods reflects the fact that there are many different kinds of problems. Experimental designs are basically ways of arranging the conditions of an experiment in order to identify relevant variables, and determine causes of events. Since causation is one of the key concepts involved in experimental design, it will be helpful to indicate briefly what is meant by this term.

THE CONCEPT OF CAUSALITY

There have been many discussions by philosophers and scientists concerning the concept of causality and many subtle issues are involved. A few of the important notions will be described here.

In the eighteenth century, David Hume, the philosopher, presented a very important analysis of the concept of causality. He pointed out that there seem to be three important criteria that people use to judge (explicitly or implicitly) that one event is the cause of another. First, it is usually assumed that the cause and the effect are very closely related in space or are *contiguous*. One of the reasons that Newton's concept of gravitation was not immediately accepted is that his gravitational law seemed to imply some kind of action-at-a-distance. This idea was so completely inconsistent with the notion of causality accepted even by Newton himself that many physicists tried to develop modified gravitational theories which did not require this assumption.

Second, it is assumed that the *cause must precede the effect* in time. So strongly has this idea influenced scientists that the great French mathematician, Laplace, early in the nineteenth century, claimed that if he could know the present conditions of the universe he could predict its future course for all time.

The third assumption often made in connection with the idea of causality is that there is a *necessary connection* between a cause and its effect. To understand this notion requires a definition of two important terms: *necessary* and *sufficient conditions*. When it is said that event A is necessary for event B to occur, it means that B cannot occur unless A has occurred, but it does not mean that B must occur whenever A occurs. This is because event A may be necessary for B but not sufficient; that is, other conditions must also be present. When it is said that event A is a sufficient condition for event B, it implies that A can cause B, but so can other events, C, D, E, etc. In other words, A is simply one "cause" among several possible ones.

To illustrate: suppose a man is injected with a drug which produces symptoms of hallucinations thirty minutes later. If this finding is a consistent one and can be shown to occur with great uniformity, then the drug is a sufficient condition for the production of hallucinations. It is, however, not a necessary condition, since other drugs could conceivably produce similar effects, and the effects may even occur in the absence of any known administrations of drugs, as in some psychotic patients. Is it possible to say what some necessary conditions are? In a general sense, this would mean such things as the fact that the subject is an adult who can verbalize his reactions, that he is in "normal" health, that the drug gets into the bloodstream so it may be distributed to various parts of the body including the brain, etc. Although each of these conditions may be necessary, none are sufficient in themselves to cause hallucinations. One may only *assume* that there is some basic biochemical reaction in the brain, which can be triggered by several different drugs or even by modifications of diet, or certain environmental conditions, which is both *necessary* and *sufficient* to cause hallucinations in an adult.

It should be obvious from this illustration that there is a big difference between finding some of the sufficient or necessary conditions which may affect some aspect of behavior, and finding the one single necessary and sufficient condition. Typically, most research is concerned with finding sufficient conditions which affect various phenomena, while the so-called "basic, underlying cause," that is, the necessary and sufficient condition, is usually inferred, or developed, in a theory.

An interesting illustration of the ambiguity of the word *cause* is given by Morison (1960) in a discussion of the history of concepts concerning malaria.

Whatever the reason, medical men have found it congenial to assume that they could find something called *The Cause* of a particular disease. If one looks at the history of any particular disease, one finds that the notion of its cause has varied with the state of the art. In general the procedure has been to select as *The Cause* that element in the situation which one could do the most about. In many cases it turned out that, if one could take away this element or reduce its influence, the disease simply disappeared or was reduced in severity. This was certainly desirable, and it seemed sensible enough to say that one had got at the cause of the condition. Thus in ancient and medieval times malaria as its name implied was thought to be due to the bad air of the lowlands. As a result, towns were built on the tops of hills, as one notices in much of Italy today. The disease did not disappear, but its incidence and severity were reduced to a level consistent with productive community life.

At this stage it seemed reasonable enough to regard bad air as the cause of malaria, but soon the introduction of quinine to Europe from South America suggested another approach. Apparently quinine acted on some situation within the patient to relieve and often to cure him completely. Toward the end of the last century the malarial parasite was discovered in the blood of patients suffering from the disease. The effectiveness of quinine was explained by its ability to eliminate this parasite from the blood. The parasite now became *The Cause,* and those who could afford the cost of quinine and were reasonably regular in their habits were enabled to escape the most serious ravages of the disease. It did not disappear as a public health problem, however; and further study was given to the chain of causality. These studies were shortly rewarded by the discovery that the parasite was transmitted by certain species of mosquitoes. For practical purposes *The Cause* of epidemic malaria became the Mosquito, and attention was directed to control of its activities.

Entertainingly enough, however, malaria has disappeared from large parts of the world without anyone doing much about it at all. The fens of Boston and other northern cities still produce mosquitoes capable of transmitting the parasite, and people carrying the organism still come to these areas from time to time; but it has been many decades since the last case of the disease occurred locally. Observations such as this point to the probability that epidemic malaria is the result of a nicely balanced set of social and economic, as well as biological, factors, each one of which has to be present at the appropriate level. We are still completely unable to describe these sufficient conditions with any degree of accuracy, but we know what to do in an epidemic area because we have focused attention on three or four of the most necessary ones.

Research scientists in the laboratory constantly make interpretations about causes of things. How, in fact, is this done? Early in the nineteenth century John Stuart Mill, a British philosopher, described several general methods for establishing cause-effect relations. Mill tried to set down certain rules or canons that could be used as a basis for experimentally identifying causes. These methods should be understood since they provide a basis for understanding many of the currently used experimental design methods. Therefore, they will be briefly described and illustrated.

METHOD OF AGREEMENT

If several instances of some event being observed have only one circumstance in common, then that circumstance is the cause of the phenomenon. Thus, if a group of delinquent boys are all found to come from broken homes, it is sometimes said that the existence of broken homes is a "cause" of delinquency. This situation is like the frequently cited case of the man who wanted to find out in a "scientific" way, why he got drunk. The first night he drank rye and water and became drunk; the second night he drank scotch and water and became drunk; after getting drunk on bourbon and water the third night, he concluded that he had better give up water.

Obviously, in any complex situation there may be many more common factors present than the observer is aware of; and, in addition, a given effect may be produced by many different causes. Thus delinquency may be related not only to broken homes, but to economic status, value conflicts, possibilities of social mobility, or biochemical factors, any one or more of which may simultaneously be present.

The method of agreement is thus inadequate as a way of unequivocally identifying causes. However, it often provides a clue or suggestion about important variables to be looked at or examined in more experimental ways. Much of clinical practice, in both psychology and medicine, relies on this method, and at least in the case of psychoanalysis, a whole theoretical edifice has been erected on the basis of observations common to diverse patients. The existence of many rival schools and the frequent disagreements among practitioners attests, at least in part, to the unreliability of the method.

METHOD OF DIFFERENCE

If two situations differ in only one respect, and an effect is observed in one situation and not the other, then the effect is due to the factor which is different. In psychology this can be illustrated by experiments in which the investigator tries to equate two groups in as many respects as possible, and then subjects one of the groups to an experience or condition which is expected to influence some phenomenon being measured. For example, two groups of rats of an inbred strain may be established by separating litter mates randomly. One group is then required to learn a maze while it is under the influence of some drug; the other group learns the maze under identical conditions except that no drug is administered. If it turns out that maze-learning ability of one group is different from that of the other group, it is usually concluded that the difference is due to the drug (the one different factor).

Although this method is the basis for a great deal of experimental work in psychology as well as in the other sciences, it poses certain serious problems. For one thing, it requires that the two groups be equated, i.e., equal in all respects at the start of the experiment. How can one know or justify this? Even a chemist working with two samples of a purified chemical knows that certain impurities exist in one that do not exist in the other, or do not exist to the same degree. This is much truer of complex biological organisms such as rats, monkeys, or men, who differ not only in genetic endowment but in life experiences as well.

The answer usually given to this objection is that groups are equated not on all possible conditions, but only on *relevant variables*, that is, variables known or believed to influence the effect being measured. The problem then arises: how does one know what variables are relevant? This can only be determined by another experiment using the very method which one is trying to justify, and thus a vicious cycle is established.

A tentative answer to this dilemma can be given by pointing out that science develops only by a series of successive approximations. At any one point in the history of science, certain variables are judged to be of major relevance on the basis of experiments which are more or less limited. If at a later time inconsistencies appear or theoretical difficulties arise, it may require changes in the variables which are studied until a better approximation is obtained. This may be illustrated by the many studies of the *galvanic skin response,* or GSR. This term refers to the small electrical changes that take place in the skin under a variety of conditions. Two of the most outstanding characteristics of these reports are their inconsistency and variability. This is due not only to the great differences between subjects, but also to variations in instrumentation and methods of collecting and analyzing data. Such factors as electrode placement, type, size and pressure of electrodes, polarization effects, type of current (AC or DC), and amount of current, as well as the basal resistance of the subject, all have been found to affect the size of the GSR; thus the conception of what is a *relevant variable* has gradually been enlarged and may be taken into consideration in future research.

Similarly, it has been demonstrated that the effect of punishment on behavior depends upon such factors as the strength of the punishment, the time interval between the response and the punishment, and the strength of the response to be punished. It took a great deal of research to clearly identify even these factors and it is reasonably certain that there must be others as well. Thus, even if it were possible to take all of these factors into account in any one experiment, the results would still be tentative and conditional. It is in the nature of science to always proceed by successive approximations. An interesting analysis of this process is given by Churchman in his book *Theory of Experimental Inference* (1948).

There is a second problem which is often associated with the method of difference when one is trying to identify the one factor which is presumably responsible for an effect. This may be illustrated most clearly with drug studies. If two groups of subjects are made equal in certain respects and one group is injected with a drug while the other group is not, any differences which are found may be due to at least three different factors: (a) the chemical effect of the drug itself, or (b) the extra attention the subjects are getting, or (c) a desire to show a reaction because it is expected. If the experiment is an animal study, perhaps the pain of the injection or the extra amount of fluid in the bloodstream might have an effect independent of the drug itself. In such experiments, generally, additional groups may be studied in order to take into account these possible factors. Often a so-called placebo, or harmless material, is also administered in the same way as the drug in order to keep constant as many of these extraneous variables as possible.

This problem is one of the many reasons that research in clinical psychology is so difficult. If one of two groups of subjects presumed equal on at least a few relevant variables is exposed to therapeutic counseling while the other is not, there is no simple way of selecting the factor or factors from this complex situation which may produce a change.

JOINT METHODS OF AGREEMENT AND DIFFERENCE

Sometimes, observations using the method of agreement will enable certain hypotheses to be formulated. An hypothesis is an assumption about a possible causal factor influencing some behavior. An experiment may then be performed using the method of difference in order to determine whether the hypothesized factor actually produces an observed change.

One of the contributions of the psychoanalytic movement was its emphasis on infantile determinants of later adult behavior. This hypothesis stemmed from clinical observations. Eventually, a number of studies using the method of difference were done with lower animals in an attempt to examine some of these hypotheses. Hunt (1941), for example, exposed a group of young rats to a feeding stress (i.e. limited access to food) during the first weeks of their lives, while another group of litter mates had unlimited access to food during the same period. In later adult life, when both groups were tested for hoarding behavior under a mild deprivation stress, the previously frustrated group was found to hoard significantly more. Many other similar attempts have been made to experimentally test hypotheses developed by clinical observations. It should be obvious though that the general problem raised earlier would apply here as well.

METHOD OF CONCOMITANT VARIATION

Mill stated this canon in the following way: "Whatever phenomenon varies in any manner whenever another phenomenon varies in some particular manner, is either a cause or an effect of that phenomenon, or is connected with it through some fact of causation."

In a sense, this method is an extension of the method of difference in that instead of two equal groups being used with a certain factor present or absent, three or more groups or conditions are used, and the factor being studied is varied over a range of values. Thus, in certain studies of learning, the length of a list of syllables is varied in order to determine the effect of length on recall, or changes in the brightness of a radar screen are made in order to determine its effect on the accuracy of identification of signals. All these kinds of studies are what are usually called functional or multivalent experiments.

Some writers have interpreted this canon as also including correlation studies in which "naturally occurring" variations in some condition are correlated against some other condition. This would be indicated by correlations between IQ and school grades, or childhood training practices and adult personality traits. This last type of correlation is illustrated in an interesting way in the book by Whiting and Child (1950). Obviously, a simple correlation does not in itself give any adequate evidence for cause-effect relations. But, in general, when the method of concomitant variation is conceived as a functional type of experiment, it is more satisfactory than any of the other types thus far described. It is no surprise to discover that one of the signs of advancement in a science is an increasing use of this method in the form of multivalent experiments.

A review of this list of Mill's rules of experimental inference should make it evident that all are limited in one way or another and all involve certain assumptions which can never be completely met in practice. This is not a cause for despair; it simply reflects the fact that empirical science will *always* have an element of doubt in its findings and conclusions and will always be capable of extension and correction. As science progresses, however, we gradually move closer to an increasingly complete understanding of the nature of the universe.

OTHER METHODS FOR IDENTIFYING CAUSES

Since John Stuart Mill first formulated his canons, many extensions and developments have been made. The detailed application of these ideas to psychology will be the subject of a later chapter; at this point, however, one other general schema for identifying causes is pertinent. In a contemporary book dealing with research problems in the physical sciences, Wilson (1952) described various methods which can be used to identify causes of difficulty in equipment which does not work properly. These methods will be described here, using psychologically related illustrations.

METHOD OF ARTIFICIAL VARIATION

If a piece of equipment does not function properly, vary a *suspected* cause by an amount greater than normal and see if the troublesome effect correlates closely with these variations.

An example of this might be the following. Suppose an investigator wishes to determine the number of trials it takes to learn lists of nonsense syllables of a given length. He discovers that there is a great deal of variability in the results, not only from subject to subject but also from one list to another. After considering the matter, he suspects that a possible reason for the variability is that the nonsense syllables vary a lot in the degree to which they suggest actual words, a property called *association value*. Some lists seem to have many words with high association value and some have only a few such words.

Using the *method of artificial variation* as a guide, the experimenter makes up several lists with syllables which vary systematically in association value, and he then measures the number of trials it takes to learn each list. If he finds that this varies with association value, he concludes that it is possible that this factor produced the large variability in his original study.

This conclusion is at best tentative since there are several other alternatives. It is possible, for example, that although the large changes in association value that were actually tried may affect rate of learning, the smaller ones present in the original experiment may have had little to do with the variability of the findings. Even if association value is a real variable affecting learning, it may still be the wrong variable in this particular case.

Another problem that may arise with this method is that it is sometimes difficult or impossible to produce the artificial variations one believes are responsible for the effect. If it is suspected that changes of the weather affect moods or that childhood experiences of frustration affect an adult's frustration tolerance, it is extremely difficult to actually manipulate these suspected causes outside their normal range of variation in order to test the hypotheses. Thus, this method, although useful, is not without limitations.

METHOD OF STABILIZATION

Another method for determining whether a suspected cause is operating in a given situation is to *reduce* the variation in the suspected cause. In the previously discussed example, if the experimenter suspects that the association value of the syllables varies from list to list, he might then prepare a series of lists which are deliberately made equal in association value. Of course, this has to be done by some independent method, using other subjects. If this can be done, and the variability in the data decreases, it is possible that this factor had originally produced the large variability. This, again, is not entirely certain, since other factors might have been varied in the new lists of syllables. The method, though useful, is never conclusive.

METHOD OF CORRELATION

This method simply requires the recording of naturally occurring changes in a suspected variable and correlating them with changes in some observed effect. This kind of procedure is, of course, frequently used in psychology as well as in some other sciences. Some of the limitations have already been described, but a few additional comments will be made here.

One of the difficulties sometimes encountered in correlational studies is the existence of time lags between cause and effect which greatly obscure or minimize the correlation between them. This may be illustrated by studies concerned with the medical effects of new drugs. Not uncommonly the undesirable side effects do not occur immediately but only weeks or even years later, or they occur only under special circumstances. A case in point is thalidomide, one of the tranquilizers. A large number of people had used the drug without any apparent ill effects. Then it began to be noticed that pregnant women who had used it gave birth to defective infants. Subsequent research showed that the drug is relatively harmless for all users except pregnant women during a certain critical period. These complex relationships obscured any simple correlation between drug usage and side effects.

The other point to be made about correlation studies is an old one: correlation does not necessarily imply cause. If two events are causally related, then there will be a correlation between them, but a correlation between two events does not necessarily mean that they are causally related. In other words, a correlation may be a *necessary* condition for causation but not a *sufficient* condition. However, correlation studies are valuable for suggesting hypotheses about possible causes which can be investigated by other design methods.

THE FACTORIAL METHOD

If several suspected factors are operating simultaneously to produce some observed change, it is possible to determine their relative contributions and interactions in the following way. Arrange to give each suspected variable a high and a low value. With three variables there are eight combinations possible. One observation is made under each of the eight conditions, and then the results for comparable high values and low values are averaged and compared.

To take a psychological illustration, suppose that an investigator studying the galvanic skin response (GSR) suspects that there are several sources of variability affecting his data: one is the size of the electrodes which are attached to the skin, another is the amount of current going through the subject, and the third is the subject's skin temperature. The experimenter then sets up an experiment in which he makes eight observations as follows:

Conditions		Suspected Variables	
1	small electrode	low current	low skin temperature
2	small electrode	low current	high skin temperature
3	small electrode	high current	low skin temperature
4	small electrode	high current	high skin temperature
5	large electrode	low current	low skin temperature
6	large electrode	low current	high skin temperature
7	large electrode	high current	low skin temperature
8	large electrode	high current	high skin temperature

By averaging the four large electrode conditions and comparing the mean with the mean of the four small electrode conditions, the effect of electrode size on GSR may show itself in spite of fluctuations due to the other variables. The same can be done for the other two suspected variables.

Although this method is important and is being increasingly used in research, it does have some limitations. One kind of limitation concerns the choice of "high" and "low" values for each of the suspected variables. Since these terms are completely relative, the experimenter may make a choice which is not different enough to show an effect or, on the other hand, too different. This latter condition will occur if there is a U-shaped relation between the variable and the effect, as described in Chapter 4. In a sense the factorial method can be thought of as several bivalent experiments carried out simultaneously. It is a relatively efficient means for identifying relevant variables, but gives little information on the functional relation between the cause and the effect.

SUMMARY

A number of different procedures have been suggested for identifying cause and effect relations. The basic ideas behind most of them were described over a century ago by John Stuart Mill, an English philosopher. These methods have been called: *the method of agreement, the method of difference, the joint methods of agreement and difference,* and *the method of concomitant variations.* Most experimental inquiry uses these methods in various guises. Each method has its limitations, and each provides only an approximation, more or less adequate to the "truth."

THE NATURE OF

BIAS AND CONTROL

The study of error is not only in the highest degree prophylactic but it serves a stimulating introduction to the study of truth. . . . We see vividly, as normally we should not, the enormous mischief and casual cruelty of our prejudices. And the destruction of a prejudice, though painful at first, because of its connection with our self-respect, gives an immense relief and a fine pride when it is successfully done.

—WALTER LIPPMANN

Experimental design methods have the purpose of eliminating or minimizing sources of error or bias so that unequivocal causal connections can be established. It is therefore necessary to examine the nature and sources of bias in research before discussing the different kinds of procedures that have been developed to deal with them.

GENERAL TYPES OF BIAS

Since experiments are always performed to answer specific questions, a bias or source of error may be thought of as any fact or factor which contributes to an erroneous conclusion or which makes the conclusion ambiguous. Another way of describing bias is to define it as any *unspecified* factor which affects one condition or one group of the experiment differently than others.

Biases may occur in connection with the overlooking of relevant variables, the analysis of data, or through inadequate sampling procedures. The following sections will illustrate some of the more important of these sources of bias.

BIAS DUE TO OVERLOOKING RELEVANT VARIABLES

A great deal of research in psychology, particularly in the field of learning, has been done using rats as subjects. Although certain important generalizations have been attempted, there have been many disagreements and conflicting reports concerning the findings of particular kinds of experiments. One investigator has suggested that a possible explanation for the differing results is due to the fact that rats vary greatly in the experiences they have had before being used in an experiment. Many articles published in the literature dealing with learning do not mention the source of the rats used, the maintenance schedule, or the caging and handling procedures even though evidence has been accumulating that each of these factors has an influence on later learning performance. Thus it is possible that some of the contradictory findings in the literature are related to the variability of preexperimental treatment in different laboratories (Christie, 1951).

A second example concerns the use of the pursuit rotor apparatus in connection with the study of human learning. In a review of apparatus variables, Ammons (1955) notes that there have been numerous instances of disagreement of results probably due to failure to standardize such variables. Factors such as target size, rate of target rotation, target distance from center of rotation, stylus characteristics, size and height of turntable, and scoring devices are all known or believed to affect performance, yet many studies do not specify the values used for most of these variables. If such factors are ignored or overlooked, biases may occur.

Still another illustration of the need to identify and control relevant variables concerns the effect of early mother-child separation on the development of the child. Several clinical reports had appeared during the 1930s which remarked on the high frequency of delinquencies among children who had very disturbed relations with their mothers in their early years. Since retrospective clinical reports are subject to serious biases, several studies were begun to investigate this hypothesis. These studies reported that children raised in an institutional environment showed marked declines in indices of development during their first year of life and that children living in a residential treatment nursery showed more signs of behavior disturbance than a group in a day nursery. As research continued, however, it was seen that these findings were by no means consistently confirmed and that many children apparently show no signs of disturbance even though hospitalized at an early age. As a result, it was finally explicitly recognized that there are many relevant variables operating to affect child personality in addition to separation. The age at separation, the relationships to adults during the period of separation, the age at which substitution or replacement appears (if at all), as well as constitutional factors all seem to be relevant (Group . . . , 1959).

A final illustration comes from the recent research on the biochemistry of schizophrenia. In one experiment it was found that hospitalized schizophrenic patients tended to excrete less of a certain hormone in their urine than normal control subjects. It was hoped that this fact might provide a biochemical basis for distinguishing between them. A repetition of the experiment using control subjects on the same diet as a schizophrenic group showed no significant differences in the excretion of the hormone. Further observations seemed to indicate that control subjects, when on the same diet as schizophrenic subjects, did not differ from them in the amount of the hormone secreted.

What all this implies is that no research can be adequately done without knowing the relevant variables and taking them into consideration. Serious biases may enter into an experiment as a result of ignoring the influence of such variables. The more we know about the factors operating to affect a given phenomenon the more adequately can we plan research. This is why a literature review is so important *before* an experiment is done. Although at any time we may not know all the variables which may influence a measurement in which we are interested, we can still take into account those that are known and use design methods that tend to distribute unknown effects more or less equally. These methods will be described later.

BIAS RESULTING FROM INADEQUATE ANALYSIS OF DATA

It is surprising how often biases enter into an otherwise adequate experiment through errors in the analysis of data. There is first of all the more or less obvious matter of the need for computational accuracy. Until the 1940s there was a relatively infrequent use of statistical procedures beyond simple measures of central tendency and variability, and the clinical literature and even a sizeable part of the studies dealing with animal behavior tended to be largely descriptive. But as the science of psychology grew, more and more elaborate apparatus, experimental designs, and mathematical and statistical procedures were developed and put to use. With this increased sophistication has also come the greater possibility of computational errors. Computational errors and statistical inconsistencies are occasionally noted in the psychological literature. This important source of error can best be handled by having at least two experimenters analyze the data independently and check for consistency at each stage of the analysis.

Of far greater importance as a source of error associated with the analysis of data is the question of the adequacy and appropriateness of the statistical procedures used. Lewis and Burke (1949), for example, examined all the experimental papers published in one of the psychological journals for a three-year period, to determine the types of application made of the chi-square test, a statistical procedure used in assessing the significance of the discrepancies between expected and observed frequencies of events under various experimental conditions. Fourteen such papers were found, but in only three were the applications judged to be acceptable.

Sometimes, a reexamination of published data leads to conclusions that are quite different from those of the original investigator. Chapanis (1963) demonstrated this by reanalyzing two studies dealing with problems in the field of engineering psychology. In both cases, he found that incorrect statistical methods had been used and that contrary to the authors' claims, proper analysis showed *no* significant differences between the various conditions.

Reanalysis may work in the opposite direction as well. One investigation reported that the Minnesota Multiphasic Personality Inventory (MMPI) could not discriminate between psychotics, psychopaths, neurotics, and chronic alcoholics. Aaronson and Welsh (1950), however, showed that the data had been inadequately analyzed. Reexamination of the same data by using other more appropriate techniques apparently indicated that a differentiation of these groups was clearly evident.

One last example will be given of the biases that may occur through inadequate analysis of data. In a review of the literature in which statistical methods are applied to the Rorschach Test, Cronbach (1949) gives illustrations of many inadequate uses of statistics as well as several unsolved statistical problems. He notes that critical ratios instead of *t*-tests have been used for small samples, that chi-square has been applied to small numbers of cases without suitable corrections, that the test of significance for proportions has been consistently misused. He notes also that checklist scores have been developed to discriminate between two groups without validating on new samples where many signs often do not discriminate, that statistics implying equal units are often used on Rorschach scores even though clinical experience implies that score units are not equal, and that highly unreliable ratio scores are often used for analysis.

Cronbach concludes his analysis by making a number of recommendations for improving the statistical analysis of this kind of material and adds the following statement:

The analysis also shows that the studies have been open to errors of two types: (1) erroneous procedures have led to claims of significance and interpretations which were unwarranted; and (2) failure to apply the most incisive statistical tests has led workers to reject significant relationships. So widespread are errors and unhappy choices of statistical procedures that few of the conclusions from statistical studies of the Rorschach Test can be trusted. . . . Some of the most extensive studies and some of the most widely cited are riddled with fallacy. . . . Perhaps ninety per cent of the conclusions so far published as a result of statistical Rorschach studies are unsubstantiated—not necessarily false, but based on unsound analysis. . . . With improvements in projective tests, in personality theory, and in the statistical procedures for verifying that theory, we can look forward to impressive dividends.

These examples illustrate some of the biases that may arise through inadequate analysis of data, ranging from computational errors to incorrect use of statistical tools. It is important that considerable thought be given to this problem by researchers.

BIAS DUE TO INADEQUATE SAMPLING

Since one of the aims of experimentation is to be able to make general statements on the basis of laboratory research, the question of adequate sampling naturally arises. If generalizations are to be made, then the subjects used must somehow represent in a known way the larger population to which the data is to be related. This is often very difficult to do and biases frequently enter into an experiment as a result of the sampling procedures. We may illustrate this point with several different kinds of examples. They will be kept brief since a detailed discussion of sampling problems has already been given in Chapter 5.

Many studies have reported that people who are willing to respond to mail questionnaires are usually different on a number of variables from those who do not respond. This has also been found in connection with the self-selection of male volunteers for the Kinsey study of sexual behavior (Maslow and Sakoda, 1952). Differences have also been reported between those who volunteer as subjects for hypnosis experiments and those who do not. At the National Institute of Mental Health, an evaluation of 83 subjects who had volunteered as normal control subjects for medical experiments showed that about half the members of the group had marked signs of psychiatric maladjustment (Perlin *et al.*, 1958). Such findings have been reported with enough frequency in recent years to indicate that inadequate selection of subjects could become an important source of bias.

A related criticism has been raised about research in the area of propaganda. In a review of 34 attitude change experiments, one group of investigators found that 28 used college or other students as subjects. While this practice is quite common in psychological research, it may contribute bias in studies of attitude change where the eventual aim is to apply the results to different social groups.

In very recent years, some interesting experiments have been reported showing how an experimenter's expectations may inadvertently affect the kind of results he obtains. In one study, a number of students were used as experimenters in a laboratory course in psychology. Some of the students were told that the rats they would be experimenting with had been specially bred for intelligence as measured by maze-learning ability. Other students were told that their rats had been specially bred for dullness in maze learning. The animals actually given to all the experimenters were standard laboratory animals and were randomly assigned. The results showed that those experimenters who believed their animals to be "bright" had rats who showed significantly better learning than the other group. Many other examples of experimenter bias are described by Rosenthal (1963). In order to deal with such biases, Rosenthal (1964) suggests several possible courses of action. First, wherever it is possible, contact between the experimenter and subject should be minimal. Second, *double blind* procedures should be generally used. This means, in essence, that the experimenter who does have direct contact with the subject should not know, if possible, what outcome is expected. In drug studies this is done through the use of coded but otherwise unidentified drugs, and by the use of placebos, that is, harmless materials such as plain water. Third, replication of the experiment by different investigators is one of the best ways of dealing with inadvertent biases.

THE NEED FOR CONTROLS

The illustrations given above have indicated in part how many different possible sources of bias there are in connection with research. Problems of bias are by no means confined to psychology but are more or less general and are relevant to all sciences. Even a cursory examination of the history of science would show how many erroneous conclusions have been drawn as a result of unrecognized sources of bias. In current medical research we find the same problems. To illustrate: an analysis of 100 consecutive articles in a medical journal, dealing with a procedure or a type of therapy, revealed that 45 percent of the studies made no attempt to compare the results of the specific therapy with results obtained from a control group. In an additional 18 percent the control used was judged as inadequate (Ross, 1951). A similar review of the studies reported in 11 psychiatric journals in 1949 and 1950 led to the following conclusions: (a) there was either inadequate or no definition of the hypotheses used in the research, (b) there was poor or inadequate use of statistical methods, and (c) there was a failure to establish adequate experimental controls in many instances

(Hughes, 1953). The author concluded that special training in research methods is required if research is to be adequately performed.

To be able to draw meaningful conclusions from research, the source of bias must be dealt with in some manner. In general, the problem of bias may be approached in three possible ways: (a) sources of bias may be *avoided,* (b) the effects of bias may be *distributed* evenly among the various conditions being measured, or (c) the bias may be *measured* and its relative contribution evaluated. *One of the purposes of experimental design methods and controls is to accomplish one or more of these aims.*

THE NATURE OF CONTROLS

The word *control* has come into use relatively late in the history of science and has already acquired several different meanings. The following historical summary is based upon a paper by Boring (1954).

Examples of controlled experiments are recorded at least as far back as 1648 when Pascal showed that the height of a column of mercury in a tube was dependent upon the altitude. The controls he exercised in this case were examination of the height of a mercury column at several places along a mountain path, and regular checking of a similar tube at the foot of the mountain.

By 1843, John Stuart Mill had made implicit the notion of control, primarily in the sense of a verifying check. In the 1870s the word control began to be used in the sense of a standard of comparison in regard to which a difference may occur, and by 1893, the New English Dictionary defined control as "a standard of comparison used to check the inferences deduced from an experiment by application of the Method of Difference." Darwin had used the word control in an 1875 publication also in the sense of a standard of comparison to describe some of his experimental studies of insectivorous plants.

In psychology the word control was used in the sense of a calibration by Wundt in the 1870s, and several other investigators of psychological problems used controls in their experiments. By 1901 Thorndike and Woodworth had recognized the need for a control group in experimental studies of transfer of training, but it was not until 1908 that control groups began to be used for the first time. In 1933, 11 percent of the articles in psychological journals indicated that control groups had been used, and in 1951, 52 percent of the studies used control groups. Over the same period there has also been an increase (although less consistent) in the use of control observations.

This brief survey has shown that the word control has been used primarily in the sense of a basis of comparison between two or more conditions or two or more groups. Another way of saying this is that the control represents a reference point in relation to which a comparison is made. If, for example, an investigator is concerned with the effect of drugs on behavior or IQ, then a condition without drugs would represent a reference point or norm against which to evaluate a change.

Controls, however, have been used in at least two other senses in experimental research. One sense refers to the manipulation of variables or conditions; that is, we control the independent variable in an experiment by causing it to change in a specified and known manner. We might control the amount of deprivation in an experiment on drive, the meaningfulness of a list of syllables in a study of transfer, or the type of verbal reinforcement in a study of verbal conditioning.

The other meaning of the term control is in the sense of restraint of variables or the keeping of constant conditions. Just as we manipulate certain variables in an experiment, an attempt is made to keep all other relevant variables constant. In a study of visual sensitivity in humans, for example, the color and size of the light stimulus as well as the position of the eye are kept constant. Quite typically, head and chin rests are used to keep the head steady, sometimes even a mouth bite is used to further prevent movement, and a fixation point or circle is generally put into the visual field. All these procedures plus some constant period of dark adaptation are used to maintain all variables known to be relevant at constant values. In human learning studies, the variables kept constant in most cases include the type of material, the amount of practice, and the distribution and length of trials.

From these illustrations it should be evident that the factors kept constant or controlled are the very factors which can affect the variable being measured. But since it is not possible to know *all* the variables which can operate at any given moment, we can only control those factors which we believe are relevant to the research at hand and this, in turn, depends, at least in part, on the state of knowledge in the field. As the illustrations cited earlier in this chapter have shown, a frequent source of error in research is the overlooking of relevant variables and the failure to control them in the sense of keeping them constant. The use of controls, therefore, presupposes considerable knowledge.

In summary we may note that the word control has been used in at least three different ways: (a) as a reference or comparison point, (b) in the sense of manipulation of independent variables, and (c) in the sense of restraint or the keeping constant of variables not under investigation. Therefore, in the broadest sense, *controls are procedures used in research which are designed to test or limit probable sources of error.*

One further point should be made: the very fact that sources of error exist and that inadequate controls are used in research implies that it is not always obvious to the investigator what variables require controlling or how the control may be carried out. This depends partly on knowledge of the field under investigation, on general knowledge of research designs, on economy or feasibility in terms of time or money, and on the ingenuity and imagination of the investigator. It should be evident also that these problems are by no means limited to the field of psychology but apply to all experimental science.

WAYS OF HANDLING BIAS

This chapter will conclude with some illustrations of ways of dealing with bias in research. As was pointed out earlier, there are three general approaches: (a) to avoid the source of bias, (b) to distribute the bias, or (c) to measure the amount of bias.

If the problem being investigated, for example, is whether a certain type of drug produces a persistent drop in blood pressure in hypertensive patients, it is recognized that several possible factors may produce such an effect in addition to the drug being studied. One of these factors is the doctor-patient relationship. The importance of this relationship is demonstrated by a study which found that the attitude of the physician affected efficacy of the drug when the physician administered *known* hypotensive (i.e., blood-pressure reducing) agents. During the period when an observer classified the physician's attitude as enthusiastic, the drug produced a marked decrease in blood pressure, but when the physician's attitude was classified as unenthusiastic or negative, the drug effects were much smaller. The way to *avoid* this source of bias is to use a double-blind design, i.e., the administration of the drug, and placebos of identical appearance, in a sequence unknown to both the patient and the doctor.

In learning experiments it is often necessary to *distribute* the effects of bias over two or more conditions. Suppose an experimenter wishes to investigate the ability of an observer to learn nonsense syllables in lists of different lengths. The experimenter will usually present the subject with several conditions, each of which is identical except for the length of the lists. Since the ability to learn this kind of task is affected by practice and experience, the conditions that come later in the experiment would be more affected by practice than those that come earlier. The way this variable is usually controlled is to present the conditions in random order; while this does not eliminate the practice variable, it does distribute any practice effects equally over all conditions.

The problem of the measurement of amount of bias is particularly evident when various types of equipment are used as part of the research. If, for example, a timer is utilized, the manufacturer will usually indicate how precise the timer is by specifying a tolerance range. It might be stated that the timer measures to the nearest one-tenth of a second plus or minus one one-fiftieth of a second. This tolerance range represents the possible error associated with any recorded time value. Frequently the error is stated as plus or minus 3 percent or some other specified value. This kind of error cannot be avoided or distributed; in such a case it is sufficient to *measure* it and include it in the reported findings. Such an estimate should be made, as far as possible, whenever any equipment is being used, whether it be electronic, mechanical, or optical.

SUMMARY

This chapter has attempted to show that sources of bias operate in many different ways in experimental work. It has illustrated how errors may arise in the analysis of data, or by overlooking relevant variables, or through inadequate sampling.

The concept of control was explored and shown to have several meanings as used in contemporary psychological research. Illustrations were given of how sources of error may be avoided, distributed, or measured. An important notion that was considered is that the development of adequate controls depends to a large degree on the state of knowledge that the experimenter has acquired in relation to a given problem.

10

EXPERIMENTAL DESIGN METHODS

Owing to the historical accident that the theory of errors, by which
quantitative data are to be interpreted, was developed without reference to experimental methods, the vital principle has often been
overlooked that the actual and physical conduct of an
experiment must govern the statistical procedure of its
interpretation.

—RONALD A. FISHER

The expression *experimental design* may be defined in several
ways. On the one hand, experimental designs are thought of as
ways of arranging the conditions of an experiment in order to
answer the questions we are concerned with. These questions
generally deal with the identification of relevant variables, the
determination of causes of events, and the evaluation of conditions in order to produce an optimum result. These aims, however, are statements of ideals or goals, and it is not always easy
to achieve them in practice. On the other hand, experimental
design methods have the purpose of eliminating or minimizing
sources of error or bias so that unequivocal causal connections
can be established. Sources of bias are generally handled in one
of three ways: by avoiding them, by distributing their effects
over all conditions, or by measuring them.

This chapter will describe some of the more commonly used

design methods and will indicate the kinds of difficulties that may attend their use. The methods to be described are not simple rote formulas into which experimental groups can be neatly plugged and answers run off by computer. On the contrary, there are often difficult decisions to be made concerning which of a number of alternate designs should be used. Since only a minimal amount of statistical background is presupposed of the reader, the analyses will be largely qualitative.

THE RANDOM GROUPS DESIGN

This design method is basically the same as Mill's *method of difference* described earlier. Ideally, in this design two large groups are selected randomly from some defined population, and one of the groups is subjected to the experimental treatment (e.g., reinforcements, drugs, teaching methods, shock, and so on). Both groups are then tested on one or more measures to see if there are any differences. Symbolically, the procedure is as follows:

	Experimental	
Random group I	treatment	Test
Random group II	No treatment	Test

The group given no treatment is usually called the control group; it represents a reference level for deciding if the experimental treatment had any effect.

The basic assumption of the random groups design is that the random selection procedure will produce groups which are alike initially and which do not differ, on the average, on any variables which are likely to affect the behavior which is to be measured. This is a reasonable assumption to make theoretically, but from a practical point of view, it rarely happens that all its prerequisites are met.

For this method to enable us to make generalizations to a large population, a basic population must be defined and two random samples taken from it. If the population of interest is all the schizophrenics in a mental hospital, then the samples should be randomly selected from the entire hospital and should not be simply a group of convenient or tractable patients. If the population of interest is all the students in one college, then a couple of classes is not a random sample. These considerations are even more relevant if the population of interest is all the schizophrenics in the United States in 1966, or all college students.

Even if the assumptions are met initially, difficulties often arise because subjects are lost during the course of experiment and/or because control groups, if small, are not always equivalent. Let us look at some actual examples.

In a study concerned with conflict resolution, a group of children were asked to make ratings of how much they liked different toys and were then allowed to choose one for themselves (Brehm and Cohen, 1959). A week later similar ratings were again made by the children. Groups having different numbers of alternatives were compared and certain predictions made. However, of the 203 children originally tested, only 72 were used in the analysis, because most of the children did not meet various conditions that were set up. In addition, the discarding of subjects was made after the data had been examined. Such a procedure limits the randomness of the samples and makes the use of classical tests of significance (e.g., t-tests) questionable. Chapanis and Chapanis (1964) give a number of other examples in the area of social psychology of studies where subjects were discarded after the collection of the data because certain requirements were not met.

This problem sometimes arises in certain types of educational research. In recent years the problem of the "underachiever" has prompted a number of experiments which have tried to show the effect of some educational procedure on underachievement. The basic design is simple. Two groups of underachievers are chosen on some criteria, and one is exposed to a special educational environment for a period of time. Both groups are then tested on various measures to see if any significant differences have appeared.

Thorndike (1963) has pointed out that the simplicity of the design is deceptive and may cause investigators to overlook some important possible sources of error or bias. For one thing, the special attention given to the experimental group is likely to increase the motivation of those students relative to the ones in the control group. Second, it is quite likely that a certain number of students will drop out of the program so that the ones who complete it are a biased sample of the initial group.

Sometimes the random groups method has been interpreted to mean that several large intact groups are selected to represent the experimental and control groups. For example, one class of students might be exposed to a massed learning condition while another class would be exposed to a distributed condition. Although the results might show that the groups did not differ initially on the learning task, the method of choosing the groups is still questionable. This is because the classes might differ on other relevant factors, such as motivation or age, which could modify the rate of improvement even though they did not affect initial level of performance. As an alternative, the random placement of subjects into the various groups presumably distributes all relevant factors equally.

This problem connected with the use of intact groups can be illustrated by reference to a clinical study (Brockway *et al.*, 1954) concerned with EEG differences in several groups. In this study, 40 patients whose dominant symptom was anxiety were compared on a variety of EEG and personality measures with several groups of normal subjects. However, instead of simply using a single control group of subjects who were convenient, they obtained data on four different normal groups. Group I was a miscellaneous collection of young men, mostly from a local National Guard unit ($N = 59$); Group II consisted of Army officers ($N = 30$); Group III was university students ($N = 38$); and

Group IV consisted of seminary students ($N = 39$). The officers and patients had a median age around 29 years, while the median age for the other three groups was about 21 years. The four nonpatient groups were paid volunteers with no history of psychiatric illness.

Analyses of variance of results for the four normal control groups showed they differed significantly on Rorschach anxiety and maladjustment ratings, on figure drawing maladjustment ratings, on vocabulary mental age, and on several other measures. Some of the control groups were not significantly different from the patients on some of the measures. The distribution of overall EEG patterns was about the same in all the groups, but the amount of alpha (10 cps) activity was greater in the controls. The authors of the study drew two general conclusions: (1) "controls from different occupational, social, and economic sources may vary greatly in their psychiatric and psychological characteristics and thus a single source cannot be considered a random sample of the normal population"; (2) the fact that certain responses frequently occur in an abnormal population does not necessarily mean they are pathological since certain normal control groups will also show these same responses to the same degree.

Although this study is not an experimental one in the sense that the different groups were not exposed to various new conditions and their responses measured, it does suggest an important point. If the aim of an experiment is to enable generalizations to populations larger than the actual one used in the experiment, then some sort of random selection or random assignment of subjects is necessary.

The examples given have been chosen to suggest that the random groups design method as it is actually used in practice is no certain method for identifying variables or establishing causal relations. In summary, the main reasons for this are (1) groups used in research are not often random samples; (2) some studies lose a certain number of subjects during the course of the experiment; and (3) when the random groups design is used in a bivalent study, it shares in the various difficulties already described in Chapter 4.

These are practical difficulties which do not necessarily imply that the design method is at fault. On the contrary, when randomization is carefully used for the selection and assignment of subjects, and relatively large numbers are used, it is one of the best methods for enabling generalizations to be made.

In order to deal with the problems connected with bivalent experiments, the basic solution is to expand the number of randomly selected groups used and to expose each to a different value of the independent variable, in some such fashion as follows:

Random group I	No treatment	Test
Random group II	X amount of treatment	Test
Random group III	2X amount of treatment	Test
Random group IV	3X amount of treatment	Test
Random group V	4X amount of treatment	Test

The different amounts of treatment refer to different levels of the independent variable, although obviously the amounts need not be exactly those listed as X, 2X, 3X, etc. Any increasing set of values could be used.

In analyzing the data of an expanded random groups design, two general approaches are used. One is the analysis of variance which has been briefly described in the chapter on statistical methods. The other involves plotting the data on a graph and finding the type of curve which best fits the points. This latter method has been outlined in the chapter on functional methods and curve fitting. In general, the expanded random groups design is much to be preferred over the simple two group design, but in any case, generalizations should depend upon the congruence of results from many experiments done by different investigators using different kinds of subjects and different design methods.

MATCHED GROUPS DESIGN

A design often used in psychological research is one based upon matched groups rather than random groups. This design eliminates some of the sampling problems mentioned previously, but it creates other problems instead. As an example, experiments concerned with transfer of training may be considered. Although there are a number of different approaches, one frequently seen uses a matched groups design somewhat as follows:

	Pretest on	Training on	Retest on
Control group	A	—	A
Experimental group	A	B	A

Assume that task A is mirror tracing with the right hand (i.e., tracing a complex pattern by means of a mirror image) and that task B is training on the same pattern with the left hand.

Equating on the pretest A is usually done by giving a group of subjects one trial on the A task and recording the amount of time it took each subject to trace the complete pattern. The subjects are then ranked and two groups are created such that the mean performance time and standard deviation of the performance times are as close as possible.

Once this is done (and it may sometimes take days or weeks to get the initial trial on a large number of subjects), the subjects in the experimental group return to the laboratory for the training trials on B. Then both groups are retested on the original A task. The amount and direction of transfer depends on the difference in performance between the experimental and control groups on the retest.

In actual practice, matching of groups may be done in four other ways.

Matching on Correlated Variables. Sometimes the matching is done not on the task being studied, but on some other task or variable believed to be related to the one under investigation. Thus, in the example given for transfer of training, the subjects might be matched on some pattern other than the one finally tested, although a task would be chosen which produced performance scores correlated with those on task A. Sometimes the subjects are matched on several other variables (age, sex, education, etc.) believed to be correlated with the task performance to be measured.

Matching by Pairs.   In some studies matching is effected by selecting out pairs of subjects with similar characteristics. For example, in twin studies one member of each pair of twins might be assigned randomly to the experimental group, the other to the control group. In educational research, in order to take into account variations among teachers, two students (or some multiple of two) might be selected from each of a number of classes, with the students from each class matched on age, sex, or achievement level. This kind of matching will always produce groups of equal size. When matching on mean and standard deviation, it is not necessary that the experimental and control groups be of equal size.

Matching by Yoked Control.   A number of studies have been reported in recent years which have used a special type of matching procedure called the yoked control. One such study was an attempt to solve a problem created by a prior experiment in which rats who were hungry and thirsty were given an electric shock whenever they tried to eat or drink. Under these conditions, they developed more ulcers than rats in an unshocked control group (Sawrey and Weisz, 1956). The problem raised by this experiment is that the ulcers might have been due to the electric shock per se, or they might have been due to the severe conflict set up between the desire for food and the desire to avoid the shock. What was needed was a control group of rats that experienced the same magnitude and temporal sequence of shocks, but which had little or no conflict.

Such a study was reported by Brady (1958) using a yoked control design. In this experiment monkeys were trained to press a lever to avoid an electric shock which was automatically delivered to the animals' feet every 20 seconds. The shock could be avoided if the monkey pressed the lever at least once in each 20-second interval. This technique is usually learned quickly by monkeys, and they continue to press the lever at a fairly regular rate; only occasionally do they miss a 20-second period and thus get a shock.

Monkeys who did this on a schedule of six hours "on" and six hours "off" (i.e., rest) developed ulcers. Therefore, to check on the possibility that the ulcers resulted from the shock rather than from the frustration associated with having to avoid it, another monkey was "yoked" to the first. He sat in a restraining chair which was exactly the same as that of the other monkey, but only the experimental subject could control the onset or frequency of shocks. Any shocks that did occur were delivered to both animals simultaneously. Thus the control animal had the same number of shocks and in the same sequence as the experimental animal, but he was not involved in the conflict. This kind of yoked control design has also been used in studies of conditioning, secondary reinforcement, and effects of shock (Church, 1964).

Matching on a Performance Criterion. The first method of matching described, which was in terms of mean and standard deviation, has at least one obvious limitation. If only one trial is given on the matching task, it is quite likely that large individual differences will be found. If all subjects are used, then it may turn out that large variabilities occur, which in turn increase the unreliability of the data and make the matches less adequate on subsequent trials. For this reason many experimenters will use two or three trials as a basis for matching and may even eliminate subjects whose initial performance is too different from that of the rest of the group.

There is, however, an alternative method for matching that

has been used occasionally (Lewis *et al.*, 1952). This involves testing the subjects until they reach a predetermined performance level within a predetermined number of trials. For example, on the basis of a pilot run it might be decided that the performance level for matching on the mirror tracing task is to be 60 seconds ±5 seconds, and that this criterion is to be reached within three trials. If a subject reaches the criterion (55–65 seconds) on the first, second, or third trial, he stops and then goes on to the next task (the B task if he is in the experimental group). As subjects reach the criterion, they are randomly distributed to the two groups. If any subject does not reach the criterion performance in the three trials, or if he exceeds the tolerance limits on any of the three trials, he is simply not used in the experiment.

This method has three advantages. (1) The groups are equated both in terms of the number of trials to reach a criterion as well as in terms of the criterion level reached; therefore, implicitly, their learning curves are matched. (2) Equating at a fixed performance level ensures that the variability of the data is very small and increases the chances that the equality of groups will continue on subsequent trials. (3) Since the performance criteria are selected in advance, it is unnecessary with this approach to postpone the experiment while means and standard deviations are being computed after a certain trial. If the experimenter wishes, each subject can be run through the entire experiment without waiting for the results of other subjects to come in.

ADVANTAGES AND LIMITATIONS OF THE MATCHED GROUPS DESIGN

One of the principal advantages of the matched groups design is that it tends to eliminate any ambiguity about whether the groups are equal or not at the start of an experiment. Whereas the random groups design usually requires large numbers of subjects to ensure equality, matching can often produce reliable differences between control and experimental groups with Ns as small as 5 or 10. Generally speaking, matching on a pretest reduces variability because it creates a correlation between the groups on the measures which are later compared; experimental effects can therefore be identified more readily. Tests of significance based on matched groups have a smaller standard error due to the existence of this correlation. The formula for the standard error of the difference between means for correlated data depends upon the type of matching procedure that has been used. But in all cases the larger the correlation r due to matching, the smaller the number of cases needed to show a significant difference; or alternately, the larger the r, the smaller a difference in means necessary for the detection of significance. Guilford (1965) has an excellent discussion of this problem.

Despite these advantages of the method, there are also some limitations. One minor disadvantage is that in most cases the procedure usually requires a lapse of time between the actual matching, ranking, and establishment of groups, and the conduct of the rest of the experiment. The longer the wait, the less adequate the matching is likely to be simply because of the possible unreliability of any test score.

A second problem concerns the yoked control design. Church (1964) has criticized the method on the grounds that it does not control for the effects of individual differences. To illustrate his point, we may take the experiment mentioned earlier on the production of ulcers in monkeys. In any given pair of monkeys, it is quite possible that either the control animal or the experimental animal is much more sensitive to the effects of shock than is his yoked mate. If such is the case, then it is possible that one of the monkeys will develop ulcers before the other and that this will not be due to the conflict in the situation, but simply to the shock. However, if large numbers of pairs are used and assignment to each pair is random, then consistent results in favor of one group probably indicates a real effect.

Another problem with the yoked control design is that the procedure in many cases does not allow control over the number and distribution of stimulus events. It is quite possible for one experimental monkey to allow many shocks to be given to his yoked control and for another experimental monkey to allow very few shocks to be given. If only a few pairs of animals are used, there is no way of knowing how much the absolute frequency of occurrence of the stimulus event determines the results. Here again, only by using large numbers of pairs of animals will this variable be distributed more or less equally over a range of values.

Of much greater importance as a limitation of the matched groups design is the fact that the more careful and circumscribed the matching of groups, the less general are the results of the experiment. This is related to two points. The first is that careful matching generally produces a loss of subjects. This may vary from the loss of three or four individuals with extreme scores in a college group being tested for bilateral transfer, to the loss of hundreds of subjects in studies of hospital patients. An example of the latter situation is found in a study by Kellerman (1964) where an attempt was made to obtain two matched groups of mental hospital patients with 20 subjects in each group. In order to approximately match the patients on age, sex, IQ, and education, over 300 hospital records had to be examined and rejected. Although this procedure produces closely matched groups, it is evident that the characteristics of the rejected subjects are not represented in the experiment. The conclusions may be valid for the matched subjects and others like them but not for the type of subjects not tested. The ideal random groups design, in contrast, because of its sampling of an entire population, produces results which have a potentially wider range of generalization.

However, and this is the other point, whether or not subjects are rejected, the matching process necessarily produces a loss in generality, since matching is always done on one specific value of a variable out of a large range of possible values. If college students are matched in the transfer of training experiment on a 60-second performance, then it is simply indeterminate how much the results apply to other classes of subjects or to different equating levels. Thus, although the matched groups design is more sensitive to small effects, it is less capable of providing data which permit broad generalizations to be formed.

The best way of dealing with this problem is to do a series of experiments of a parametric type in which each of the major variables of interest is explored systematically. This means, as was noted in connection with the random groups method, that studies using this design method should not be limited to two conditions of a variable but should use many matched groups, each of which is exposed to different levels of some independent variable. In the context of a transfer design, it might look something like this (where the B's refer to different levels of practice):

	Pretest on	Training on	Retest on
Control group	A	–	A
Experimental group I	A	B_1	A
Experimental group II	A	B_2	A
Experimental group III	A	B_3	A
Experimental group IV	A	B_4	A

Data of the sort obtained here is then handled by means of analysis of variance (see Ray, 1960) or by means of curve fitting techniques (Lewis, 1960).

RETROSPECTIVE RESEARCH

There is a type of research design called *retrospective* or *ex post facto*, which has certain similarities to the matched group design and is frequently used in clinical investigations. This kind of research usually begins with an observation which suggests that people with one kind of illness or symptom are different from other people without the illness in terms of some previous life history experience. For example, it might be noticed that people who develop lung cancer smoke a great deal; this suggests an hypothesis about *cause*; namely, that smoking produces lung cancer. Or, it might be observed that many delinquents who are caught and brought before the court come from homes where the parents are either separated or divorced. This suggests the hypothesis: broken homes cause delinquency. As a final example, a psychotherapist might notice that several of his patients have ulcers and form the hypothesis that ulcers are caused by conflicts between feelings of dependency and feelings of aggression.

In each of these cases, an observation of a patient group suggests an hypothesis about possible causes. How can these hypotheses be tested? This is obviously not a simple problem since the hypothesized cause has occurred in the past and the experimenter has no direct control over it. The best he can do is to try to evaluate its presence in some way.

Notice that the problem is the inverse of what is usually the case in a matched groups experiment. In that situation, two (or more) groups are matched on some variable, one is exposed to a possible causal factor, and then both groups are measured on some variable believed to be affected by the independent variable. The statistical tests we use are designed to tell us whether a "real" difference is now apparent.

The retrospective design starts by assuming that a real difference does exist between two groups: one has lung cancer, the other does not; or one is delinquent and the other is not; or one has ulcers and the other does not. The problem is to justify the idea that some situation (or variable) in the past life of these individuals or some personality characteristic has caused this present difference.

It should be obvious that such an inference is not an easy one to make with any certainty. Suppose, for example, that an investigator was able to find 20 patients in psychotherapy who had ulcers. He then obtains 20 college students as normal controls. Both groups are then interviewed extensively and life history data relating to feelings of dependency and aggression are obtained. Suppose that some index of conflict between dependency and aggression is found to be very high in 15 of the 20 ulcer patients and in only 3 of the normal controls, and that a test of significance shows that the difference is significant. What conclusions can be drawn?

One is tempted to say that conflict produces ulcers, but before reaching this conclusion several problems must be solved. For example, to what extent are the ulcer patients in therapy a good sample of ulcer patients in general. We know that people who go into therapy are mostly of middle and upper class status and that disease rates generally vary with social class level. Therefore, many ulcer patients are not represented in this group. The college students, likewise, are not a representative sample of the total population and most likely would not even be a good sample of college students since they are willing to allow detailed personal questions to be asked about their past life.

Another factor to be considered is age, since ulcer rates are highest in the decade between 40 and 50 years. This suggests that the ulcer patients are probably older than the college sample with which they are being compared. In addition, there may be differences between the two groups on dozens or even hundreds of life history factors, any one of which might have much greater relevance to the production of ulcers; to cite just a few: marital state, diet, general health, normal level of gastric acid secretion, feelings of inadequacy, and hospitalization per se.

Theoretically, it would be necessary to rule out every one of these factors as possible causative agents before deciding that conflicts alone produce ulcers. To some extent this is done; in actual research practice, groups that are compared are usually matched on such variables as age, sex, IQ, and education. Sometimes, they are matched on a variable such as hospitalization experience or presence of a different type of illness.

Now, although the matching of a few broad social or personal variables may make a case seem more plausible, it still does not deal with the multitude of possible causes that could produce the illness being studied, and therefore any statement about cause and effect solely on the basis of a retrospective study is highly questionable. This is particularly true when one considers that the statistics that are typically used (e.g., *t*-tests) are not validly applied in situations where the samples compared are not randomly selected.

Let us consider two specific examples. Hecht (1952) had the impression that ulcer patients are ambitious, driving, independent, self-sufficient, perfectionistic, and very aggressive. In order to test whether this was true, he compared 30 ulcer patients with a control group of 30 ulcerative colitis patients. Here is an example where the control group is clearly not a "normal" one, but is defined by the presence of ulcers in a different part of the gastrointestinal system. The groups were not equated on age, education, or any other variable, but only right-handed subjects were used. Subjects in both groups were given the Purdue Pegboard test as a measure of level of aspiration. In this task each subject was asked how many pins he thought he could place in the holes, and comparisons were made between performance and estimates. A group of psychologists and psychiatrists rated the verbal statements associated with the estimates for passive or assertive quality. The conclusion reached on the basis of these comparisons was that, in contrast to the passivity displayed by the ulcerative colitis group, individuals in the peptic ulcer group were ambitious, hard driving, and assertive, and they maintained a high goal in spite of realities of actual performance. In this study, even if the single test used could reveal all these characteristics, it is extremely doubtful that any implication can be made about these factors as causes of the ulcer.

In another study, the investigator hypothesized that ulcer patients have a high need for achievement and a high sense of responsibility in comparison to other people (Marshall, 1960). With this as the starting point, 40 peptic ulcer patients were compared with 20 other patients with "psychosomatic" disturbances other than gastrointestinal, and with 40 hospitalized patients without "psychosomatic" illness. The groups were equated on age, sex, educational level, socioeconomic level, and intelligence. All patients took a personality test and filled out a self-rating scale. The ulcer patients were found to be more emotionally inhibited and more conformist than the other groups, and they did not show a strong need for achievement. T-tests were reported as showing that the differences were significant.

Even if we disregard the apparent disagreement of the results with the original hypothesis and with those of Hecht's experiment, we simply do not know what other important variables might have distinguished the groups in addition to the few that were tested. This is always the problem with retrospective research.

In summary, retrospective studies attempt to argue backwards, so to speak, from effect to possible cause. Basic problems concern decisions about what the control group or groups should be, and about what should be matched or held constant. But even under the best conditions, many possible factors are left uncontrolled so that conclusions are always tenuous. However, the method is sometimes useful when only a limited number of important causes are believed to exist and when these can be evaluated in some way. Those who would like a more detailed analysis of the usefulness of this method when employed under these restricted conditions might find rewarding a paper by Hammond (1958) concerning research on smoking and death rates.

COUNTERBALANCED DESIGNS

This type of approach has sometimes been called a crossover, randomized-block, or Latin Square design. The details of the method vary somewhat, but the basic idea is that one subject or group is tested in one sequence of conditions while another subject or group is tested in a different sequence. In all cases, the subjects must be assigned at random to the different sequences.

This may be illustrated by two studies. One was concerned with the comparability of mean scores on two different IQ tests, the Revised Stanford-Binet (S-B) and the Wechsler Intelligence Scale for Children (WISC). It is evident that if one test were given first to all the children, there might be a practice effect that enabled each child to do better than he might ordinarily do on the second test. To deal with this possible sequence effect, the children were all divided into two groups at random so that one group received the S-B first followed by the WISC, and the other received the WISC first followed by the S-B, as shown in the following Latin Square:

	Test	
Group I	S-B	WISC
Group II	WISC	S-B

In analyzing the results, the major interest is in comparing the mean score on the S-B with the mean score on the WISC, regardless of sequence; in other words, the data for the two groups on comparable tests are combined. This means that if there is a practice effect of some kind, it is not eliminated but simply averaged out. This design method assumes that the practice effects in the different sequences used are approximately the same. The improvement in the WISC score due to taking the S-B first is assumed to be about equal to the improvement in the S-B score due to taking the WISC first. If analysis of variance is applied to the data, then it becomes possible to actually test whether this assumption is appropriate (Stanley, 1955).

The second illustration is taken from the field of psychosomatic medicine. A number of investigators had reported that hospitalized patients who showed high anxiety had larger secretions of hydrocortisone (one of the hormones secreted by the adrenal cortex) than matched normal subjects. In light of these reports, an experiment by Weiner *et al.* (1963) was designed to see if injections of this hormone into volunteer medical students would produce increases in subjective feelings of anxiety.

Sixteen subjects were injected with one dose level of the hormone and immediately tested with the Rorschach, as well as with tests designed to measure both immediate feelings of anxiety and persistent levels of anxiety. Three months later the same subjects returned to the laboratory, were injected with a placebo, and retested with the same tests presented in a different order.

Another 16 subjects were handled in the same general way, except for the fact that they were injected with the placebo first and then with the hormone three months later. Analysis of variance was used to compare the test results obtained after hormone injection with the results obtained after placebo injection, regardless of order of testing. One of the interesting things that was found was that there was a definite difference in results due to the order of testing. When the hormone was given first, test scores associated with the drug were higher than when it was given second. All the differences found were dependent entirely on this order of testing.

ADVANTAGES AND LIMITATIONS OF COUNTERBALANCED DESIGNS

One of the advantages of the counterbalanced design is that each subject serves as his own control. Since the performance of an individual on two different tasks, or on the same task repeated, tends to be highly correlated, the size of standard errors in tests of significance is reduced and thus it is easier to detect small effects. From this point of view, the design is more sensitive than a random groups design, or even a matched groups design. No pretest is necessary to equate groups since the basic comparison is of each individual with himself. In addition, statistical analysis enables the effects of order as well as those of the major variable to be evaluated.

The extent of the limitations of the method depend on how much the order of testing affects the results, and how much one position in the sequence affects, or interacts with, later positions in the sequence. If, for example, there is a large effect related to the order of testing (e.g., going from the drug to the placebo condition), then this tends to greatly increase the variability of the results and decreases the sensitivity of any tests of significance used. This loss in sensitivity may offset any advantage gained by using each subject as his own control.

There are, of course, definite limits on the ability to generalize if only two conditions are compared in a bivalent experiment, but this is not a necessary fault of the method. The Latin Square can be used with any number of conditions. If, in addition to the placebo, there were two dose levels of hydrocortisone used in the experiment mentioned in the previous section, the Latin Square might look like this:

	Dose Level		
Group I	Placebo	Low dose	High dose
Group II	High dose	Placebo	Low dose
Group III	Low dose	High dose	Placebo

From such data it would be possible to plot a dose-response curve so as to establish functional relations between the dose level and the subjects' responses.

A problem remains, however. It is obviously possible to arrange the sequence of tests in a different way and still meet the general requirements of the Latin Square—that is, that each condition appear once and only once in each row and each column. Thus we might have the following sequences:

	Dose Level		
Group I	Placebo	High dose	Low dose
Group II	Low dose	Placebo	High dose
Group III	High dose	Low dose	Placebo

If there were four conditions being tested, there would be many more possible orders that could be used. Yet, in any experiment only one particular set of sequences is actually used. Thus in cases where several conditions are being compared, the sequence is a sample from a population of sequences, and it is not known how good a sample it is. The effect of using one particular sample rather than another is probably small, but there is no certainty about this.

Finally, it should be remembered that the Latin Square was first used in agricultural research for reducing the effects of variations in soil in different parts of a test field. The field was laid out in blocks within rows and columns, and each block was given a different kind of experimental treatment. In this setting there is no necessary relationship between what is done in one block and what is done in adjacent ones. Mathematically, this statement means that there is no interaction effect between blocks. In psychological research, however, the blocks (the different conditions tested) are not independent of one another since ordinarily they are treated in sequence. This would mean that there is an interaction between them, and if there is reason to believe that this interaction is appreciable in any given case, then some other design method, such as random or matched groups, would probably be more suitable.

An example of this problem has been reported in connection with the study of one of the variables influencing conditioning—namely, the intensity of the conditioned stimulus (CS). Although several studies with human subjects have shown that the intensity of the CS has little effect on conditioning, a few experiments have indicated large effects (Grice and Hunter, 1964). A close examination of these studies and some follow-up research has shown that the probable reason for the discrepancies is the type of design method employed. When several independent groups are used so that each subject is exposed to only one intensity level, the effect of intensity is minimal. However, when each subject is exposed to all intensities in some counterbalanced sequence, the effect of CS intensity is much greater. Thus, it appears that there is a substantial interaction effect with this variable. It would be interesting to study other problems by comparing different design methods as was done in this case.

COUNTERBALANCING WITH A SINGLE GROUP

There are certain areas of psychological research where order effects are relatively negligible. This is true, for example, in studies of visual or auditory discrimination. In such situations the tradition that has developed over a century of research is to use very few subjects, but to study them intensively; sometimes thousands of judgments are required from a single observer. The data are therefore obtained from highly practiced subjects.

One result of this is essentially to eliminate any practice effects. With such subjects it is possible to expose them to the experimental conditions in any order and to expect that different results that are obtained will be due largely to the differences in the experimental variable and not to the effect of practice.

To take a concrete example, suppose two highly practiced observers were to be used in an experiment to study the keenness of hearing at different frequencies, and suppose that two frequencies were to be used: 1,000 cps, and 10,000 cps. If the observers are highly practiced, it will make no difference if the 1,000 cps condition is given first or last. However, sometimes, if a long series of judgments are required, fatigue effects gradually become apparent and these effects, though usually small, can be balanced out by repeating the conditions in reverse sequence. Thus, in this example, the subjects would be exposed to the 1,000 cps condition first, then the 10,000 cps condition, followed by the 10,000 cps condition and the 1,000 cps condition. If we let the letters A and B stand for the two different conditions, the sequence then is ABBA. In analyzing the results, the two A conditions are combined and the two B conditions are combined. It is assumed that fatigue or practice effects, if they exist, are linearly related to trials or exposures.

Sometimes this *ABBA* sequence of testing is used in studies where a definite practice effect is known to exist; where, for example, it is known that the second time the A condition is presented the subject will perform much better than the first time. In such cases, if this design method is used at all, the A and B conditions are usually broken down into small units so that the sequence can be repeated many times over. Thus instead of giving 100 trials in the first A condition and 100 in the second, these 200 trials may be broken down into groups of only 10 trials each, and the whole sequence is repeated somewhat as follows:

Sequence of trials	A B B A	B A A B	B A A B	A B B A etc.
Number of trials	10 10 10 10	10 10 10 10	10 10 10 10	10 10 10 10

All the As are eventually combined and the mean value is compared with the mean for the combined Bs.

One example of the use of an *ABBA* design will be briefly described. Stanley and Schlosberg (1953) were interested in finding the influence of tea on a variety of tests. As subjects they obtained 22 housewives who were habitual tea drinkers. On the first of five days of testing, the subjects (in pairs of two) were given an opportunity to gain experience with each of the tasks to be used (e.g., hand steadiness, reaction time, strength of grip, attention, long division, and subjective ratings of fatigue and tension). The first day was simply for practice.

On the second and fifth day 14 of the women were exposed to the same tasks after a cup of tea, while on the third and fourth days the same tests were given, but without the cup of tea. For the remaining women the order was reversed (third and fourth days, tea; second and fifth days, no tea). Analysis of data was concerned with gains or losses between tea and no-tea days. It is interesting to note that the experimenters reported that practice effects appeared absent during the last two experimental periods. The only effect found in the experiment was an improvement in reaction time which lasted about an hour after drinking the tea.

ADVANTAGES AND LIMITATIONS

The "ABBA method" as it is sometimes called is useful in situations where it is desirable to use a single subject and to compare two conditions. Since each subject is his own control, it reduces variability of the type due to differences between subjects and makes it somewhat easier to detect significant differences than when the random groups method is used.

However, it is not at all evident how much generalization is possible from the results of one or just a few subjects. This issue does not usually arise in most psychophysical research because the aim of such research is not to study the characteristics of the "average" person, but rather the characteristics of the eye or ear of the highly trained observer. It is this difference in aim that usually enables these investigators to ignore issues connected with subject sampling.

A second problem involved in the use of this design method relates to the assumption that practice or fatigue effects are small and linearly related to trials or exposures. If this assumption is not true, then it is necessary to break up the sequence into smaller units and repeat them many times. But how small is each small unit to be? This depends on prior knowledge of what the practice curve looks like, and such data are often not available. That is why most studies using this method give the subjects a good deal of practice before collecting any data. In essence, this makes negligible any further effects due to practice.

The use of highly practiced subjects, however, creates a problem in certain situations. The difficulty is that the subject's performance is likely to be close to his maximum possible performance, and any variable that is introduced is unlikely to improve it any further. The design method may thus reveal variables that produce decrements in performance but is less likely to show the effect of incremental factors.

A fourth issue related to this design method concerns the question of how to adapt it so that more than two values of some independent variable can be used. Suppose we wanted to test for keenness of hearing not only at 1,000 cps and 10,000 cps, but at 500, 2,000, and 5,000 cps as well. If we were to have a single group exposed to all conditions, there are several ways this could be done. Following the plan of calling the different conditions by different letters, we could arrange the sequence in ascending and descending order:

$$A\ B\ C\ D\ E \qquad E\ D\ C\ B\ A$$

Here again the two As would be combined to provide a single mean, the two Bs, etc. If there was evidence of large practice or fatigue effects, the units of testing might be made smaller and the whole sequence repeated. The other alternative is to randomize the trials of $A\ B\ C$ . . . etc., using a table of random numbers. If there are enough repeated trials, then any sequence effect will be balanced out. This is an approach which is generally recommended.

THE CONCEPT OF BASELINE BEHAVIOR

The previous discussion of counterbalancing with a single group of subjects has brought up some points which are very similar to those made by Sidman (1960) in his book on the tactics of research. One of the fundamental ideas he presents is that there are many experimental situations where elaborate group designs and statistics are irrelevant or misleading in connection with the basic purposes of research, namely, to identify the variables affecting behavior and to show what effects they have.

The kind of behavioral measures Sidman has been mostly concerned with are rates of response (usually bar pressing in a Skinner-type box or setting). In such cases it is often possible to find some schedule of reinforcement (positive or negative) that produces a highly constant rate of response from the animal for hours or even days. As one example, he presents a shock to an animal once every 20 seconds. If the animal presses on a bar during the 20-second interval, he postpones the shock for the next 20 seconds. By responding at a constant and fairly high rate, the animal can postpone the shock indefinitely. This method establishes a steady baseline rate of response. If the experimenter now introduces some variable such as a drug or a loud noise, and the rate of response changes, he is fairly certain that his manipulation caused the change. If the effect is reversible, and removal of the imposed stimulus is followed by a return to the same baseline in the animal's rate of response, then the experimenter can continue to introduce other conditions (more of the drug or other drugs, louder noise, etc.) to determine their effects on the response rate. In such a case the sequence of testing is irrelevant and any order can be used.

One of the difficulties with this general approach is that it is not always possible to establish constant baseline rates of response, especially if the research is being done with humans. Even when animals are used as the subjects, it may require extremely long periods before constant baseline rates are established. Sidman gives an illustration of a study using rats in which seven six-hour sessions were run with each animal. The results for the first 18 hours were discarded because the behavior was not stable enough, and only the average rates for the last 24 hours were used.

A second difficulty is that a good deal of behavior is not reversible, which means, in essence, that there are baseline shifts for reasons that are related to the life history of the particular individual. A third problem is that many investigators are not interested in rates of bar-pressing response as measures but are concerned with other classes of behavior. The general approach, however, is worth examining since it has produced some important insights into the nature of learning.

THE PROBLEM OF SAMPLE SIZE

A major decision that experimenters must make concerns the number of subjects to use. This problem has no simple or general answer, and each solution depends upon a variety of factors that usually cannot be specified in advance. However, it is clear from the research literature that, depending on the kind of problem studied, anything from one to 1000 subjects is appropriate. What are some factors that must be considered?

In general there are three types of considerations: (1) the traditions that have developed in an area of research; (2) the kind of variability in results which is expected on the basis of previous experience; and (3) the kind of statistical analysis that is planned. Let us take these in reverse order.

If the investigator is planning a bivalent experiment, he will usually expect to use a t-test to determine the significance of any difference he obtains. It is obvious that the larger the difference found, the easier it is to get a significant t-value; and since t is proportional to N, the larger the N, the larger the t (other things held constant). This means that if an investigator decides on a value of t for significance in advance (and almost everyone takes the 5 or 1 percent level), and if he can specify in advance a difference in means that he thinks is important as well as the amount of variability to be anticipated, then the value of N is determined. Note that three prior decisions must be made in order to fix the value of N. One is the significance level to be used, a second is the size of a difference between the means that is to be considered important, and the third is the variability to be expected. But this also has a large element of arbitrariness about it. It looks almost as if we are substituting three arbitrary decisions for one. It is certainly evident that decisions about the *importance* of a finding are not statistical decisions at all but relate to judgments about the implications of certain findings. Thus it is apparent that some very subtle factors enter into the choice of N in the context of testing for significance of differences.

There are three other important points to be made in relation to statistical considerations. First, Dixon and Massey (1951) point out that if groups are equal in size, it is relatively easier to find a significant difference than if they are unequal in size. Thus an experimenter who has 100 subjects available will have a more sensitive significance test if he divides the group into two equal halves rather than if he puts 90 into one group and 10 into the other. This observation is simply a consequence of the definition of a *t*-test.

Second, in an illuminating discussion of experiments in which two groups are compared, Ryan (1959) poses the following hypothetical situation:

An experimenter is convinced that a certain factor should produce a difference in learning rate. He tries it once and fails to get a significant difference. He is so sure that the experiment should have worked that he reconsiders his experimental technique for possible errors. He decides that some actually irrelevant feature of the experiment is responsible, changes it, and tries again. Finally after many different revisions of the conditions, all actually irrelevant, he obtains a "significant" difference and publishes the result. We assume that, as an honest scientist, he will mention in his report that several other trials failed, but this will not usually affect his test of significance, and he will usually explain away the earlier, unsuccessful trials as due to errors in technique. Clearly, all his data should be tested as a single experiment, otherwise obtaining a "significant" difference will depend only upon the experimenter's stubbornness and patience, or upon the number of his research assistants.

An important implication of this example is that experiments do not exist in isolation but are part of a more or less continuous sequence of interrelated observations. If one considers an experiment in this way, the question of the number of subjects to be used in any one study becomes relatively less important. We shall return to this point later.

Another aspect of the problem raised by Ryan can be illustrated by reference to the concept of the significance of a correlation. Suppose that an investigator reports that in a group of 20 subjects he found a correlation of +0.20 between the average number of cigarettes they smoke each day and the number of months they were breast fed as infants. For this N the correlation is not significantly different from zero at the 5 percent level. If the experimenter is not discouraged by this finding and starts to increase the size of his group, he will eventually reach a point where the same correlation *is* significantly different from zero. This will occur when he has increased his group size to 100 subjects. In fact, it is generally the case that as N increases, the size of the correlation coefficient needed for significance decreases, so that with very large Ns very small differences will be judged as significant. With very large Ns a correlation may be significant even though it enables almost no improvement in prediction from one variable to the other. A statistician has written: "Virtually any study can be made to show significant results if one uses enough subjects, regardless of how nonsensical the content may be" (Hays, 1963). *This would suggest that we need additional criteria for judging the meaningfulness of a finding beside the criterion of statistical significance.*

This notion of whether prediction is improved or not is usually described by the expression "the proportion of variance in Y accounted for by X." Another way of saying this is that knowledge of the value of X (the independent variable) decreases our uncertainty by some amount of the estimated value of Y (the dependent variable).

Hays presents a simple equation which can be used to provide an estimate of the amount of uncertainty that is reduced by knowing X, or, to state it in other terms, the proportion of variance in Y accounted for by X. The equation is

$$\text{est. } \omega^2 = \frac{t^2 - 1}{t^2 + N_1 + N_2 - 1} \tag{1}$$

where est. ω^2 (read "estimated omega squared") is the proportion of variance in Y accounted for by X, t is the t-value obtained in the usual test of significance, and the Ns refer to sample sizes.

Using this equation, Hays shows that in two different experiments, the same approximate level of significance is associated with very different estimates of the improvement in prediction. In the case where N is large, the improvement in prediction is much less than in the case where N is small. Hays concludes: "Statistical significance is not the only, or even the best, evidence for a strong statistical association. . . . It seems far more reasonable to decide to follow up a finding that is *both* significant *and* indicates a strong degree of association that to tie this course of action to significance level alone."

TRADITIONS AND VARIABILITY

We shall now examine the other two criteria for deciding on the number of subjects, i.e., experience with the amount of variability to be expected with a given type of subject or problem, and the traditions that have developed in the field.

It should be obvious that these two criteria are not unrelated since traditions develop because of certain kinds of experiences. If we look at the research done in psychophysics concerned with the measurement of sensory acuity and sensitivity, we discover that most of the published research is based on only two or three subjects per experiment. If we examine the studies concerned with the effects of different schedules of reinforcement, we discover that many of the reports are based on two or four animals per group. If we peruse the journals where social psychological research is published, we find that much larger groups are typically used with Ns ranging from 20 to many hundreds.

In order to get some data on what these traditions are, the present author examined three journals for the year 1960 and simply recorded the number of subjects used in each of the different experiments published in that year. Of the 169 experiments published in the *Journal of Experimental Psychology*, five experiments used only two subjects, one experiment used only one subject and 26 used 10 or fewer subjects. The median number of subjects per experiment was about 45. In the *Journal of*

Comparative and Psysiological Psychology for that year, there were 38 experiments out of 145 that used 10 or fewer subjects. The median for this journal was about 20 subjects. The *Journal of Clinical Psychology* for that year published 125 experiments; 8 used 10 or less subjects, and the median was about 90. (The medians given here are only approximate since four experiments in the *Journal of Comparative and Physiological Psychology* did not list the number of subjects used and 11 experiments in the *Journal of Clinical Psychology* did not.)

These figures, approximate as they are, certainly suggest a range of policies in regard to choice of sample size, even though some overall trends are apparent.

The role of experience may be illustrated by two concrete examples. Sidman (1960) reported that "it had been the usual experience in this laboratory that when as many as four animals (usually less) yielded the same data, subsequent experimentation rarely failed to achieve replication." Chapanis (1956) who has had considerable experience with human engineering studies writes: "As a general rule, psychophysical experiments on simple sensory functions . . . generally require fewer subjects than most other kinds. Learning experiments, experiments involving motor performance, and so on, may give erratic results unless a minimum of about 20 or 30 subjects is used."

These quotations imply that the investigator actually uses as his criterion for choice of N the consistency and reliability of his results from subject to subject and experiment to experiment. In some areas of research variability is inherently much greater than in other areas, and larger numbers of subjects must therefore be used. But implicit in this criterion of consistency is the idea that each experiment is part of a sequence of related experiments and not an entity unto itself. Replication of results is a more convincing sign of reliability of data than significant *t*s obtained in a single experiment. In fact, a number of statisticians have begun to develop so-called sequential designs in which the number of subjects to be used is not stated in advance, but depends on the nature of the data as it is collected (Anderson, 1953).

CAN N=1?

One final point. Are experiments using a single subject meaningful? The answer given by Dukes (1965) in an interesting paper on this question is definitely "yes." He points out that experiments on single subjects have played a very significant role in the history of psychology, and that there are several general situations where they do occur.

The basic studies of memory by Ebbinghaus around 1885 were done with one subject, himself, and his methods and findings have influenced the course of research in this area up to the present time. Watson's famous study of conditioned fear (1920) was done on a single child and prompted hundreds of subsequent experiments. In the early 1930s the Kelloggs raised a chimpanzee with their son as if he were their own child; this provided some important insights into the relationship between nature and nurture.

Occasionally, a phenomenon occurs so rarely that a single example of it is of great significance. This is true, for example, of the very few people who are apparently born with a total insensitivity to pain, or the rare person who is color blind in one eye but not in the other. Careful study of such single cases sometimes reveals facts of fundamental importance.

In a survey of 11 journals of psychology, which are *not* clinical journals, during the years 1939 to 1963, Dukes found that a total of 246 reported studies used only a single subject, thus suggesting that such experiments are still considered meaningful at the present time. These were of four main types: (1) psychophysical, where intersubject variability is usually found to be low; (2) the study of rare events such as a person with congenital insensitivity to pain; (3) the study of "negative" cases showing that an assumed universal relationship does not hold (e.g., feeblemindedness does not necessarily occur as a result of prolonged congenital hydrocephaly); and (4) the development of new approaches to a problem, such as the stabilizing of images on the retina. Studies of the single case are thus important aspects of contemporary research. Chassan (1960), a statistician, has also discussed the value of studies of the single case.

The examples and discussions that have been presented in this chapter have been meant to highlight two important implications. One is that there is no simple formula for handling all experimental design problems. Each method has advantages and disadvantages and each is best used in certain contexts. The second is that there are many issues to be considered in making a choice of design method, and that the issues are not all statistical. One well-known statistician has put the matter this way: "I have always felt that the statistician has at least as much and possibly more to learn from the good experimenter than the experimenter from the statistician" (Box, 1957). The world around us sometimes presents us with problems that the statistician does not have models for, but they are real problems nevertheless.

AN INTRODUCTION TO

PSYCHOPHYSICS

By *psychophysics* . . . I mean a theory which, although ancient as a
problem, is new here insofar as its formulation and treatment are
concerned; in short, it is an exact theory of the relation of
body and mind.

—GUSTAV FECHNER

Classical psychophysics—the psychophysics of the last century—was primarily concerned with the study of sensory thresholds. These thresholds were of two general types: *absolute* and
differential. The absolute threshold refers to the minimum
energy needed to elicit a response; the differential threshold
refers to the minimum energy needed before a difference is noticed relative to some fixed level. The determination of the
dimmest light the eye can see would be an example of an absolute threshold, while the smallest pitch difference the ear can
detect would illustrate the differential threshold. In order to
determine these various kinds of thresholds with minimum possibilities of error, several standard procedures were developed,
called psychophysical methods. Although these methods were
first proposed in the context of the study of the threshold, they
have been adapted to many other kinds of problems including

the construction of intelligence and attitude tests. In this chapter some of the basic psychophysical methods and concepts will be introduced.

THE BASIC ISSUES

Modern psychophysics has considerably expanded the range of questions to be studied. Galanter (1962) suggests that there are four basic problems implicit in the analysis of sensory function: (1) the detection problem ("Is anything there?"); (2) the recognition problem ("What is it?"); (3) the discrimination problem ("Is this different from that?"); and (4) the scaling problem ("How much of X is there?"). Another way of describing the modern task of psychophysics is by comparing man's sensory system with that of a complex machine such as a television camera. We might then ask such questions as: (1) How sensitive is the system? (2) How accurate is it? (3) How reliable is it? (4) How small a change can it detect? (5) What is its speed of response? (6) What is its range of response? (Granit, 1955.)

Perhaps the simplest way of describing the basic issues of concern to psychophysics is in terms of the following three problems: (1) the matching problem (when are two things equal?); (2) the discrimination problem (how small a difference is detectable?); and (3) the scaling problem (how much of the stimulus is judged to be present?). We will use these three questions as a basis for an introduction to some psychophysical methods and concepts.

THE MATCHING PROBLEM

Suppose a piano tuner is called to your home. One way he might go about his job of tuning would be by matching the tones produced by the piano to the tones produced by a standard set of tuning forks. Similarly, in order for a physicist or psychologist to calibrate the intensity or luminance of a light source, he tries to match it against a standard known illumination. When an artist paints the colors of the sunset, he is usually dealing with the problem of matching.

All of these situations have several elements in common. First, there is a reference or *standard stimulus* (e.g., frequency, luminance, or wavelength). Second, a *variable stimulus* is matched as closely as possible to the standard. The value of the variable at the point where the observer considers that the two quantities are matched is called the *point of subjective equality* (PSE). For example, if the tuning fork produces a tone with a frequency of 256 cycles per second (cps), and the piano tuner sets the piano key at 258 cps, this latter value is his point of subjective equality.

Once the PSE is determined it will usually be found that it differs from the standard by some small value. This difference between the PSE and the standard represents an error of judgment in matching and is called the *constant error* or CE. In symbolic terms, by definition, CE = PSE − Standard.

If, as is usually the case, a series of matching settings are made, then the PSE will vary somewhat from trial to trial and the constant error is then defined as the average value of the different PSE's minus the standard. The different matching settings (i.e. the different PSEs from trial to trial) can be used to determine a measure of how consistent the subject is in his judgments. Such a measure of variability is called the *variable error* or VE and is usually measured by a standard deviation or by the interquartile range of his series of settings.

To summarize: when making matching judgments we have a standard stimulus and a variable stimulus which is compared with it. The value judged equal to the standard is called the point of subjective equality. The difference between the mean point of subjective equality and the actual value of the standard stimulus is called the constant error. The standard deviation of a series of judgments (PSEs) is called the variable error. All these measures can be obtained when a variable stimulus is matched against a standard stimulus.

THE METHOD OF ADJUSTMENT

The usual procedure followed when matching is called the method of adjustment. This simply requires the observer to manipulate the variable stimulus, changing it gradually (like tuning in a radio station), until he considers it matched to the standard. Sometimes a bracketing procedure will be used with the observer making the variable alternately larger and smaller than the standard until it appears exactly equal.

Let us take a simple example. Suppose a subject (S) is presented with a standard line exactly 10 inches long. He is requested to draw a series of lines on several separate sheets of paper which he judges to be equal to the standard in length. Assume the results of four trials are as follows: 9¼ inches, 10⅛ inches, 9¾ inches, and 9⅞ inches. These judgments are actually points of subjective equality, and the mean of them is 9¾ inches. Since the constant error is defined as PSE − Standard, it is therefore 9¾ inches − 10 inches = − ¼ inches. The S thus shows a slight tendency to underestimate the length of the standard line or to overestimate the length of the drawn line. The variable error is defined by the standard deviation (or any other measure of variability), and thus the PSE, the CE, and the VE are all easily determined.

Although the method of adjustment is a simple and obvious procedure for making matching settings, it has sometimes been criticized on several grounds. First, since it requires the S to physically manipulate some object, we are inadvertently studying not only perceptual characteristics of the S, but also his motor skills. It would seem desirable to find a method that would separate these two factors. Second, different Ss will manipulate the variable stimulus at different rates (like tuning a radio quickly or slowly) and this has been found to influence judgments. It was because of problems of this sort that other standard psychophysical methods were developed.

One last point. The method of adjustment can be used not only for matching studies, but for studies of discrimination as well. This will become obvious after a discussion of the discrimination problem.

THE DISCRIMINATION PROBLEM

Several new concepts are introduced when we go from the matching problem to the discrimination problem. As an illustration we might consider the musical aptitude test developed a number of years ago by Seashore. Although there are many aspects to it, we shall consider only the pitch discrimination subtest.

In it, the S is presented with a randomized series of paired tones, and he is asked to judge whether the two tones of each pair are the "same" or "different." Sometimes the tones differ by a relatively large frequency and sometimes by a relatively small one. The Ss keenness of discrimination is measured by the smallness of the frequency difference in tones which he can consistently detect.

This kind of testing procedure is essentially an example of a well-known psychophysical method called the *method of constant stimuli* which we shall now examine.

THE METHOD OF CONSTANT STIMULI

This method is often used to determine an S's differential threshold. In order to do this the S must be presented with a standard stimulus, which is to be the fixed reference point, and a series of other stimuli which are slightly different in magnitude from the standard. The smaller the difference he can consistently detect, the smaller is his differential threshold.

Since an S's threshold is never absolutely constant, but varies slightly from time to time, we cannot expect his responses to be entirely consistent. In other words, if two stimuli which differ slightly are presented to an S many times, it is perfectly reasonable to expect that his judgments concerning them will vary. Sometimes, he will judge one stimulus as larger, sometimes the other. Such inconsistency of judgment usually occurs only over a small range of values. This range is called the *interval of uncertainty*, and outside of this interval, the S is always correct in his comparative judgments of the two stimuli. The method of constant stimuli is only concerned with stimuli in this interval of uncertainty.

The method has several general characteristics: (1) two stimuli are compared at a time, either simultaneously or successively; (2) the stimuli used are all selected from the interval of uncertainty; (3) the paired stimuli are presented in random order; (4) the pairs are presented many times; and (5) the S's responses are usually limited to two categories of judgment such as "larger" and "smaller," or "higher" and "lower."

This may be illustrated with the following hypothetical example. Suppose we wish to determine a person's keenness of hearing, or to put it another way, his differential threshold, at a frequency of 1000 cycles per second. Our procedure might be as follows. We would first do a pilot study to quickly and roughly estimate the S's interval of uncertainty. We might discover that when the tone was at 1010 cps he seemed to consistently recognize it as higher in pitch than the standard of 1000 cps, and when it was at 990 cps he consistently recognized it as lower in pitch. When the second tone was placed somewhere between 990 and 1010 cps the S had difficulty in making his judgment and sometimes he was incorrect. This then roughly determines his interval of uncertainty.

Our second step would be to select at least five stimuli within the S's interval of uncertainty to be used as comparison stimuli. For example, we might choose 992 cps, 996 cps, 1000 cps, 1004 cps, and 1008 cps as our comparison stimuli, with 1000 cps as the standard. Notice that it is perfectly possible and valid to use a 1000 cps tone as a comparison stimulus.

We would then arrange all these pairs in random order and would present each pair to the subject many times. Reports in the literature suggest that 100 repetitions of each pair are sufficient in most cases for reliable results, although reliable data have been obtained with as few as 40 or 50 repetitions of each pair. This means that if five comparison stimuli are used and 50 repetitions of each pair are given, the S must make 250 judgments.

The type of judgment the S makes is limited to two categories; in this case he would be asked to simply state whether the comparison tone was "higher" or "lower" in pitch than the standard tone. When such data are compiled they tend to look somewhat as represented in Table 11–1. It is typically found that

Table 11.1. The distribution of "higher" (H) and "lower" (L) judgments in a pitch discrimination experiment using the method of constant stimuli (the standard tone is 1000 cps)

| Trials | Comparison Tones (cps) | | | | |
	992	996	1000	1004	1008
1	L	L	H	L	H
2	L	L	L	H	H
3	L	H	H	H	H
4	H	H	L	L	H
5	L	L	H	L	H
.	.	.	.	.	.
.	.	.	.	.	.
.	.	.	.	.	.
49	L	H	H	L	H
50	L	L	H	H	H
Number of Hs	2	6	28	46	50
Percent of Hs	4	12	56	92	100

the percent of "higher" judgments increases as the frequency of the comparison tone becomes higher. Similarly, as the comparison tone becomes lower, the percent of "higher" judgments becomes lower. If these data are plotted on a graph, they produce an S-shaped curve which is called the *psychophysical function*. The curve approximates an ogive and is illustrated in Fig. 11–1.

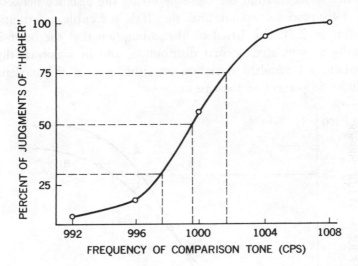

Fig. 11-1. Hypothetical ogive obtained in a differential threshold experiment.

From the figure it is evident that the ogive is relatively linear in its middle portion and sharply curved near both ends. This means that the most accurate estimates and interpolations can be made from the middle portion of the curve.

Based on the ogive it is possible to estimate the PSE, the CE, and the VE as well as one additional measure called the *just noticeable difference* (JND), or *difference limen* (DL). The PSE is interpolated from the 50 percent point of judgments of "higher" and turns out in this example to be approximately 999.6 cps. This means that the constant error is 999.6 − 1000 = −0.4 cps, indicating that the S has a slight tendency to underestimate the 1000 cps tone when judging. The variable error is usually estimated from the ogive by the interquartile range; that is, the difference between the 75th percentile point and the 25th percentile point. In this case it turns out to be 1001.7 cps − 997.7 cps = 4.0 cps. In general, the smaller the VE the more consistent are the judgments of the S. Sometimes, the standard deviation can be estimated from the ogive by taking the distance between the 84th percentile point and the 16th percentile point and dividing by 2. This is based on the assumption that the ogive is actually a cumulated normal distribution, and in a normal distribution, ±1 standard deviation on either side of the median, includes 68 percent of the cases.

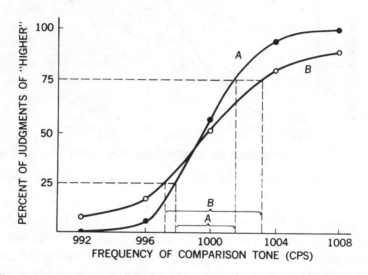

Fig. 11-2. Hypothetical ogives from two **S**s differing in relative sensitivity.

The concept of a just noticeable difference is a little more complex. What is the smallest increment in frequency which is just detectable? A little reflection will convince you that no one answer is possible, simply because there is always some probability that any increment in frequency, however small, will be correctly identified. This means that the value we choose for the JND is somewhat arbitrary. As a result, it has become fairly conventional to take as the JND, the stimulus value between the PSE and the 75th percent point. This distance, however, is actually the semi-interquartile range and is simply a measure of variability. Therefore, any one of the variability measures can be used as a measure of the JND.

This notion can perhaps be made clearer another way. Fig. 11–2 shows two hypothetical ogives obtained from two Ss, A and B. Ogive A is steep and ogive B is relatively flatter.

It should be evident that subject A is more accurate in his judgments than subject B. A is closer to having "perfect pitch" than B since he is far less likely to make errors in his comparisons. A thus has a smaller JND than B. One way to measure the slope of the ogive is to find the difference in frequency that corresponds to the difference between the 75th and 25th percent points, and this value, of course, is the interquartile range. In general, any measure of variability could be used as an index of the relative slope of different ogives, and thus could be used as an index of the JND. It is important, however, that investigators be consistent in their choice.

There is one further point that should be commented on and that concerns the use of only two categories of judgment in this method. In the past, there have been reports published in which investigators allowed Ss three categories of judgment, such as "larger," "equal," "smaller," or "higher," "equal," "lower," etc. This would seem perfectly natural since there are undoubtedly many situations that arise where the S believes the comparison stimulus to be equal to the standard one. In such cases, why force him to choose either "higher" or "lower?"

There are two main reasons. The first is that Ss usually turn out to be better judges than they realize when forced to guess. Their guesses are always better than chance. The other reason for a two-category system is that the "equal" judgment has been found to be very sensitive to attitude and personality factors. Because of the method used for computing the JND, sometimes an observer uses the equal category when he has even the slightest doubt, while another observer might use it only rarely. It turns out that the first observer will have a large JND and the second a small one. The size of the JND in this case will reflect the S's attitudes about the task, or their criteria of judgment, more than it will reflect the sensitivity of their auditory system. The two-category procedure seems to be less affected by such variations in criteria of judgment and is therefore used more frequently by experimenters.

THE METHOD OF LIMITS

Another of the classical psychophysical methods used in studies of discrimination is called the method of limits. It can be illustrated by describing its use in determining a person's absolute threshold of hearing, that is, the softest tone he can hear.

The basic procedure involves the presentation of a given tone to an S at lesser and lesser discrete intensities until he can no longer hear it. The intensity of the tone at the point where his response changes from "Yes" (I hear it) to "No" (I do not hear it) is approximately his absolute threshold. Once this is determined, the tone is presented in reverse order, that is, starting at intensities well below what he can hear, the intensity is increased in a series of steps until he just hears it. The series of alternating descending and ascending intensity are continued so as to get several estimates of the absolute threshold.

If an audiometer test were being run on an S to get the absolute threshold the procedure would be somewhat as follows: (1) A particular frequency would be selected, e.g. 1000 cps. (2) Series of tones of this frequency would be presented at decreasing intensity levels until the S could no longer hear the tone. (3) A fixed time for each exposure of the tone would be used. (4) Series of different intensity would be presented alternately in ascending and descending order, starting in each case well above or well below the estimated intensity threshold. (5) In order to avoid errors due to the S's expectations about the length of the series, each sequence of intensities would be started at a different value. Another way to avoid expectation errors is to occasionally repeat a given step. Sometimes "check" trials are used; that is, no tone is given at a time the S expects one, to see if he reports a "false positive." (6) The S is requested to simply state whether the tone is present or absent, using "Yes" or "No" as responses (or he may be requested to hold a key down for as long as he hears each tone). Each sequence is discontinued when the response changes from "Yes" to "No" or vice versa. The threshold is defined at the midpoint of the change from one response to the other.

Table 11-2. Hypothetical data showing how the method of limits might be used to determine the absolute threshold. Descending and ascending series are alternated (Y stands for "Yes" and N for "No").

Intensity of Tone Decibels	Series					
	1	2	3	4	5	6
40	Y				Y	
35	Y				Y	
30	Y		Y		Y	
25	Y	Y	Y		N	Y
20	N	N	Y	Y		N
15		N	N	N		N
10		N		N		N
5		N				N
Estimated thresholds	22.5	22.5	17.5	17.5	27.5	22.5

Table 11–2 gives an illustration of the kind of data that might be obtained from an S during such threshold determinations. On the first trial the response changed in going from 25 decibels (db) to 20 decibels and we therefore estimate the threshold on that series as 22.5 decibels. (Decibels are a measure of sound intensity.) The absolute threshold is simply defined as the mean based on a number of determinations. A measure of variability can be obtained which is usually the standard deviation of the individual estimated thresholds.

One word of caution about the method. Several studies have shown that the actual threshold which is obtained depends upon both the step-interval size and the rate at which trials are given. Brackmann and Collier (1958) have reported that the brightness threshold based on a series of increasing light intensities is lower than that based on decreasing intensities, and that this difference increases as the step interval increases. In addition, the variability of the data was directly proportional to the size of the step interval. Day (1956) has reported that successive responses to a repeated near-threshold stimulus tend to be serially correlated if the time interval between them is less than about three seconds. If intervals longer than this are used, the responses tend to be more nearly independent. These studies indicate that such factors should be carefully controlled if these sources of variability are to be avoided.

Although the example which has been given is concerned with the absolute threshold, it is important to recognize that the method could be used to determine a differential threshold as well. In the latter case there would be a fixed reference stimulus, and the variable stimulus would be increased and decreased in a series of steps. The S would be required to indicate whether each value of the variable stimulus was larger or smaller than the standard one. As a matter of fact, the point cannot be too strongly emphasized that each of the psychophysical methods described can be used for matching studies, for absolute threshold determinations, or for the measurement of differential thresholds. The basic measures that are obtained are one or more of the following: PSE, CE, VE, and JND. Over the years variations in these methods have been reported (e.g., the use of the method of limits with only ascending series), but the basic concepts are those described above (Stevens, 1958a). For a more detailed discussion of these and other classical psychophysical methods, the interested student should see Guilford (1954).

THE SCALING PROBLEM

People constantly make subjective estimations of the magnitude of things or events. We estimate heights, weights, personality traits, and degrees of conservatism, as well as the brightness of lights, the loudness of sounds, and the softness of textures. Ever since the middle of the last century a controversy has existed on the nature of the relationship between the magnitude of physical quantities and the magnitude of the corresponding subjective sensations. It is known, for example, that doubling the physical intensity of a light does not make the light appear twice as bright and that, in general, there is no linear relation between physical magnitudes and the corresponding subjective sensations.

Early in the nineteenth century, E. H. Weber made a number of observations on the relative sensitivity of our sense modalities under different conditions. He tried to measure the differential threshold, or JND, at different frequencies of sound, different intensities of light, different weights of objects, and so on. An interesting generalization seemed to emerge. As the initial frequency, intensity, or weight increased, the JND also increased, roughly in proportion. This meant that the ratio of the JND to the standard was approximately constant for different-sized standards. The actual value of the constant varied from one modality to another.

In 1860, Fechner published his book on psychophysics in which he named this generalization Weber's law, and then went on to use it as the basis for a statement about the relation between subjective sensations and physical stimuli. Fechner proposed that the subjective sensation was proportional to the logarithm of the physical intensity and was defined mathematically as given in Chapter 7.

Over the past century, considerable debate has existed over the question of whether Fechner's logarithmic relation was the "true" one, and a number of alternatives have been proposed. The alternative which has achieved the greatest prominence is Stevens' *power law* (1957), which states that the magnitude of the subjective sensation depends on the intensity of the physical stimulus raised to some power.

Is there any way of determining empirically which of these two laws—the logarithmic law or the power law—is more consistent with empirical data? To do this we need to be able to measure subjective sensation in quantitative terms; that is, we need to be able to apply numbers reliably to our sensations. There are a number of different ways of doing this, but, unfortunately, when they are compared, they do not provide us with equivalent answers. The issues involved in this problem are deep and subtle and only some of them will be mentioned here. First, however, we will examine one of the methods used in establishing subjective scales.

THE METHOD OF MAGNITUDE ESTIMATION

In this method, the S is presented with a standard stimulus to which a number is arbitrarily assigned. For example, he might be given a tone at 90 decibels and told that this was to be called "100." The S is then given a series of tones and he is asked to numerically judge their intensity relative to the standard. If the variable tone sounds one half as loud as the standard, S is to call it "50," if it sounds one tenth as loud, he is to call it "10," etc.

In one experiment using this method (Stevens, 1958) the Ss were asked to estimate each variable against a 90-db standard arbitrarily called "100," and then asked to estimate each variable against a 45-db standard arbitrarily called "1." The results were like those shown in Fig. 11–3, where the logarithm of the magnitude estimations is plotted against the sound intensity in decibels (which is a logarithmic scale). Two parallel curves were obtained with identical slopes, implying that a power function fits the data nicely. As a matter of fact, the method of magnitude estimation has become a preferred method for demonstrating that the data on many of the senses show a power function.

In using this method, there are a number of "rules" that

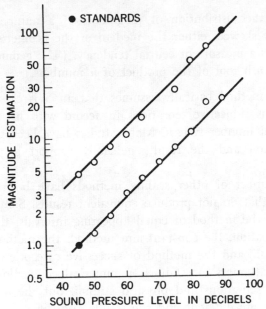

Fig. 11-3. Loudness estimations based upon two different standards. In upper curve 90 decibels equals "100." In lower curve 45 decibels equals "1." (Adapted from J. C. Stevens, 1958.)

should be followed if the data are to be of maximum consistency. These rules have been summarized by Stevens, Herrnstein, and Reynolds (1965) and are paraphrased here.

1. Do not require too many judgments from each S; two or three per stimulus is usually sufficient.
2. Each S should be presented the stimuli in a different and irregular order.
3. The S is asked to choose a number to stand for the subjective intensity of the first stimulus. He assigns numbers to the other stimuli in proportion to the first one. Sometimes, the first stimulus is assigned a number by the experimenter, but this is not a necessary aspect of the method.
4. It is not necessary to present a "standard" before each stimulus.

5. Since the distribution of judgments of a number of Ss is usually skewed, either the median or the geometric mean is used as a measure of central tendency. (The geometric mean is the nth root of the product of n numbers.)

This method basically assumes that an S is capable of arranging his subjective sensations in accord with his knowledge of the real number system. Many studies have been done using this method and the results generally support a power law concept.

A number of other scaling methods have been proposed, however, that do not produce equivalent results. Some of these are called the method of equal appearing intervals, the method of fractionation, the constant-sum method, the method of multiple stimuli, and the method of successive categories. These all represent attempts to establish a numerical connection between subjective sensations and physical stimuli, but the assumptions they make are different and the results also differ. Some of the basic issues are discussed in Stevens (1958b), Garner (1959), Warren and Warren (1963), and Poulton and Simmonds (1963).

A RECENT DEVELOPMENT: SIGNAL DETECTION THEORY

In a recent study college students, naive with respect to the purposes of the experiment, were asked to taste some samples of water and to report if each was salty or not. Unknown to the students, the samples in each case consisted only of distilled water. The results showed that 82 percent of the Ss made at least one "salt" response, and that the median "salt" response was 24 percent (Juhasz and Sarbin, 1966).

This study simply illustrates the existence of so-called "false alarms" in perception, that is, an erroneous statement that a stimulus exists, when in reality it does not. Such false alarms are well known in psychophysical studies and are more likely to occur when the limits of a person's sensitivity are being explored.

If a person is intently listening for a very faint tone, he may occasionally report a tone present when none exists. Some Ss are more likely to do this than others. This fact raises a very important issue for psychophysics. It suggests the possibility that the actual threshold which is measured for a given S will depend partly upon the sensitivity of his sensory processes *and* partly on his response criterion. The response criterion is simply the basis an S uses for deciding whether he should report whether he has heard a faint tone or seen a dim light.

As an illustration of this point we may consider the testing procedure for visual threshold. The S is usually presented with brief, circular flashes of light that are very dim. He is to report whether he sees the light or not. Some Ss will report the light as present only if they see a complete circle of light. Other Ss will report the light as present even if they see a faint flash with no definite contours. The sensitivity of the two Ss might be equal, but one has a more liberal response criterion for reporting when the light is present, and he will show up as apparently having a lower threshold. Therefore, the usual methods for testing thresholds confuse, to some degree, the S's response criterion and his actual sensitivity.

One way in which this problem has been handled in the past is by inserting "catch" trials into the testing series, that is, random trials in which a stimulus is not presented. If the S reports the stimulus as present, he is usually warned by the experimenter to be more careful, or, if the S persists, his data may simply be disregarded.

The result of this procedure is that a good deal of the psychophysical data of the past have been obtained from a small number of highly trained observers, who have established consistent but high response criteria.

During the past ten years or so, a new approach to this problem has been developed (Swets, 1961) called *signal detection theory*. Although the details are complex and depend upon the mathematics of statistical decision theory, a few general ideas may be presented here.

A basic aim of detection theory is to separate, by experimental procedures, the response criterion of the S from his actual sensitivity. One of the ways this can be done is by presenting the observer with a large number of "catch" trials so an independent estimate can be made of his response criterion (i.e., his probability of saying "yes" when no signal is given). Another approach to this problem is to use a different kind of psychophysical method—what Swets (1961) has called *the second-choice experiment*. In this procedure, the S is told that a signal will be presented during one, and only one, of four time intervals during each trial. His task is to judge in which of the time intervals the stimulus is present. He is also asked to make a second choice. This kind of data can be analyzed in such a way as to minimize the effects of response criterion and maximize the effects of sensitivity alone (Swets, Tanner and Birdsall, 1961). The analysis of "false alarms" in this approach—which were usually considered simply as errors—has led to some interesting ideas concerning sensory function.

Let us consider a few examples. Suppose that an auditory stimulus is chosen that is close to the limits of hearing and that this tone is presented 100 times along with 100 randomly interspersed trials in which no tone is given. The S is asked to report on the presence or absence of the tone. The results of this series of observations can be summarized in a simple 2 x 2 table in which the number or proportion of "Yes" and "No" are indicated for the condition when the tone is presented and for the condition when the tone is not presented. This is shown in Table 11-3.

Table 11-3. Proportion of Responses of "Yes" and "No"

		Yes	No
Stimulus	On	0.60	0.40
	Off	0.25	0.75

These results would indicate that 60 percent of the time the S said "Yes" when the tone was presented (i.e., showed a "hit") and 40 percent of the time he missed the stimulus. These values reflect his sensitivity under these particular conditions. When the tone was not presented, S correctly said "No" 75 percent of the time, but showed a "false alarm" 25 percent of the time. The number of "false alarms" reflects the S's expectations. Thus it is possible to find separate measures of the S's sensitivity and of his expectations.

The results presented here, however, were obtained under conditions in which the stimulus was given on 50 percent of the trials. If the tone is presented on (say) 80 percent of the trials, a different set of proportions would be obtained for the table. In order to carry through a signal detection experiment using this approach, four or five different stimulus probabilities would be used at several intensity levels. From these data separate estimates may be made of the S's perceptual sensitivity and of his response criterion. An alternative method that has been used requires the S to make a rating of his confidence that the stimulus is present on each trial. This is described by Price (1966).

What are some implications of this general approach for the study of sensory function? One observation that has been made is that the use of the PSE did not discriminate between schizophrenic patients and normals on a size-constancy task, although the use of a separate measure of perceptual sensitivity, unaffected by the S's response criterion did discriminate between some of the groups (Price and Erickson, 1966). This approach helped to clarify some of the inconsistencies reported in this area of research.

Another important implication relates to studies of motivation and perception. It has been noted that many such studies have confounded the S's sensitivity with his response criterion. For example, if an S shows a higher threshold to certain kinds of words (e.g., sexual) it does not follow that his needs or values influence his perception. The difference may be due to a change in sensitivity or to a change in his criterion for reporting a perception or to a change in both. An S may be unwilling to report a particular type of word until he is quite confident that he knows what it is. This means that his false-alarm rate would decrease even though his sensitivity might remain constant. Since the usual threshold measure does not enable us to obtain an independent estimate of these two factors, the interpretation of a difference obtained between two thresholds is unclear. The theory of signal detection has thus provided important new insights into some of the traditional problems of psychophysics.

SOME APPLICATIONS OF PSYCHOPHYSICS

Almost all the examples thus far given have utilized situations where an observer is presented with a simple, usually discrete stimulus and required to make some kind of judgment about it. However, psychophysical methods have also been applied to much more complex situations where there is no simple relationship between the stimulus as physically measured and the observer's judgment.

One of the important uses of such methods is in the construction of attitude scales. For example, Ss may be presented with pairs of nationalities and asked to state their preferences. This method of paired comparisons enables a systematic scaling of preferences for each S for all nationalities tested. Such scales have been used for evaluating the effects of propaganda on attitudes. The method of paired comparisons has also been used to establish scales for the judgment of the relative seriousness of crimes.

Other psychophysical methods have been used to measure the emotional meanings of words in contrast to their cognitive meanings, the relative similarity of different types of packaging in retail stores, the optimum inventory for mail order houses in certain items in order to please the majority of customers, the most desirable menus to use in certain types of restaurants, the esthetic value of paintings, and the effects of running certain kinds of candidates in political elections (Thurstone, 1954). In fact, it should be evident by now that psychophysics deals with the general nature of human discrimination.

12

THE NATURE OF MEASUREMENT

Science is an art. There are no *ab initio* principles to tell us how to be
clever in devising procedures of measurement. The way to empirical
discovery lies not through mathematics, even, but through the
exercise of uncommon experimental sense and ingenuity. We
invent mathematical models, but we discover measures
in the laboratory.

—S. S. STEVENS

WHY MEASURE?

Most of the events or objects that scientists are concerned
with vary in magnitude. The basic dimensions of physics—
length, mass, and time (from which most other dimensions are
derived)—can vary from zero magnitude to indefinitely large ones,
and although dichotomies are sometimes used for convenience,
they are recognized as crude approximations.

Many of the variables studied in psychology are also continuous. People are not extroverted *or* introverted any more than
minerals are hard *or* soft. Although practice is often described
as massed *or* distributed, and reinforcements are categorized as
continuous *or* partial, it is recognized that such dichotomies are
simply convenient names representing the extremes of continuous
variables.

In their effort to represent the fact that events or objects
vary in magnitude, scientists utilize numbers, partly because

225

numbers are a well understood system of concepts that involve magnitude. To say this another way, numbers (plus the operations associated with them) can be considered to be a general analogue or model of the relationships existing among many events that occur naturally. If people vary in intelligence from low to high, we can represent this idea with numbers that also vary from low to high. If some people are slightly prejudiced and others highly prejudiced, we can also represent this idea by numbers that vary from low to high. Generality obtains because the very same numbers are used to represent the magnitudes of very different kinds of events. In fact, one of the purposes of assigning numbers to events is to provide a common and universal language for describing the magnitudes of many different kinds of things.

There is another reason for assigning numbers to events. When this is done, it becomes possible to make fine distinctions in situations where only broad or vague verbal distinctions were previously possible. The assignment of numbers enables us to distinguish between "dull normal" intellects and "normal" ones, as well as between "normal" and "bright."

Thus, if we define measurement as *the assignment of numbers to objects or events according to certain rules*, it appears that there are at least two good reasons for doing this. One is that numbers represent a universal language for describing many different kinds of things; the other is that numbers enable us to make finer magnitude distinctions than would otherwise be possible.

DO EVENTS MATCH NUMBERS?

Once the value of measurement is recognized several other important questions may be raised. Since numbers are considered to be similar to many events that occur in the "real" world we may ask whether the events and the numbers correspond in all respects. For example, the real number system not only includes the property of magnitude, but also of additivity. In the number system 40 plus 40 is always equal to 80. But the question arises as to whether events also operate in this way, or to put the matter differently, whether events have the property of additivity as defined in the number system.

If two 1-foot rulers are placed end to end, their combined length is 2 feet; if two 100-ohm resistors are placed in series, their combined resistance is 200 ohms. These findings are thus in accord with our number system analogy.

But suppose the two 100-ohm resistors are added in parallel instead of in series; then their combined resistance is 50 ohms rather than 200 ohms. If water is boiling at 100°C, and more boiling water is added at 100°C, the temperature of the combined water is still 100°C.

One point being made here is that many events occur in nature which can be described with the use of numbers, but which do *not* show all the properties of the number system. Another point that is implicit is that the word *addition* must be defined anew each time we deal with a new physical or psychological system.

Let us examine a problem from the field of audition. Suppose we produce a pure tone of 1000 cps whose intensity is 40 decibels. Assume we then play a second 40-decibel pure tone of 1000 cps from a loudspeaker adjacent to the first. Do the two sounds add arithmetically from the point of view of a listener? It turns out that they do not add arithmetically although there is some increase in apparent loudness. The problem is much more complicated for the addition of frequencies. Two 1000 cps tones played at the same time do not sound like a 2000 cps tone, but only a 1000 cps tone. If a 1000 cps tone is played at the same time as a 2000 cps tone, the result is a complex mixture of tones and harmonics. Two people, each with an IQ of 100, and working together on a given problem, do not function equally as well as one person with an IQ of 200.

It should thus be evident that some of the ways events may

be added in the real world do not always match the addition of numbers in our theoretical model, the real number system.

SCALES OF MEASUREMENT

The preceding observations lead to an important concept, the concept of scales of measurement. Although the properties of numbers and the properties of events do not always match exactly, it is often possible to indicate the *degree* to which they agree or disagree. For example, sometimes numbers can be used simply to designate different events or objects without regard to the magnitude of the object or event. This is done when numbers are used to indicate different football players or when numbers are used to indicate items in a catalog. In such cases order is of no significance; numbers are used only as labels. It is debatable whether this use of numbers should be considered measurement, but Stevens (1958b) has called this a *nominal* scale.

Situations of greater significance to the psychologist are those in which it is possible to rank-order a group of objects or events. When an expert rates beef as "prime," "choice," or "good" this represents a rank ordering on estimated fat content, but no attempt is made to indicate that "prime" has twice as much fat as "choice" or five times as much as "good" beef. The numbers 1, 2, and 3 could be given to these three grades, but any other set of increasing numbers could just as well be applied, e.g., 2, 7, and 10 or 4, 15, and 25. Since the relative differences between rankings are not specified, any set of numbers of increasing rank could be used. Such a scale is called an *ordinal* scale, and it is evident that adding or multiplying such arbitrary ranks could lead to misleading results. In psychology, ratings of personality traits, ratings of sales ability, ratings of creativity and the like are usually rank-order or ordinal scales.

There are certain events which match the number system more closely; not only do they show increasing order of magnitude, but they imply that equal differences in the magnitude of the events are associated with equal intervals between numbers applied to the events. The difference between 10°F and 20°F is the same difference of temperature as that between 40°F and 50°F, or 80°F and 90°F. If we convert scores on an intelligence test for a group of students into percentiles, then we have equal numbers of students between the 10th and 20th percentile, the 40th and 50th percentile, or the 80th and 90th percentile. But this does not mean that intelligence as theoretically conceived is equally distributed among these percentiles. The difference in intelligence between students in the 40th and 50th percentile (the middle portion of the normal distribution) is not as great as the difference in intelligence between students in the 80th and 90th percentiles (the upper tail of the normal distribution). If intelligence test data are converted to standard scores, the *assumption* is usually made that equal standard scores represent equal differences in intelligence. This is, however, an assumption and not directly verifiable. Scales of this type are called *interval* scales.

Finally, certain events occur which match the number system not only in terms of increasing order of magnitude and equal intervals, but also in terms of the existence of a meaningful zero point. In the Centigrade temperature scale the freezing point of water is arbitrarily called zero degrees. This same physical occurrence is 32 degrees on the Fahrenheit scale. Since the zero point is arbitrary it is not correct to speak of 40°F indicating twice as much heat as 20°F (since 40°F is equal to 4.4°C and 20°F is equal to −6.7°C). The actual numerical ratio between any two numbers will depend on the choice of a zero point.

If, however, a meaningful and unique zero point exists, then all ratios between numbers are meaningful and unique, and most mathematical operations appropriate to the number system can be performed. Such scales are called *ratio* scales and can sometimes be achieved in psychology by the use of special scaling methods, some of which will be described later.

The concept of scales of measurement described above has been presented most fully by Stevens in several papers (1946; 1958b; 1959). There are, however, several problems relating to the generality of this viewpoint about the nature of measurement.

The first problem concerns the fact that in practice it is extremely difficult to know whether or not we have an equal unit, interval scale. The examples of equal unit scales given by Stevens are taken mostly from physics; he lists temperature, time, and potential energy; he then adds "intelligence test standard scores (?)." Stevens gives no other psychological examples and no formal rules for determining whether we have obtained such a scale or not.

Guilford (1954), in discussing this same problem, points out that one way of determining whether or not an equal unit scale exists is by demonstrating additivity. If 10 units of intelligence plus 20 units of intelligence are equal to 30 units of intelligence then additivity is shown. However, Guilford notes that

> The property of additivity is rarely experimentally demonstrable, even in the physical sciences. . . . On the ordinary temperature scales there is no operation for the summation of two temperature levels. Even in the realm of length or distance there are very serious limitations to the proof of addition by experimental operations. No one has ever placed light-years end to end, nor has anyone demonstrated the addition of atomic distances. . . . In all the sciences, then, the assumption of applicability of number properties rests on very limited empirical proof.

Despite the limited proof of additivity of measures there is no doubt that physics and technology in general have made remarkable progress in the last century. This at least raises the question of whether additivity and equal unit scales must be proven at all. To anticipate a point to be made in the next section, physicists seem to be far less concerned about the existence of equal unit scales than are psychologists.

A second problem concerns the claim that a simple mathematical transformation may change a scale from a "lower" type to a "higher" type. For example, Guilford states that the Pearson product-moment correlation coefficient r has a meaningful zero point, but lacks equality of units and is therefore only an ordinal scale. He adds, however, that theories of reliability and factor analysis assume that the simple process of squaring r changes the ordinal scale to a ratio scale. Since, in general, an infinite number of mathematical transformations are possible, this raises the possibility that any kind of scale can be made into any other kind of scale if the appropriate transformation can be found. If this is true, then the whole notion of higher and lower types of scales seems of little value.

A third problem that has been mentioned in discussions of scaling concerns the question of "context" effects. In an effort to obtain ratio scales in psychology, Stevens has used a method called *fractionation.* This requires the subject or observer to adjust one light until it is one-half as bright as another light, or to adjust one tone until it is one-third as high in pitch as another. Any fraction can be used and the technique can be applied to any sense modality. The essential requirement is that the subject make direct ratio estimates of the numerical relationships between subjective magnitudes.

Although this technique has been widely used, a number of criticisms have been raised against it. For example, Garner (1954) reported a study in which three different groups of subjects were given the same standard reference auditory intensity, but varying ranges of comparison stimuli. The results showed that the mean half-loudness judgment for each group was approximately at the middle of the range of comparison intensities that were used, thus indicating that the stimulus context had a marked effect upon the subjective scales obtained from subjects by the fractionation method. As a result of a subsequent experiment, Garner (1959) concluded that half-loudness judgments mainly reflect individual response sets typical of ambiguous situations and are therefore of doubtful validity.

Poulton and Simmonds (1963) have also shown in connection with the visual modality that fractional (or multiple) estimates of sensory magnitude are considerably modified by the ranges of stimuli used and by the ranges of numbers available to the subjects. They also conclude that numerical estimates of sensory magnitude are of doubtful validity. Other criticisms of direct scaling methods have been made by Warren and Warren (1963) and by Graham and Ratoosh (1962).

HOW PHYSICISTS MEASURE THINGS

In England in A.D. 965 a law was passed stating that the standard of length was to be kept at London and a series of copies were to be used throughout the kingdom. This standard yard was defined to be 36 inches. The yard that had been used until then was 39.6 inches and this standard was eventually prohibited by law.

In 1760 a new standard was made consisting of a brass bar a little over a yard in length with gold studs near the ends. The yard was then defined as the distance between the center of two dots, one punched in each of the gold studs, when the temperature of the bar was 62°F.

In the middle of the nineteenth century, five bronze bars were made as nearly alike as possible and used as the new standards. Every ten years these five standards are compared with one another, and it has been observed that one of them showed a gradual decrease in length over the first 40 years amounting to 228 millionths of an inch.

In France, a standard meter was made in 1801 and replaced in 1889. It is made of a platinum-iridium alloy with two engraved lines near the ends defining the length of the meter. This is true, however, only when the temperature of the bar is that of melting ice and the bar is supported in a certain standard way.

This bit of history has been given to emphasize the fact that what we take to be the unit of measurement of any quantity is essentially an arbitrary convention. Another important point to be made is that stable units, in a practical sense, require considerable knowledge of the nature of the world, in this case, of the nature of physical properties of bodies. A physicist puts the matter this way: "Much of this knowledge depends upon observations which involve measurements of length based on an earlier and less satisfactory standard. In general, science advances through stages of successive refinement" (Feather, 1959).

There is one other point of fundamental significance for an understanding of the nature of measurement, and this concerns the question of addition of units. When a person wants to measure the length of something, he lays a ruler or yardstick down end over end until some subdivision of the ruler is lined up with the end of the object. In doing this, he implicitly makes two assumptions: (1) that the length of the ruler remains the same no matter where it is moved, and (2) that the mathematical operation of addition is to be represented by the process of placing rulers end to end.

Now the fact is that neither of these assumptions can be proven to be logically necessary. Euclid recognized this first point in relation to geometry and simply made the assumption that figures may be moved freely in space without change of shape or size. The second assumption is not necessary either since it is perfectly possible to imagine measuring the length of objects in other ways. For example, in a treatise on measurement Ellis (1966) suggests that we imagine measuring lengths by placing the measuring rods at right angles to one another. In such a case, the length of an object is the diagonal of the triangle formed by this "right-angled addition," and it turns out to satisfy all the logical requirements of length measurement.

The basic reason this method of addition or any one of the other logically possible ones is not used is that the results of such measurements would make the laws of science more complicated than they are now. This means that the problem of how best to add units is at least partly a question of convenience.

The same sort of considerations apply also to the measurement of time. Because every process occurring in nature involves duration, any recurrent process can be used as a clock. The rising and setting of the sun, the movement of a pendulum, the vibrations of a tuning fork, and the speed of radioactive decay have all been used to measure the passage of time. But one fundamental *assumption* must be made—that the unit of time tomorrow is the same length as the unit of time today. In short, equality of units is assumed and not proven.

THE PHYSICAL MEASUREMENT OF ROUGHNESS

Let us look at another example of measurement in an area which is less clear-cut. How might a physicist develop a technique for measuring the roughness of surfaces?

According to Wilson (1952), four basic steps are necessary for developing a measurement scale. The first requires some kind of *intuitive feeling* for the quality to be measured. The second requires the development of a method for *comparing* two samples so that it can be said that one has more of the quality than the other. The third involves setting up *standards,* and the fourth requires the development of a set of *rules* for relating the standards.

When we apply these criteria to roughness, it is evident that we can usually make subjective judgments about the roughness of surfaces on the basis of touch. Alternately, it would be possible to move a phonograph needle and pickup across the surface and record the magnitude of the electrical signals produced by the vibration of the needle. The magnitude of the signal could be used to compare two surfaces.

As a third step, a set of standard plates could be prepared having different degrees of roughness as measured by the phonograph needle system. Copies of the plates could then be prepared and used in different places.

Finally, a scale of roughness might be defined in terms of

the voltage outputs produced by drawing the needle over different surfaces under standard conditions.

The physicist does not generally concern himself with the question of whether his scale has equal units. However, he is very concerned about the *consistency* and *reliability* of the data resulting from his method. He is also concerned with their relations to other kinds of data, for example, with measurements of coefficient of friction. The physicist may also try some practical tests. He may actually determine whether surfaces with higher roughness indices actually wear out faster than those with lower measures. In general, he does not expect simple linear relations between his roughness measure and wearability or coefficient of friction. But, so long as the relationship is a consistent one, he can work with it. If, however, some other method of measuring roughness, e.g., a reflected light technique, shows mathematically simpler relations to other types of measures, he is inclined to drop the phonograph needle technique and adopt the mathematically simpler one.

The preceding description is obviously an oversimplified account of the development of a measurement scale. It does suggest, however, that the physicist is not generally concerned with whether he is dealing with an ordinal, interval, or ratio scale. He does not measure equality of units in any direct way, but on the contrary, simply assumes it. His major concerns are with the consistency of the data and their relations to other kinds of measures. These same considerations can meaningfully apply to the psychologist as well.

SOME IMPLICATIONS

There are some interesting implications of the views that have been presented. If we examine the physicist's apparently successful approach to the problem of measurement, we find that the basic requirements are the establishing of standards and specification of rules for comparing the things to be measured with the standards so that numbers may be assigned. It has not been shown that addition of scale values is either a necessary or a sufficient condition to ensure meaningful measurement. In fact, many fundamental physical quantities do not show additivity of the sort implied by the arithmetic number system (e.g., temperature, density, hardness). What is essential is that the results obtained by applying a particular measurement procedure be consistent and related in an orderly fashion to other kinds of measures.

These considerations apply also to the measurement of quantities of concern to psychologists. This includes measures used in the study of learning, intelligence, motivation, stress, and even psychophysics. No one has seriously tried to show that rate of response, number of errors, trials to reach a criterion, probability of a response, or proportion of animals responding (to name a few) are based on an equal unit scale or show the property of additivity. Some of these measures of learning may turn out to be more useful than others, but the grounds for this assertion have nothing to do with whether or not the measures are additive. On the contrary, the criteria refer to such matters as ease of making the measurement, generality of the measurement approach to many situations, consistency of the data obtained by it, and responsivity of the measure to important experimental variables. In relation to this issue Ehrenberg (1955) has commented that, "no reasons seem ever to have been suggested, let alone shown to be cogent, why an empirical correspondence with arithmetical addition, which is only one out of all the many mathematical operations which have been defined and studied, should be *the* criterion of 'measurability.'"

It is perfectly possible and practicable for psychologists to attempt measurement using whatever measures are available or whatever measures can be invented, without concern in advance as to whether or not an equal unit scale is implied. Consistency of data obtained, relation to other variables and other considerations will eventually indicate whether the measure is useful or not.

Let us briefly examine one final illustration. If an investigator was interested in measuring the strength of hunger motivation, a variety of measurement approaches would be available. One approach is to record some event designed to produce the state being measured, for example, the time the animal is deprived of food. A second approach would be to use some measure of the animals' behavior as an index of the degree of hunger, for example, the speed of running a maze to get food might be one such index. Another might be the rate of bar pressing for pellets. Still a third approach would be a measure based on the degree of noxious stimulation needed to prevent a response; thus, we might measure the strength of hunger by the magnitude of shock just needed to stop the animal from crossing an electrified grid to food, or we might find the amount of quinine that must be added to the food to prevent the animal from eating. These examples are actually illustrations of general approaches that can be used in a large variety of settings. Whether or not a particular type of measurement is useful depends on various considerations unrelated to the problem of additivity of units.

SUMMARY

Measurement is concerned with the assignment of numbers to objects or events according to certain rules. This is useful because numbers represent a universal language for describing many different kinds of things, and because they enable fine distinctions to be made. Unfortunately the addition of events in the real world does not always match the addition of numbers in the arithmetic number system. This, however, does not prevent measurement from being valid or useful. What is essential to measurement is the existence of standards and rules for comparing things with the standards so that numbers may be assigned. The major concern of the investigator should be with the consistency of his data and with their relations to other important variables.

13

THE ROLE OF INSTRUMENTS

IN RESEARCH

Biological instrumentation cannot be separated from biological theory, for
the meaning of each measurement must be sought in the instrument,
the measuring process, and the nature of the material being
measured.

—HAROLD J. MOROWITZ

SCIENCE WITHOUT INSTRUMENTS

Instruments are not essential to all of science. Many parts
of biology and geology are basically descriptive and require nothing more than observational skill and knowledge for the acquisition of fundamental data. This is also true of classical genetics
which was based upon the careful observation of certain characteristics in many generations of plants. A whole body of fact and
theory was developed on the basis of observations of such simple
things as color and texture of peas and the color of eyes and
shape of body parts in fruit flies. Measuring instruments were
not used and yet a complex science evolved capable of predicting
many facts of hereditary transmission.

There are also areas of psychology where instruments play
a small role. This is true, for example, of most of clinical psychology and large parts of the study of child development and

even social psychology, where often the only tools used are rating scales or attitude questionnaires.

These examples are given simply to emphasize the fact that observation of naturally occurring events is the fundamental starting point of science. Yet, as we look around today, the impression is unavoidable that science is characterized by the use of gadgets and equipment of increasing degrees of sophistication. At what point in the development of science do instruments become of central significance? Or, to put the question in a slightly different way, what is the role of instruments in research?

WHAT INSTRUMENTS DO

Although some aspects of science will always rely relatively more on careful observation alone, the tendency is toward increasing use of instruments. There are several reasons for this.

The first is that instruments help acquire data under known conditions. Observing the behavior of fish in their natural environment has provided many interesting kinds of information about such things as schooling behavior, migrations, social interaction, and predation. However, most of this information suffers from one defect; it is often difficult, if not impossible, to determine the causes of the observed behavior. If, however, the fish are raised in a large tank and such conditions as illumination, temperature, and salinity are varied systematically, it becomes possible to determine what factors produce changes in the events that are observed. The instruments enable us to know the conditions under which the observations are made.

When an animal is placed in a maze or a Skinner box, or when a human subject is placed in an iron lung in a sensory deprivation experiment, the instrument is designed to limit the environment so that whatever data are collected are obtained under known conditions.

This fact suggests a second purpose of instruments; they can be used to standardize data acquisition procedures from experiment to experiment. Once an instrument has been designed to limit the environment in a certain way, it sometimes becomes apparent that it can be used in the acquisition of data in a large variety of situations. This is true, for example, of the Skinner box which is used routinely in all sorts of learning studies, in drug research, and in physiological research. This is also true, to a lesser degree, of the Wisconsin General Test Apparatus, developed by Harlow and his associates for use with all types of animals in the study of learning. In Russia, the Pavlovian conditioning techniques have become standardized to a considerable degree and many kinds of experiments have been done in the same basic setting. This standardization due to the use of instruments enables a large body of information to be built up within a common framework, simply because different investigators are using the same equipment.

The third major reason for the increasing use of instruments is that they enable the permanent recording of events. This is done with cameras and tape recorders, as well as inkwriting polygraphs. In clinical research, for example, there is an increasing reliance on tape recordings of interviews and therapy sessions, on motion picture records of psychotherapy interactions, and on physiological recording of such variables as heart rate and respiration rate. These instruments do not reveal anything which cannot be observed, but they provide permanent records so that repeated observations may be made of any and every aspect of the events by the original observer as well as others. Needless to say, there are often things discovered about the interactions that were not immediately obvious to an observer. Through these methods, detailed analyses have been made of the facial expressions and postures of patients, and of their idiosyncratic uses of language, including such things as inflections, pauses, interruptions, and other aspects of the speech pattern.

There is one other and probably most significant purpose of instruments—to enable us to measure and record things not available to our unaided senses. In any living organism there are literally thousands of chemical, electrical, and thermal events that occur at all times, and yet they are not directly perceptible. Only by interposing special instruments does it become possible to record or measure them.

Brain waves can only be recorded with special, highly sensitive amplifiers. Skin resistance changes (or the GSRs) require electrical measuring devices. Blood pressure can be measured in an animal by probes placed directly into arteries, or indirectly in man in a variety of ways. Reaction time in man is measured in tenths of a second, while nerve action potentials are measured in thousandths of a second. The loudness of sounds is measured by pressure changes in the atmosphere, while psychophysical research on color vision requires the accurate specification of colors. Microscopes and telescopes extend the range of action of our sense organs, just as the various measuring instruments mentioned above make all kinds of events potentially available to our senses. It is thus obvious that many areas of science would be largely inaccessible without special measuring instruments.

The points that have been made may now be summarized. Instruments are important to science because: (1) they enable data to be obtained under known conditions; (2) they standardize data acquisition procedures from experiment to experiment; (3) they enable information to be permanently recorded for future analysis; and (4) they enable measurement of events which are not directly observable by the senses.

It is obvious that these are important values, but as is so often the case, the blessings are not unmixed. There are many problems created by instruments that require considerable caution and thought concerning their use.

PROBLEMS CREATED BY INSTRUMENTS

The very fact that instruments allow the collection of information under standard conditions means that a sampling process has been utilized. This is true simply because the conditions that are standardized by the instrument are only a few out of a potentially large number of conditions that could have been used.

The first maze used in this country was designed in 1900 by Willard Small. It was designed for rats and was 6 by 8 feet in size with wire netting for walls. Several years later, J. B. Watson reduced the size of the maze to 5 by 7 feet and made his alleys of wood. Since that time a large number of modifications have been introduced in the details of the construction of the maze (Lyons, 1965). Now, although this meant that the conditions of an experiment were probably constant for any one experimenter, they were not constant for all researchers in a given field. Differences in results obtained by different investigators could then be attributed at least partly to differences of procedure and equipment. To take a simple example, no one knew the influence of the width of the alley in the maze on learning ability in rats.

In light of these problems it would seem at first glance that one solution to the problem would be to standardize equipment so that all investigators in a field used the same instruments. This solution creates a difficulty too, namely, that it may artificially limit the direction of research and prevent creative innovations. For example, by the middle 1920s, multiple T-mazes and multiple U-mazes had become fairly standard devices used in studies of learning, but it often took hundreds of trials for the rat to learn to discriminate between simple visual patterns. Around 1930, Karl Lashley developed an alternate method for studying discrimination, a device which he called a "jumping stand." In this device, the rat was placed upon a small stand, a foot or two off the floor, and was forced to jump toward one of two doors, each marked with a different visual pattern. If the rat hit the "correct" pattern, the door opened and a food pellet became available; if he hit the "wrong" pattern, the door remained shut and the rat fell into a net. With this equipment, a rat could often learn the same discrimination in 20 or 30 trials. Thus the study of learning became much more efficient.

The same considerations also apply to the invention of the Skinner box. This was, in some ways, a simplified version of Thorndike's 1898 "puzzle box" in which an animal had to open a latch in order to escape from a small cage. The Skinner box is simply a small closed chamber in which the animal must press a lever or peck a key in order to receive some kind of reward such as food, water, or escape from electric shock. One of the major values of the instrument is that all of the procedures used with it can be made automatic so that rewards can be given in any kind of sequence and responses may be recorded on moving strips of paper. Large numbers of animals can be run simultaneously and the response records can be examined at the convenience of the experimenter. This instrument has therefore made many kinds of studies possible which would have been almost inconceivable a few decades ago.

It is thus evident that standardization is not necessarily a desirable thing. This is even true of the Skinner box. Because of the discrete (on-off) characteristics of the response measure, problems related to use of continuous responses, such as the degree of force with which an animal presses the bar, were ignored until quite recently. Another difficulty created by the Skinner box is that it limits the kinds of problems that can be studied. For example, Harlow (1953) has criticized the use of the Skinner box partly on the grounds that such phenomena as "curiosity," "exploratory drive," and "affection" are not readily observable in that setting.

The picture that emerges from all this is that although standardization is often desirable, it should never limit or prevent innovation. Researchers constantly strive to develop instruments which are simple, adaptable to many kinds of problems, and which allow information to be gathered reliably and in permanent form. The danger in all this is that the results of the experiment may reflect certain arbitrary properties of the apparatus, such things as size, lighting conditions, types of responses that are required, etc.

The physicists have also faced this problem and they have arrived at two general approaches to a solution. One approach is to conceive of instruments as ways of measuring theoretically important variables whose properties are inferred from the instrumental results, but are not equivalent to them. In other words, they are concerned with instruments as measures of hypothetical constructs (see Chapter 3). Physicists who tried to measure the charge on the electron could do this in half a dozen different ways using as many different kinds of instruments. But in every case, there were theoretical links between the readings obtained on dials and the concept "charge on an electron." Similarly, it is possible to measure breathing characteristics in a person by means of a pneumatic system, a strain gauge, a variable resistance device, and a variable impedance device, all of which are based on different physical principles, but all of which (under proper conditions) can produce identical answers.

The other approach to the problem of equating different instruments is through *calibration*—a set of procedures of fundamental importance in all research. Calibration refers to the process of exposing the instrument to precisely known inputs or standard conditions, so that its readings under those conditions can be determined. This enables different instruments to be set or adjusted to produce equivalent results. For example, whenever an EEG machine is used to record brain waves, a calibration check is usually made at the beginning. This means that a carefully controlled 50-microvolt electrical signal is fed into the device and the size of the output on the record is noted. This is then used as a reference for evaluating the magnitude of the EEG changes during the experiment itself. Variations in the accuracy of the instrument over time may be compensated for by knowledge of the calibration values.

The various standards used for calibration of electrical, mechanical, thermal, etc. instruments are kept at the National Bureau of Standards in Washington, D.C. Copies of these standards are made available to scientists and instrument manufacturers for calibration of their instruments. In addition, scientists meet periodically to discuss the establishment of standards for all nations as well as to consider new and more refined ways of defining the fundamental standards. These facts give some idea of the importance researchers attach to the problem of accurately calibrating their instruments. It is a good rule to periodically check the calibration on all instruments in use.

HOW TO SPECIFY THE PROPERTIES OF INSTRUMENTS

When an instrument is used as a measuring device there are many requirements which it must fulfil. For example, it should provide a faithful reproduction of the event measured without introducing any distortion. It should also be sensitive enough to record events which are either very rapid or very small. These criteria (among others) are not always easily satisfied, so that it becomes necessary to have ways of describing, in quantitative terms, how close an instrument comes to providing satisfactory measurement. Some of these ways will now be outlined. Many of the concepts used will be taken from the language of electronics simply because electrical instruments are being used more and more for all types of recording. It should also be noted that it is now generally possible to change the energy in any given system into an electrical signal which can then be easily measured.

Sensitivity. This refers to the minimum energy, signal, or input which the instrument can reliably distinguish. If the device is an electrocardiograph, the sensitivity is usually measured in terms of a few millivolts that it can record. If the device is an electroencephalograph, its sensitivity is measured in microvolts or millionths of a volt. If the device is designed to measure skin resistance, its sensitivity might be given in terms of the smallest change in resistance (ohms) that it can reliably record.

When an investigator considers the purchase of some measuring equipment it is important for him to have some idea of the approximate size of the input signal he wants to measure so that he can check it against the manufacturer's sensitivity specifications.

Range. All measuring instruments have a range within which they are designed to normally operate. This range includes an upper maximum value of the input energy or signal as well as a lower maximum sensitivity value. For example, a sound level meter used for measuring the intensity of sounds might be designed to operate within the range of 40 to 110 decibels, which roughly covers the range of sounds normally encountered in the environment. However, for special purposes, a sound level meter might be used to record sounds up to 130 decibels, which is approximately the auditory pain threshold.

Similarly, light meters are designed to work in different ranges. If an investigator is concerned with measuring the absolute threshold, he might use a very sensitive meter with a small range of action. If he was studying differential thresholds at higher intensities he would use a light meter with a larger range of response.

Linearity. Another characteristic of a good measuring instrument is called linearity, which means that there is a simple and direct relationship between the size of the signal entering the instrument and the size of the response or output of the instrument.

Most recorders used in psychophysiological research have three major elements. There is first an electrode or a transducer, which either picks up small electrical signals coming from the body (e.g., the electrocardiogram) or transforms another form of energy into an electrical signal (e.g., blood pressure into an electrical change, or a volume displacement, as in breathing, into an electrical change). These small electrical signals are then fed through an amplifier which is simply designed to greatly increase the size of the signal so that it can operate a recording device of some sort. For example, the 10 to 100 microvolt signals picked up as the EEG of the human brain are amplified until they may be as large as several volts which is an increase of about 50,000 times. Finally, the output of the amplifier is sent to a recording device which usually consists of a galvanometer with an ink writing pen attached to it. When current flows through the galvanometer, it causes the pen to be deflected by an amount which is proportional to the amount of current flowing. If the pen deflection in millimeters (or any unit of distance) is directly proportional to the amount of current flow (in milliamperes or other appropriate unit), the recorder is said to be linear.

Similarly, if a strain gauge produces an electrical output which is directly proportional to the volume displacement of the chest during breathing we describe it as linear. If the resistance change of a thermistor (a small bead of semiconducting material used for temperature measurement) is directly proportional to the temperature change, it is operating as a linear device. Linear devices are desirable because they are easier to calibrate and work with.

However, in practice most pens on ink writing recorders are not linear and this is due partly to the fact that the pen is fixed at one point of the galvanometer and swings in an arc when current flows. This has two undesirable effects: (1) the tip of the pen becomes slightly displaced from the true time axis, and (2) the speed of rise of the pen gets slower, the further up it gets. These facts introduce some errors and the errors get larger as the deflection of the pen increases. Figure 13–1 shows what happens to a square wave or a sine wave as a result of the arcing of the pen in a recorder. It indicates that the shape of any signal will be distorted to some degree by this kind of recording.

How can this problem be dealt with? There are several approaches to a solution. (1) Some recorders do not use an ink writing pen, but use an electron beam instead, as in cathode ray oscilloscopes. The electron beam deflection is usually fairly linear with respect to the input. To get permanent records, however,

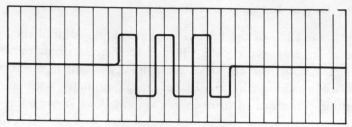

SQUARE WAVE INPUT

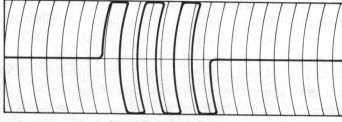

PEN RECORDER OUTPUT

(a)

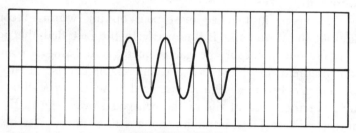

SINE WAVE INPUT

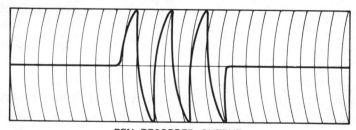

PEN RECORDER OUTPUT

(b)

a photograph must be taken of the pattern shown on the face of the oscilloscope. (2) Certain special pens have been built which do not swing in an arc. If the input is a sharp rise, ideally the pen will show a sharp rise. The major difficulty with this method is that it adds considerable expense to the recorder, and it also slows the speed of the pen. If the event to be described is a rapid one, this kind of pen might not record it accurately. (3) The most common solution is to use a pen with a relatively long arm so that the arc described by the point is a reasonable approximation to a straight line. In other words, if we have a circle with a 5-inch radius, then an arc of two inches on the circumference will be almost straight. Most manufacturers will specify how much of a deflection is tolerable in order for the record to remain approximately linear. In addition, the degree of linearity *within that range* is specified by a percent figure such as 1 or 5 percent. Obviously, once that range is exceeded, these linearity specifications no longer apply.

Accuracy. Every measuring instrument has a certain accuracy which can be specified. For example, if a timer is used to measure the speed of an event such as a reaction time, the result is usually expressed in terms of fractions of a second, e.g., 0.24 seconds. However, such an answer implicitly assumes that the instrument is absolutely accurate whereas, in reality, *all* instruments are in error to some degree.

The degree of error is determined by a calibration procedure which uses some other instruments believed to be more accurate than the one being tested. In order to calibrate a timer, some highly reliable time signal of known duration would be fed into the timer on a large number of trials, say 100. This signal, let us say, is almost exactly 0.20 seconds and is known not to vary from this by more than one millisecond in either direction. Therefore we can specify the input duration as varying between 199 and

---

Fig. 13-1. An illustration of how a typical pen recorder tends to distort certain signal inputs because of the arcing of the pen.

201 milliseconds, or, as the engineers would put it, the input signal is 0.20 ± 0.001 seconds (read "plus or minus").

With such an input we would find that the timer did not produce exactly the same reading on every one of the 100 trials. On most trials it might read 0.20 seconds, but on some it might read as low as 0.19 seconds or as high as 0.21 seconds. We might then specify the accuracy of the timer as accurate within plus or minus 1/100 of a second or ± 0.01 seconds.

Such a calibration check would have to be made for other parts of the range of action of the timer, since accuracy often depends on the part of the scale we measure with. Because of such variation, accuracy is usually stated in terms of percent. Thus, you might buy a timer with a 1 percent accuracy. This would mean that the "true" value of the time being measured is within one percent of the reading on the instrument at the maximum value the instrument reads. This is usually called "full-scale deflection" and is the typical way in which accuracy is specified. It means that accuracy is much less at other parts of the scale. When instruments are bought, accuracy specifications should always be requested and examined.

Frequency Response. Many of the events that psychologists try to measure are periodic events, for example, heart rate, brain waves, and sound waves. All such periodic events are said to have a certain frequency, usually measured in terms of cycles per second (cps). Sound waves that are audible can vary from about 20 cps to 20,000 cps. Brain waves vary from around 2 or 3 cps to about 40 cps, and heart rates are around 1 cps, with certain parts of the complex much faster than that. The galvanic skin response is a relatively slow acting event, with one cycle taking as long as several seconds.

Measuring instruments vary greatly in their ability to record events that are periodic. Many commercial EEG machines have a frequency response from 2 cps to about 60 cps. Some manufacturers have tried to make their machines more versatile by extending the range at both ends with the lower limit designated as "DC" and the upper limit about 120 cps. "DC" refers to direct current which means a frequency of zero cps. Paradoxical as it may sound, the amplification of a steady, direct current signal is actually one of the most difficult things to amplify without distortion or drift, and psychologists had to wait until the engineers had developed reliable methods for doing this (since about 1950) before they could study certain kinds of problems. For example, there are certain kinds of eye movements that are very slow so that the electrical changes associated with them may be considered almost DC. These changes could not be recorded with conventional amplifiers but required the special "DC" amplifiers.

At the other end of the frequency spectrum, a recorder which has a good high frequency response can record events which are very rapid, such as a spike potential generated by a nerve. As another illustration, we know that blood pressure changes are relatively slow, but there is one very brief event, called the dicrotic notch, which is associated with closure of one of the heart valves. This transient spike can only be measured with a recorder that has a high frequency response. Otherwise it is simply absent from the record.

The instrument specifications which have been described are not the only ones which should be considered, but they are undoubtedly among the more important. Anyone interested in the use of equipment should certainly be aware of such factors and should examine any company brochure carefully in the light of these considerations. The potential buyer of equipment should be wary of any company that does not supply specifications on all these and other points. In addition, he should consider such things as the reputation for reliability of the instrument, the type of warranty given, and the availability of repair services. It may be taken as an axiom that the more complex the equipment to be used, the greater the likelihood that repair and maintenance services will be necessary.

One other useful word on equipment purchasing. Companies that market devices have usually spent a good deal of time and effort designing them, testing them, and getting the "bugs" out. Rarely does an individual investigator have the opportunity to check out a piece of homemade equipment to the same extent. Therefore, even though it may seem that a financial saving will occur if you build a complex piece of equipment yourself, this often turns out to be an illusion. In general, if you can afford to buy it, don't make it!

AN INSTRUMENT CAN CHANGE THE EVENT MEASURED

One of the dangers in the use of equipment that is sometimes unrecognized by the user is that the instrument may change the event being measured, and thus distort its nature. The electrical engineers have recognized this phenomenon for a long time and have called it *loading the circuit*. Psychologists have sometimes called this *backward action* (Wendt, 1938). It can be illustrated in a number of ways.

Ever since the beginning of the century psychologists have been interested in the Féré effect, or what is now usually called the galvanic skin response. If a small current is passed through the skin of a person and the resistance of the body is measured, it will be found that many conditions (e.g., noise, lights, mental arithmetic, emotions) will cause changes in the apparent resistance of the body. This effect seemed to be a valuable tool for studying psychological phenomena.

It was gradually discovered, however, that many factors, including those of no interest per se to psychologists, could cause changes in the apparent resistance of the body. These included the size of the electrodes used, their pressure, the type of electrode paste used, its concentration of salt, and the actual level of current sent into the skin. In fact, if the current used was high enough (although still below the threshold of sensation), it could cause the skin to generate a potential at the point of contact with the electrode, so that, in essence, a small battery was formed. This battery then produced a counter electromotive force, or voltage, which resulted in an apparent decrease in skin resistance. Therefore the application of a current to the skin produced a back action which changed the apparent property of the skin being measured. Recent research has therefore suggested that current levels used be below 10 microamperes per square centimeter of electrode area (Edelberg and Burch, 1962).

Another example of back action relates to the problem of measuring blood pressure in the human. The usual manual procedure employed by a physician is to use a pressure cuff on the upper arm inflated until the pulse in the lower arm is no longer heard with a stethoscope. At the point at which the lower pulse is just cut off, the pressure in the cuff is approximately equal to the maximum pressure in the artery (i.e., systolic blood pressure).

A second method, used in "lie detectors," is to inflate the cuff about midway between diastolic and systolic blood pressure and keep it there. Fluctuations in pressure around this point presumably relate to various psychological conditions. This method limits blood flow to various tissues and can have a detrimental effect if prolonged too long.

Another method that has been developed is one which uses sophisticated equipment to automatically inflate and deflate the cuff mounted on the upper arm. A device which measures the pulse in the wrist or finger, or a microphone which listens for the pulse, sends signals periodically which determine when the cuff is to inflate or deflate.

What is common to all these methods is the production of effects on both the blood pressure itself and organ systems which have something to do with the maintenance of blood pressure. Davis (1957) has shown that the sudden application of pressure to the cuff produced large increases in the finger volume of the hand opposite to the side where the cuff was placed. In some subjects, contralateral decreases in pulse volume were found. Temperature changes of the skin were also noted. Davis concluded: "The application of pressure seems to arouse widespread circulatory reflexes, changing the very thing the occlusion method is intended to measure." Thus a back action is again evident. One of the solutions to this problem is to use the artery in the wrist and measure its amplitude displacement; another is to place the pressure cuff on the finger instead of the upper arm and thus reduce the magnitude of the reflex reactions.

Backward action may appear in many different guises. If a student's motivation is being measured and he is put into a frustrating problem-solving situation, he might redouble his efforts as a result of the frustration so that it is not at all typical of how he would usually behave. Some people seem to improve their performance over normal in competitive situations and some deteriorate. From all the examples given it is evident that the possibility of backward action exists in almost any measurement situation and should always be considered by the experimenter.

SUMMARY

Certain areas of psychology are primarily descriptive and do not depend to any important extent on the use of instruments. In many other areas of psychology instruments are being used to an increasing degree. This is because they standardize the conditions of an experiment, they make different experiments more comparable, they record data in a permanent form, and they measure events not accessible to man's senses. These values are partly offset by the fact that experimental findings sometimes reflect the arbitrary properties of the equipment used and sometimes innovation is stifled in the interests of comparability of results.

When measuring instruments are used intelligently, many specifications have to be considered, such as: sensitivity, range, linearity, accuracy, and frequency response. Sometimes the very act of measurement creates a condition which modifies the event measured. This "backward action" has to be carefully watched for.

Finally, we should always remember that instruments are always sampling devices, and that only part of a process is usually explored. It is important to be cautious about overgeneralizing on the basis of limited situations or limited measures.

BIBLIOGRAPHY

Aaronson, B. S., and Welsh, G. S. The MMPI as diagnostic differentiator: a reply to Rubin. *J. consult. Psychol.*, 1950, **14**, 324–326.

Adler, F. Operational definitions in sociology. *Amer. J. Sociol.*, 1947, **52**, 438–444.

Ammons, R. B. Rotary pursuit apparatus: I. Survey of variables, *Psychol. Bull.*, 1955, **52**, 69–76.

Anderson, R. L. Recent advances in finding best operating conditions. *J. Amer. Stat. Assoc.*, 1953, **48**, 789–798.

Andrews, T. G. *Methods of psychology*. New York: Wiley, 1948.

Attneave, F., and Arnoult, M. D. The quantitative study of shape and pattern perception. *Psychol. Bull.*, 1956, **53**, 452–471.

Baldwin, A. L. The study of child behavior and development. In P. H. Mussen (Ed.) *Handbook of research methods in child development*. New York: Wiley, 1960.

258   Foundations of Experimental Research

Barker, R. G., and Wright, H. F. *Midwest and its children.* New York: Harper & Row, 1955.

Beach, F. A. Experimental investigations of species-specific behavior. *Amer. Psychologist,* 1960, **15,** 1–18.

Benjamin, A. C. *Operationism.* Springfield, Ill.: Charles C Thomas, 1955.

Berg, I. A. The use of human subjects in psychological research. *Amer. Psychologist,* 1954, **9,** 108–111.

Binder, A., McConnell, D., and Sjoholm, N. A. Verbal conditioning as a function of experimenter characteristics. *J. abnorm. soc. Psychol.,* 1957, **55,** 309–314.

Boneau, C. A. The effects of violations of assumptions underlying the *t* test. *Psychol. Bull.,* 1960, **57,** 49–64.

Boring, E. G. The nature and history of experimental control. *Amer. J. Psychol.,* 1954, **67,** 573–589.

Box, G. E. P. Integration of techniques in process development. Statistical Techniques Research Group, Princeton University. Tech. Rept. No. 2, 1957.

Brackmann, J., and Collier, G. The dependence of probability of response on size of step interval in the method of limits. *J. exp. Psychol.,* 1958, **55,** 423–428.

Brady, J. V. Ulcers in "executive" monkeys. *Sci. Amer.,* 1958, **199,** 95–100.

Brehm, J. W., and Cohen, A. R. Re-evaluation of choice alternatives as a function of their number and qualitative similarity. *J. abnorm. soc. Psychol.,* 1959, **58,** 373–378.

Bridgman, P. W. *The logic of modern physics.* New York: Macmillan, 1927.

Bridgman, P. W. *Reflections of a physicist.* New York: Philosophical Library, 1950.

Brockway, Ann L., Gleser, G., Winokur, G., and Ulett, G. A. The use of a control population in neuropsychiatric research (psychiatric, psychological and EEG evaluation of a heterogeneous sample). *Amer. J. Psychiat.,* 1954, **111,** 248–262.

Bronson, F. H. Agonistic behaviour in woodchucks. *Animal Behaviour,* 1964, **12,** 470–478.

Bruner, J. S., Goodnow, J. J., and Austin, G. A. *A study of thinking.* New York: Wiley, 1956.

Brunswik, E. *Perception and the representative design of psychological experiments.* Berkeley: University of California Press, 1956.

Burke, C. J. A brief note on one-tailed tests. *Psychol. Bull.*, 1953, **50**, 384–387.

Chapanis, A. *The design and conduct of human engineering studies.* Tech. Rept. No. 14, Project NR 145–075; San Diego State College Foundation, 1956.

Chapanis, A. Engineering psychology. *Ann. Rev. Psychol.*, 1963, **14**, 285–318.

Chapanis, A. Color names for color space. *Amer. Sci.*, 1965, **53**, 327–346.

Chapanis, N. P., and Chapanis, A. Cognitive dissonance: five years later. *Psychol. Bull.*, 1964, **61**, 1–22.

Chassan, J. B. Statistical inference and the single case in clinical design. *Psychiatry*, 1960, **23**, 173–184.

Christie, R. Experimental naiveté and experiential naiveté. *Psychol. Bull.*, 1951, **48**, 327–339.

Church, R. M. Systematic effect of random error in the yoked control design. *Psychol. Bull.*, 1964, **62**, 122–131.

Churchman, C. W. *Theory of experimental inference.* New York: Macmillan, 1948.

Cochran, W. G. Some consequences when the assumptions for the analysis of variance are not satisfied. *Biometrics*, 1947, **3**, 21–38.

Conant, J. B. *On understanding science.* New Haven: Yale, 1947.

Cook, S. W., and Selltiz, C., A multiple-indicator approach to attitude measurement. *Psychol. Bull.*, 1964, **62**, 36–55.

Cronbach, L. J. Statistical methods applied to Rorschach scores: a review. *Psychol. Bull.*, 1949, **46**, 393–429.

Davis, R. C. Continuous recording of arterial pressure: an analysis of the problem. *J. comp. physiol. Psychol.*, 1957, **50**, 524–529.

Day, W. F. Randomness of threshold responses at long interstimulus intervals. *Percept. Motor Skills*, 1956, **6**, 205–208.

Delgado, J. M. R. Chronic radio-stimulation of the brain in monkey colonies. *Excerpta Medica International Congress.* Series No. 87, 1965, 365–371.

Dixon, W. J., and Massey, F. J., Jr. *Introduction to statistical analysis.* New York: McGraw-Hill, 1951.

Dukes, W. F. N = 1. *Psychol. Bull.*, 1965, **64**, 74–79.

Edelberg, R., and Burch, N. R. Skin resistance and the galvanic skin response. *Arch. gen. Psychiat.*, 1962, **7**, 163–169.

Edwards, W., Lindman, H., and Savage, L. J. Bayesian statistical inference for psychological research. *Psychol. Rev.*, 1963, **70**, 193–242.

Ehrenberg, A. S. C. Measurement and mathematics in psychology. *Brit. J. Psychol.*, 1955, **46**, 20–29.

Ellis, B. *Basic concepts of measurement.* Cambridge: Cambridge University Press, 1966.

Eysenck, H. J. The concept of statistical significance and the controversy about one-tailed tests. *Psychol. Rev.*, 1960, **67**, 269–271.

Feather, N. *Mass, length and time.* Baltimore: Penguin, 1959.

Feigl, H. Operationism and scientific method. *Psychol. Rev.*, 1945, **52**, 250–259.

Fisher, R. A. *Statistical methods for research workers.* (12th ed.) London: Oliver & Boyd, 1954.

Fitts, P. M. The influence of response coding on performance in motor tasks. In *Current trends in information theory.* Pittsburgh: University of Pittsburgh Press, 1954.

Galanter, E. Contemporary psychophysics. In *New Directions in Psychology.* New York: Holt, Rinehart and Winston, 1962.

Garner, W. R. Context effects and the validity of loudness scales. *J. exp. Psychol.*, 1954, **48**, 218–224.

Garner, W. R. The development of context effects in half-loudness judgments. *J. exp. Psychol.*, 1959, **58**, 212–219.

Ginsberg, A. Operational definitions and theories. *J. gen. Psychol.*, 1955, **52**, 223–248.

Graham, C. H., and Kemp, E. H. Brightness discrimination as a function of the duration of the increment in intensity. *J. gen. Physiol.*, 1938, **21**, 635–650.

Graham, C. H., and Ratoosh, P. Notes on some interrelations of sensory psychology, perception and behavior. In S. Koch (Ed.), *Psychology: a study of a science.* New York: McGraw-Hill, 1962, Vol. IV.

Granit, R. *Receptors and sensory perception.* New Haven: Yale, 1955.

Grice, G. R., and Hunter, J. J. Stimulus intensity effects depend upon the type of experimental design. *Psychol. Rev.*, 1964, **71**, 247–256.

Group for the Advancement of Psychiatry. *Some observations on controls in psychiatric research.* New York: Report No. 42, May, 1959.

Gruenberg, E. M. A review of: Mental health in the Metropolis. *Sci. Amer.*, 1962, **207**, 159–166.

Guilford, J. P. *Psychometric methods.* New York: McGraw-Hill, 1954.

Guilford, J. P. *Fundamental statistics in psychology and education.* New York: McGraw-Hill, 1965.

Hammond, E. C. Smoking and death rates—a riddle in cause and effect. *Amer. Sci.*, 1958, **46**, 331–354.

Harlow, H. F. Mice, monkeys, men, and motives. *Psychol. Rev.*, 1953, **60**, 23–32.

Harlow, H. F., Harlow, M. K., Rueping, R. R., and Mason, W. A. Performance of infant rhesus monkeys on discrimination learning, delayed response, and discrimination learning set. *J. comp. physiol. Psychol.*, 1960, **53**, 113–121.

Hays, W. L. *Statistics for psychologists.* New York: Holt, Rinehart and Winston, 1963.

Hecht, I. The difference in goal striving behavior between peptic ulcer and ulcerative colitis patients as evaluated by psychological tests. *J. Clin. Psychol.*, 1952, **8**, 262–265.

Hodos, W., and Valenstein, E. S. An evaluation of response rate as a measure of rewarding intracranial stimulation. *J. comp. physiol. Psychol.*, 1962, **55**, 80–84.

Hughes, J. An evaluation of contemporary research methods in the field of method disorders. In P. H. Hoch and J. Zubin (Eds.), *Current problems in psychiatric diagnosis.* New York: Grune & Stratton, 1953.

Hull, C. L. *Principles of behavior: an introduction to behavior theory.* New York: Appleton-Century-Crofts, 1943.

Hunt, J. McV. The effects of infant feeding-frustration upon adult hoarding behavior. *J. abnorm. soc. Psychol.*, 1941, **36**, 338–360.

Jones, F. N., and Marcus, M. J. The subject effect in judgments of subjective magnitude. *J. exp. Psychol.*, 1961, **61**, 40–44.

Juhasz, J. B., and Sarbin, T. R. On the false alarm metaphor in psychophysics. *Psychol. Rec.*, 1966, **16**, 323–327.

Kellerman, H. The development of a forced-choice personality index and its relation to degree of maladjustment. Ph.D. dissertation. New York: Yeshiva University, 1964.

Kelman, H. C. Human use of human subjects: the problem of deception in social psychological experiments. *Psychol. Bull.* 1967. **67**, 1–11.

Kirchner, W. K., and Dunnette, M. D. An industrial psychologist's lament: the problem of shrinking sample size. *Amer. Psychologist*, 1959, **14**, 299–300.

Lacey, J. I., and Lacey, B. C. Verification and extension of the principle of autonomic response-stereotypy. *Amer. J. Psychol.*, 1958, **71**, 50–73.

Lasagna, L., and von Felsinger, J. M. The volunteer subject in research. *Science*, 1954, **120**, 359–461.

Lashley, K. S. *Brain mechanisms and intelligence.* New York: Dover, 1963. (Original edition, 1929.)

Lewis, D. *Quantitative methods in psychology.* New York: McGraw-Hill, 1960.

Lewis, D., and Burke, C. J. The use and misuse of the chi-square test. *Psychol. Bull.*, 1949, **46**, 433–489.

Lewis, D., Smith, P. N., and McAllister, D. E. Retroactive facilitation and interference in performance on a modified two-hand coordinator. *J. exp. Psychol.*, 1952, **44**, 44–50.

Lindquist, E. F. *Design and analysis of experiments in psychology and education.* Boston: Houghton Mifflin, 1953.

Loevinger, J. Person and population as psychometric concepts. *Psychol. Rev.*, 1965, **72**, 143–155.

Lundberg, G. A. *Foundations of sociology.* New York: Macmillan, 1939.

Lyons, J. *A primer of experimental psychology.* New York: Harper & Row, 1965.

MacCorquodale, K., and Meehl, P. E. On a distinction between hypothetical constructs and intervening variable. *Psychol. Rev.*, 1948, **55**, 95–107.

Marshall, S. Personality correlates of peptic ulcer patients. *J. consult. Psychol.*, 1960, **24**, 218–223.

Maslow, A. H., and Sakoda, J. M. Volunteer-error in the Kinsey study. *J. abnorm. soc. Psychol.*, 1952, **47**, 259–262.

Mason, B., and Ammons, R. B. Note on social class and the Thematic Apperception Test. *Percept. Motor Skills*, 1956, **6**, 88.

McFarland, R. A., and Moseley, A. L. *Human factors in highway transport safety.* Boston: Harvard School of Public Health, 1954.

Melton, A. W. Editorial *J. exp. Psychol.*, 1962, **64**, 553–557.

Miller, N. E. Analytical studies of drive and reward. *Amer. Psychologist*, 1961, **10**, 739–754.

Miller, N. E. Objective techniques for studying motivational effects of drugs on animals. In S. Garettini and V. Ghetti (Eds.), *Psychotropic drugs.* Amsterdam: Elsevier, 1957.

Miller, N. E., Bailey, C. J., and Stevenson, J. A. F. Decreased "hunger" but increased food intake resulting from hypothalamic lesions. *Science*, **112**, 256–259.

Morison, R. S. "Gradualness, gradualness, gradualness" (I. P. Pavlov). *Amer. Psychologist*, 1960, **15**, 187–197.

Perlin, S., Pollin, W., and Butler, R. N. The experimental subject. *AMA Arch. Neurol. Psychiat.* 1958, **80**, 65–70.

Piaget, J. *The language and thought of the child.* New York: Meridian, 1955.

Plutchik, R. Further remarks on the hypothetical construct. *J. Psychol.*, 1954, **37**, 59–64.

Plutchik, R. *The emotions: facts, theories and a new model.* New York: Random House, 1962.

Plutchik, R. Operationism as methodology. *Behavioral Sci.*, 1963, **8**, 234–241.

Plutchik, R. The study of social behavior in primates. *Folia primat.*, 1964, **2**, 67–92.

Plutchik, R., McFarland, W. L., and Robinson, B. W. Relationships between current intensity, self-stimulation rates, escape latencies, and evoked behavior in rhesus monkeys. *J. comp. physiol. Psychol.*, 1966, **61**, 181–188.

Poulton, E. C., and Simmonds, D. C. V. Value of standard and very first variable in judgments of reflectance of grays with various ranges of available numbers. *J. exp. Psychol.*, 1963, **65**, 297–304.

Price, R. H. Signal-detection methods in personality and perception. *Psychol. Bull*, 1966, **66**, 55–62.

Price, R. H., and Erickson, C. W. Size constancy in schizophrenia: A reanalysis. *J. clin. Psychol.*, 1966, 71, 155–160.

Ray, W. S. *An introduction to experimental design.* New York: Macmillan, 1960.

Reiss, B. F., Schwartz, E. K., and Cottingham, A. An experimental critique of assumptions underlying the Negro version of the TAT. *J. abnorm. soc. Psychol.*, 1950, **45**, 700–709.

Rheingold, H. L. The measurement of maternal care. *Child Develpm.* 1960, **31**, 565–575.

Robinson, E. S., and Brown, M. A. Effect of serial position on memorization. *Amer. J. Psychol.*, 1926, **37**, 538–552.

Rosenthal, R. On the social psychology of the psychological experiment: the experimenter's hypothesis as unintended determinant of experimental results. *Amer. Sci.*, 1963, **51**, 268–283.

Rosenthal, R. Letter. *Behavioral Sci.*, 1964, **9**, 66.

Ross, O. B., Jr. Use of controls in medical research. *J. Amer. Med. Assoc.*, 1951, **145**, 72–75.

Ryan, T. A. Multiple comparisons in psychological research. *Psychol. Bull.*, 1959, **56**, 26–47.

Sawrey, W. L., and Weisz, J. D. An experimental method of producing gastric ulcers. *J. comp. physiol., Psychol.*, 1956, **49**, 269–270.

Schachter, S., and Singer, J. E. Cognitive, social and physiological determinants of emotional state. *Psychol. Rev.*, 1962, **69**, 379–399.

Scott, J. P. The place of observation in biological and psychological science. *Amer. Psychologist*, 1955, **10**, 61–64.

Scriven, M. Definitions, explanations, and theories. In H. Feigl, M. Scriven, and G. Maxwell (Eds.), *Minnesota studies in the philosophy of science*. Vol. II. Minneapolis: University of Minnesota Press, 1958.

Sidman, M. *Tactics of scientific research*. New York: Basic Books, 1960.

Siegel, S. *Nonparametric statistics for the behavioral sciences*. New York: McGraw-Hill, 1956.

Slovic, P. Assessment of risk taking behavior. *Psychol. Bull.*, 1964, **61**, 220–223.

Srole, L., Lengner, T. S., Michael, S. T., Opler, M. K., and Rennie, T. A. C. *Mental health in the metropolis: the midtown Manhattan study*. Vol. 1. New York: McGraw-Hill, 1962.

Stanley, J. C. Statistical analysis of scores from counterbalanced tests. *J. exp. Educ.*, 1955, **23**, 187–207.

Stanley, W. C., and Schlosberg, H. The psychophysiological effects of tea. *J. Psychol.*, 1953, **36**, 435–448.

Sterling, T. D. Publication decisions and their possible effects on inferences drawn from tests of significance—or vice versa. *J. Amer. Stat. Assoc.*, 1959, **54**, 30–34.

Stevens, J. C. Stimulus spacing and the judgment of loudness. *J. exp. Psychol.*, 1958, **56**, 246–250.

Stevens, S. S. On the theory of scales of measurement. *Science*, 1946, **103**, 677–680.

Stevens, S. S. On the psychophysical law. *Psychol. Rev.*, 1957, **64**, 153–181.

Stevens, S. S. Problems and methods of psychophysics. *Psychol. Bull.*, 1958a, **55**, 177–196.

Stevens, S. S. Measurement and man. *Science*, 1958b, **127**, 383–389.

Stevens, S. S. Measurement, psychophysics, and utility. In C. W.

Churchman and P. Ratoosh (Eds.), *Measurement: definitions and theories.* New York: Wiley, 1959.

Stevens, J. C., Herrnstein, R. J., and Reynolds, G. S. *Laboratory experiments in psychology.* New York: Holt, Rinehart, and Winston, 1965.

Stott, L. Parental attitudes of farm, town, and city parents in relation to certain personality adjustments in their children. *J. soc. Psychol.,* 1940, **11,** 325–339.

Swets, J. A. Is there a sensory threshold? *Science,* 1961, **134,** 168–177.

Swets, J. A., Tanner, W. P., and Birdsall, T. G. Decision processes in perception. *Psychol. Rev.,* 1961, **68,** 301–340.

Thompson, D. W. *On Growth and Form.* (Abridged edition). Cambridge: Cambridge University Press, 1961.

Thorndike, R. L. *The concepts of over- and underachievement.* New York: Teachers College, Columbia University, 1963.

Thurstone, L. L. The measurement of values. *Psychol. Rev.,* 1954, **61,** 47–58.

Verplanck, W. S. Since learned behavior is innate, and vice versa, what now? *Psychol. Rev.,* 1955, **62,** 139–144.

Wallis, W. A., and Roberts, H. V. *Statistics: a new approach.* New York: The Free Press, 1956.

Warren, R. M., and Warren, R. P. A critique of S. S. Stevens' "New Psychophysics." *Percept. Motor Skills,* 1963, **16,** 797–810.

Weiner, S., Dorman, D., Persky, H., Stach, T. W., Norton, J., and Levitt, E. E. Effect on anxiety of increasing the plasma hydrocortisone level. *Psychosom. Med.,* 1963, **25,** 69–77.

Wendt, G. R. Methods of recording action. *Arch. Psychol.,* 1938, Whole No. 228.

Whiting, J. W. M., and Child, I. L. *Child training practices and personality.* New Haven: Yale, 1950.

Wilson, E. B. *An introduction to scientific research.* New York: McGraw-Hill, 1952.

Woodworth, R. S. *Experimental psychology.* New York: Holt, Rinehart and Winston, 1938.

Woodworth, R. S., and Schlosberg, H. *Experimental psychology* (2nd ed.) New York: Holt, Rinehart and Winston, 1954.

Woolsey, T. D. Sampling methods for a small household survey. Public Health Monograph No. 40, Publication No. 480, 1956.

Wright, H. F. Observational child study. In P. H. Mussen (Ed.),

Handbook of research methods in child development. New York: Wiley, 1960.

Wulfeck, J. W., and Taylor, J. H. (Eds.) *Form discrimination as related to military problems.* Washington, D.C.: National Academy of Sciences, National Research Council, Publ. No. 561, 1957.

APPENDIXES

WRITING EXPERIMENTAL REPORTS

An experiment is never really completed until its results are communicated to other scientists and it becomes part of the total body of scientific knowledge. This is sometimes done through oral reports at scientific meetings, but the basic mode of communication is publication in scientific journals. No research develops in an historical vacuum, and the permanent record made available by publication enables anyone to trace the development of ideas, instruments, and theories.

There are over three-quarters of a million articles published each year in the scientific and technical fields. In psychology alone there are many thousands. In order to deal with this huge volume of information various policies have been established on the forms that technical reports should have. For one thing, reports have become considerably shorter. The average report now is about 10 to 15 typewritten double-spaced pages. In addition, the format of presentation has become almost standardized to facilitate rapid evaluation of the contents by both editors and readers.

The clearest and most detailed description of what these expectations are may be found in the *Publication Manual* published by the American Psychological Association. Everything is discussed there from the organization and style of the writing to the correction of proof. This appendix is not to be thought of as a substitute for that manual, but is simply a summary of some of the major points covered there.

The Introduction. The first part of the report should briefly make clear to the reader why the particular problem presented is being studied. For example, the experiment may be designed to test a theory or hypothesis, or it may simply be concerned with establishing or extending a relationship between two variables. Sometimes experiments are done in an effort to determine the reliability of some previously reported findings. Occasionally, experiments are done in an attempt to clarify certain inconsistencies in previous work. In any case the reader should have a reasonably clear idea, after reading the introduction, of the contemporary or historical framework of the experiment. A carefully selected number of related experiments should be referred to in order to help provide this framework.

(It is worth mentioning in this connection that one of the best sources of information about current research in the field of psychology is the *Psychological Abstracts*, which contains brief abstracts of articles on psychology and related subjects published in most countries of the world. For problems related to physiology and medicine the *Biological Abstracts* are helpful. In addition, the *Annual Review of Psychology* contains surveys of current research in selected areas, with each survey written by a specialist.)

The Method Section. The method should be described in sufficient detail to permit the reader to repeat the experiment. Sometimes other articles may be referred to for descriptions of specialized pieces of equipment or of certain procedures. The number and type of subjects used should be mentioned as well as how they were assigned to groups and how treatments were imposed upon them. Any special controls or calibrations used in the experiment should be presented here as well as some indication of the accuracy of the measurements being used.

The Results Section. Presentation of results is often a difficult section to write partly because the writer tends to vacillate between presenting too much or too little. Editors of journals generally prefer only a brief summary of the major findings of a particular study; there is rarely space available for all the basic data that have been collected in the experiment.

Partly because of the highly condensed nature of the published material in most journals, the Library of Congress has established an auxiliary publication service called the American Documentation Institute (ADI). Any material that is relevant to a published work, but which is too detailed for inclusion in the original article, may be filed with the ADI and will then be available to all readers for a small charge to cover the cost of microfilm or photocopies. Data of individual subjects or trials, subgroup performance, statistical analyses, and additional tables or figures may all be deposited with the ADI. This is done through the editor of the journal that publishes the original manuscript.

In the results section the author should attempt to summarize his major findings as simply and clearly as he can. Figures are usually more revealing than tables, but they are also more expensive to prepare and print. In any case, data should not be prepared in two different ways. It is unacceptable to present a table and then show the same information in the form of a graph.

The Discussion Section. In this section the author should compare the results of his experiment with those of previous investigators. If discrepancies exist, he should try to explain them. He may also elaborate on his theoretical position and suggest further implications. Sometimes an author may point out sources of error that may have operated in the experiment as well as their possible influence on the results.

References. Some journals prefer that all references cited be included in the body of the report in the form of footnotes. Most, however, recommend that references be alphabetically arranged by surname without numbering. The exact form to be used for journal and book citations may be found in the APA *Publication Manual.*

The Abstract. At one time, most articles ended with a brief summary of the main points of the paper. Since 1963 this has been superseded by a 120-word abstract that goes at the front of the report. This abstract should contain a brief statement of the problem, the results, and the conclusions.

It should be borne in mind that the preceding suggestions represent only general guidelines and that variations exist in editorial policies in different journals. These will become evident as the student begins to read widely in the psychological literature.

SOME ETHICAL ISSUES

IN RESEARCH

In 1965 the Congress of the United States conducted several investigations into the problems of the use and abuse of psychological tests, particularly personality tests. Claims had begun to increase in recent years that psychologists were "brain-watching," "brainwashing," "snooping," "spying," and invading the "rights of privacy." Some personality tests contain questions concerning a person's religious beliefs and his sex life, and these were the major subjects of the attacks during the investigation. At about the same time the medical profession was made painfully aware that there had been a number of published papers in recent years describing patients or normal control subjects who, in the interests of research, had been given drugs without their consent.

These facts led the National Institute of Health, the major research-funding agency in medicine and psychology, to reevaluate their policies governing the use of human subjects for research and to become more careful in examining this phase of any proposed new research.

Standards for the humane treatment of animals have been known and respected for a long time. It is expected, for example, that all due consideration be given the animals bodily comfort and that adequate housing facilities be made available. Surgery should be done only under suitable anesthesia and the animal should be cared for properly at all times. If an animal must be killed, this should be done in a humane way. If animals are used by students as part of their education, this work should be supervised by an experienced teacher. Since universities or laboratories must be licensed by the state in most cases, there are certain penalties which can result from infringement of these standards.

The situation in regard to the use of humans in psychological research is quite different. "It was not until 1953 that a formal statement was issued by the APA concerning the general welfare of human research subjects" (Berg, 1954). In 1959 it was formalized into a code of ethical standards for psychologists (see *American Psychologist*, 1959, pp. 279–282). In it several important standards of relevance to experimental psychologists were included.

Principle 16. *Harmful Aftereffects*. Only when a problem is significant and can be investigated in no other way is the psychologist justified in giving misinformation to research subjects or exposing research subjects to physical or emotional stress.

A. When the possibility of serious aftereffects exists, research is conducted only when the subjects or their responsible agents are fully informed of this possibility and volunteer nevertheless.

B. The psychologist seriously considers the possible harmful aftereffects and removes them as soon as permitted by the design of the experiment.

These issues are of particular concern to experimental psychologists because experimentation implies the control and manipulation of the subject and conditions of study. In the interests of research, at one time or another subjects have been shocked, threatened, made anxious, angry, hungry and thirsty, deprived of sensory stimulation, given false test results, had their tasks interrupted, been exposed to painful sounds, required to shock other people, been given drugs, hormones, false symptoms, and various kinds of propaganda. Under what conditions can these manipulations be justified; under what conditions can a subject be asked to participate in a psychology experiment? Although these questions are still the center of current controversies, some tentative suggestions have been made. For example, Berg (1954) suggested that there are three principles which should be used as guides in connection with the use of human subjects in psychological research. The first is the principle of *consent*.

The only safe procedure is to invite participation while avoiding any appearance of coercion and to make it easy for any subject to withdraw gracefully. Where the information requested is highly personal or where the experiment involves some pain, discomfort or risk, the subject should be made fully aware of what he is consenting to, at least in a general way.

Another way of saying this is that despite the sampling problems this creates, all subjects should be volunteers. The second of Berg's principles is what he calls *confidence*, and by this he means two things. On the one hand, the subjects should feel that whatever the psychologist learns about them is to be kept in the strictest confidence and is to be revealed only with their permission. The APA code of ethics puts the matter this way:

Only after explicit permission has been granted is the identity of research subjects published. When data have been published without permission for identification, the psychologist assumes responsibility for adequately disguising their sources.

The other aspect of the *confidence* principle is that the behavior of the psychologist in his work should be such that there is public confidence in the maturity and skill of researchers as well as acceptance of the scientific validity of their findings.

This issue is one which has generated considerable discussion and it generally centers around the use of deception in some psychology experiments. For example, suppose the experimenter tells a subject that some (fictitious) test the subject took reveals that he possesses several very undesirable traits. At the end of the experiment the subject is told about the nature of the deception. (In one experiment, these debriefing statements were actually used as part of a second deception practiced on the subject.)

If such deceptions become frequent the public may develop an image of the psychologist as a practicer of deceptions, so that even when he tells the truth he will not be believed. These considerations suggest the ethical concept that statements about confidentiality and trust must be followed literally by the psychologist, and all his debriefing statements must be true.

These considerations have led some psychologists to attempt to reevaluate the use of deception as an experimental technique and to look for alternatives. Baldwin (1960) has put the matter this way.

It is necessary on some occasions that the adult subject be unaware of the purpose or the procedure of an experiment. This circumstance is sometimes used to put adult subjects into experiments that they would never enter voluntarily, even when the knowledge would not affect their behavior in the experiment as much as it would lead them to refuse to participate. The general practice of deceiving the subjects of psychological experiments is roundly condemned by a large section of the psychological profession, perhaps the majority. They argue that in most cases the experiment can be done equally well without deception, that if necessary the subject can be told frankly that it is necessary for him to be ignorant of the purpose of the experiment and that the few experiments in which deception is absolutely required are better left undone.

The third principle that Berg suggested is what he calls *acceptable procedures*. This means simply that the procedures used in the experiment must be regarded as acceptable by competent psychologists. This point again emphasizes the highly social nature of the scientific enterprise. The various issues raised have also been discussed in detail by Kelman (1967).

There may come a time when these ethical issues have been solved and principles appropriate to all situations are firmly codified. Until that time it would be desirable for the experimental psychologist to be careful in his manipulations, conscientious in the establishment of safeguards, and sensitive to the interpersonal relations that develop during the experiment. In the opening words of the preamble to the code of ethical standards for psychologists:

The psychologist is committed to a belief in the dignity and worth of the individual human being. While demanding for himself the rights of freedom of inquiry and freedom of communication, he accepts the responsibilities that these freedoms imply.

APPENDIX

Table A. Areas of the Normal Curve in Terms of z-values

z	Area in Larger Portion	z	Area in Larger Portion
0.00	0.5000	1.60	0.9452
0.10	0.5398	1.70	0.9554
0.20	0.5793	1.80	0.9641
0.30	0.6179	1.90	0.9713
0.40	0.6554	2.00	0.9772
0.50	0.6915	2.10	0.9821
0.60	0.7257	2.20	0.9861
0.70	0.7580	2.30	0.9893
0.80	0.7881	2.40	0.9918
0.90	0.8159	2.50	0.9938
1.00	0.8413	2.60	0.9953
1.10	0.8643	2.70	0.9965
1.20	0.8849	2.80	0.9974
1.30	0.9032	2.90	0.9981
1.40	0.9192	3.00	0.9987
1.50	0.9332		

Table B. Distribution of **t**

df	.1	.05	.01	.001
1	6.314	12.706	63.657	636.619
2	2.920	4.303	9.925	31.598
3	2.353	3.182	5.841	12.941
4	2.132	2.776	4.604	8.610
5	2.015	2.571	4.032	6.859
6	1.943	2.447	3.707	5.959
7	1.895	2.365	3.499	5.405
8	1.860	2.306	3.355	5.041
9	1.833	2.262	3.250	4.781
10	1.812	2.228	3.169	4.587
11	1.796	2.201	3.106	4.437
12	1.782	2.179	3.055	4.318
13	1.771	2.160	3.012	4.221
14	1.761	2.145	2.977	4.140
15	1.753	2.131	2.947	4.073
16	1.746	2.120	2.921	4.015
17	1.740	2.110	2.898	3.965
18	1.734	2.101	2.878	3.922
19	1.729	2.093	2.861	3.883
20	1.725	2.086	2.845	3.850
21	1.721	2.080	2.831	3.819
22	1.717	2.074	2.819	3.792
23	1.714	2.069	2.807	3.767
24	1.711	2.064	2.797	3.745
25	1.708	2.060	2.787	3.725
26	1.706	2.056	2.779	3.707
27	1.703	2.052	2.771	3.690
28	1.701	2.048	2.763	3.674
29	1.699	2.045	2.756	3.659
30	1.697	2.042	2.750	3.646
40	1.684	2.021	2.704	3.551
60	1.671	2.000	2.660	3.460
120	1.658	1.980	2.617	3.373
∞	1.645	1.960	2.576	3.291

SOURCE: Table B is taken from Table III of Fisher & Yates: *Statistical Tables for Biological, Agricultural, and Medical Research,* published by Oliver & Boyd Ltd., Edinburgh, and by permission of the authors and publishers.

Table C. Random Numbers

	\multicolumn{20}{c}{Columns}
Rows	01	02	03	04	05	06	07	08	09	10	11	12	13	14	15	16	17	18	19	20
---	---	---	---	---	---	---	---	---	---	---	---	---	---	---	---	---	---	---	---	---
01	7	5	9	1	0	7	4	0	1	0	7	7	3	6	9	4	8	7	0	2
02	8	2	7	3	9	8	4	0	6	9	2	3	2	8	0	7	5	2	2	4
03	5	3	4	1	7	5	4	8	3	7	4	8	5	7	2	3	2	1	6	6
04	2	6	3	3	9	2	8	1	9	4	0	6	3	2	0	5	4	6	7	8
05	9	8	5	2	0	2	7	8	5	4	3	2	8	2	8	6	7	6	3	2
06	0	9	8	4	0	4	3	9	9	0	7	1	8	5	4	9	9	5	1	2
07	1	4	7	9	3	9	4	8	3	3	8	9	2	0	0	7	3	9	2	5
08	4	1	3	4	8	1	6	9	5	6	2	0	6	4	6	1	6	8	1	7
09	9	2	8	1	6	9	2	3	1	9	8	8	6	8	7	0	3	9	2	4
10	6	4	9	4	1	2	7	2	0	3	9	3	8	6	6	5	0	5	5	5
11	6	0	1	6	9	1	6	3	5	1	7	2	6	5	9	0	6	0	3	8
12	7	5	9	8	3	4	4	1	0	4	6	9	6	2	7	5	8	4	7	3
13	5	8	1	3	3	1	0	0	1	1	5	6	2	9	2	6	2	9	9	8
14	9	1	4	7	5	4	9	3	4	3	1	9	4	2	2	5	1	8	9	1
15	9	3	6	5	1	7	7	5	6	3	5	2	0	1	6	8	6	7	0	5
16	3	8	1	6	4	6	4	3	0	6	1	3	4	1	7	7	9	7	8	6
17	9	0	3	1	7	6	8	8	6	6	3	0	8	0	1	8	2	2	5	4
18	1	6	1	4	3	8	5	5	0	7	7	1	8	6	5	7	9	4	8	7
19	0	9	2	5	5	2	0	2	3	9	1	3	8	7	5	3	2	5	4	9
20	6	8	0	3	7	6	7	1	1	5	6	1	5	5	9	7	0	6	7	5

Here is an example of how the table of random numbers might be used. Suppose there are 90 classes in a University and you wish to select a sample of 10 classes to be tested. Number the classes from 01 to 90 and then pick any arbitrary starting point in the table, for example, column 08 and row 15. You may now proceed in any direction from this point, taking the numbers in pairs. Thus, if you proceeded sideways, you would select classes numbered 56, 35, 20, 16, 86, and 70. When you reach the end of a row you may change direction or begin at a new point. If you find a number repeated, or if you come upon a number over 90, then disregard the number and continue the process.

INDEXES

INDEX OF NAMES

INDEX OF SUBJECTS